PRAISE FOR

OVERCOMING PASSIVE-AGGRESSION

"Congressman Murphy and Loriann Hoff Oberlin call much-needed attention to the confusing, frustrating, and crazy-making problem of passive-aggression. With many anecdotes and thorough description, *Overcoming Passive-Aggression* is an easily accessible resource for the lay reader—helpful for the perpetrator as well as the victim."

—SCOTT WETZLER, PhD,
author of *Living with the Passive-Aggressive Man*

■

"More than an exploration of anger, this book is a prescription for overcoming hidden aggression and finding lasting happiness."

—SCOTT HALTZMAN, MD,
author of *The Secrets of Happily Married Men*

■

"You will find many of the people you work with every day described in this book, and Murphy and Oberlin explain why they behave as they do and how you should respond. *Overcoming Passive-Aggression* offers important insights and helpful advice for the business reader."

—WILLIAM C. BYHAM, PhD, chairman and CEO of
Development Dimensions International, Inc.

■

"This thoughtful and thorough understanding of hidden anger is a much-needed resource that can be helpful not only for parents, but teachers as well."

—BILL ISLER, president, and HEDDA SHARAPAN, director of
Early Childhood Initiatives, Family Communications, Inc.,
and producers of *Mister Rogers' Neighborhood*

ABOUT THE AUTHORS

Dr. Tim Murphy is a U. S. congressman and a psychologist in his hometown of Pittsburgh, Pennsylvania. With more than twenty-five years clinical experience, he has been affiliated with numerous hospitals and has had a private practice. Dr. Murphy holds two adjunct associate professor positions in pediatrics at the University of Pittsburgh School of Medicine and in the School of Public Health. He earned his PhD in psychology in 1979 from the University of Pittsburgh.

In 1996, Dr. Murphy was elected to the Pennsylvania State Senate, as one of the few psychologists nationwide elected to a state legislature. In 2002, Senator Murphy was elected to the U.S. Congress. He currently is the cochair of the Congressional Mental Health Caucus, cochair of the Congressional Health Care Caucus, and serves on the Committee on Energy and Commerce, where he works on healthcare issues. In March 2005, the American Psychological Association recognized Dr. Murphy for his outstanding leadership on mental health issues.

Following terrorist attacks and school shootings, Dr. Murphy was quoted in *USA Today* regarding anthrax anxiety, interviewed by national reporters, and wrote a paper about children's reactions, displayed on various Web sites. He's been featured on many talk shows and news programs including MSNBC, *Fox News, Focus on the Family,* and the CBS *Early Show.* He served as the discipline pro on oxygen.com and has offered commentary in *Parenting, Redbook,* the *Washington Post,* and many other leading publications. He cowrote *The Angry Child,* released in 2001, with Ms. Oberlin. Their book won the National Parenting Publications Gold Award.

Prior to his entry into public service, he became widely known in "Ask Dr. Tim" segments on regional television and radio appearances. He has a wife and daughter, and resides in suburban Pittsburgh.

Loriann Hoff Oberlin is an accomplished writer and author who contributes to major magazines and newspapers. Her successful book *Surviving Separation and Divorce,* written to encourage women, was released in its second edition in 2005, and she cowrote *The Angry Child* with Dr. Murphy in 2001. She's written five other books.

Ms. Oberlin has also contributed hundreds of articles in her career, now specializing in parenting, relationships, and health topics. She served as the divorce pro on oxygen.com. Ms. Oberlin writes a "Family Answers" column for regional parenting publications, and her column on balancing work and family appeared in the *Pittsburgh Business Times.* While working on this project, she was a graduate student pursuing her master's degree in clinical counseling at Johns Hopkins University in Maryland. She's a member of the National Council on Family Relations, a nonprofit organization devoted to family life education, and she's a member of the American Counseling Association.

In addition, Ms. Oberlin encourages others to write through bookstore workshops, online teaching, and her book *Writing for Quick Cash.* She's appeared on numerous radio and television news and talk show segments, including the CNN *Morning News* and *Sally Jesse Raphael.* She resides with her husband and two sons outside Washington, D.C. in suburban Maryland. Her Web site is www.loriannoberlin.com.

Overcoming
PASSIVE-AGGRESSION

Overcoming
PASSIVE-
AGGRESSION

HOW TO STOP

HIDDEN ANGER FROM

SPOILING YOUR

RELATIONSHIPS, CAREER

AND HAPPINESS

DR. TIM MURPHY *and*
LORIANN HOFF OBERLIN

MARLOWE & COMPANY
NEW YORK

OVERCOMING PASSIVE-AGGRESSION:
*How to Stop Hidden Anger from Spoiling Your
Relationships, Career and Happiness*

Copyright © 2005 Loriann Oberlin
and Tim Murphy

Published by
Marlowe & Company
An Imprint of Avalon Publishing Group Incorporated
245 West 17th Street • 11th floor
New York, NY 10011

AVALON
publishing group incorporated

Library of Congress Cataloging-in-Publication Data is available

ISBN 1-56924-361-1
ISBN-13: 978-1-56924-361-9

9 8 7 6 5 4 3 2 1

Designed by Pauline Neuwirth, Neuwirth & Associates, Inc.

Printed in the United States of America

The insights presented in this book stem from a variety of sources, including research of the literature already written about this topic; the former psychological practice of Dr. Tim Murphy; questions posed to us after our first collaboration, *The Angry Child;* and our own life and professional experiences.

All of the anecdotes in this book are composites, often based upon two or three persons, taken from real-life experiences, interpersonal, workplace, or school-related problems, and a few have been entirely created to help explain certain concepts. Fictitious names and details have been added, and any identifying information has been substantially changed to protect confidentiality. Any similarities between the anecdotes presented in this book and any actual person, living or deceased, is entirely coincidental.

We wish to make it clear that this book is not meant to be a substitute for professional counseling or psychological help. It's our intent to raise awareness of problematic behaviors and further every person's ability to express his or her thoughts and feelings, including anger, in appropriate, healthy, and productive ways. We hope that this book will help in that process.

To our families and friends

CONTENTS

Introduction   XV

PART 1   **WHAT IS PASSIVE-AGGRESSION AND WHY IS IT SO BAD?**   1

ONE   *Passive-Aggression and Hidden Anger*   3
TWO   *Understanding the Problems Associated*   25
          with Concealed Emotions
THREE   *The Childhood Roots of Passive-Aggression*   41

PART 2   **PASSIVE-AGGRESSION IN DIFFERENT SETTINGS**   57

FOUR   *Coping with Hidden Anger at Work and School*   59
FIVE   *Recognizing Hidden Anger in Couples and Marriage*   83
SIX   *Dealing with Hidden Anger in Families*   103
SEVEN   *Facing Hidden Anger in Fractured Relationships*   125

PART 3   **SOLVING THE HIDDEN ANGER PROBLEM**   141

EIGHT   *Understanding Anger as a Deeper Disorder*   143
NINE   *Ending All Enabling*   163
TEN   *Rewriting Your Own Anger Script*   187

APPENDIX   *Research Regarding Passive-Aggression*   211
               Chapter Notes and Additional Resources   221
               Acknowledgments   229
               Index   233

INTRODUCTION

AFTER MORE THAN twenty-five years practicing psychology, people often ask me how my work as a member of the U.S. House of Representatives compares. Beyond the challenge and great reward in my work, the two roles aren't all that different. When practicing psychology, I often listened to heartfelt concerns and mediated my share of family squabbles. Congress has its own share of squabbles as well, but when the participants share the common goal of solving problems, it functions at its best. Anyone can get dysfunctional pretty quickly with a goal to hurt, destroy, or otherwise make someone's life miserable. And that's when the system breaks down.

In Washington, there's a public perception that there is far too much anger and meanness. I can't dispute that. It's true. Most people in Washington are trying to do the right thing, despite their disagreements on how to accomplish that. Unfortunately, there are also some caught up in the politics of power.

While I can make light of sitting through, at times contentious debates, in all sincerity I'm thankful for men and women who wish to work out problems and for the debate, discussion, and open exchange of ideas because my training reminds me of the alternative.

When views aren't expressed in an atmosphere of trust, people hide their beliefs, emotions, and actions, and sometimes work to undermine progress. Games of intrigue, deception, and downright nastiness can be the tragic outcome when goals of power, destruction, and anger overcome reason. Revolution doesn't work; resolution by reason does. That's the legislator in me talking.

As a psychologist, I'd tell you that far too many people don't exercise the freedom to speak up or do so in ways that undermine hope. They lead incongruent, often miserable lives because they hide their anger and act in a way we term passive-aggressive. We've all experienced this, and we're all a bit guilty because of our own human frailties. But I honestly believe we can overcome any residual anger.

When Loriann and I wrote *The Angry Child* readers thanked us because it helped parents and educators reach out to children, turning around problematic behaviors. Adults have their own anger problems that ruin lives. Sometimes they express that anger in very visible, and horrific, ways. Portraits of anger that simmer just below the surface, however, have an equal potential to ruin relationships, disrupt school or productive work, and plummet cheerful people into irritable confusion. Disguising anger with seemingly civil words hurts just as much, even though to many, it may not be as easily recognized. The net result with those who can't talk through their anguish is years of stored grudges, negativity, ambivalence, and underhanded behavior. Think it doesn't affect you? We'll prove that it does.

Overcoming Passive-Aggression: How to Stop Hidden Anger from Spoiling Your Relationships, Work, and Happiness unravels this well-concealed bitterness. Today, it's getting far worse. It undermines the workplace, breaks up families, and just plain makes life miserable. The nastiest thing about hidden anger is that it sneaks up on you. When someone threatens to strike out at you like a poisonous rattlesnake, you have an opportunity to stay clear. But hidden anger comes at you in sneaky ways, much like a boa constrictor that gradually tightens its grip until it's too late for you to get away.

We'll define hidden anger and examine its core issues, childhood origins, and adult implications. We reach out to all angry souls regardless of age. This book is for parents troubled by angry children, and older children troubled by their angry parents. It's for those on the job who deal with coworkers who annoy or sabotage their efforts; bosses, with their hidden agendas; and clients or customers who take their anger out on us. This book is for educators because they know how, over time, teaching a passive-aggressive student becomes confusing and discouraging. Some have had their careers ruined by students' manipulative behavior.

Our goal is to further everyone's awareness of their own—and other people's—hidden anger so that we can all be more productive, free of cloaked hostility, mixed messages, and buried talent and thought. It's liberating to become assertive as opposed to conniving or concealing, not to mention, it benefits your physical and mental health.

I can tell you firsthand how liberating it feels to speak up, and yes, sometimes take risks that maybe your ideas, even your frustrations, will be rejected. But maybe you'll truly make a difference. Rather than react negatively to my own frustration with policies I deemed inappropriate in some "I'm mad as hell and I'm not going to take it any more" kind of way, I ran for office, leaving a satisfying and financially rewarding private practice behind. I look at my role in Congress as helping people in a different way. I stand up for my beliefs, and I provide a voice for my constituents. For that, I'm very glad.

So there you go. Look deep enough into any of group of people, and you'll find some semblance of inner struggle and anger. American history is filled with examples, like that between Alexander Hamilton and Aaron Burr, or between John Adams and Thomas Jefferson. Hamilton and Burr fought a duel that ended in one's death and the other's failure. Adams and Jefferson, on the other hand, resolved their problems. In each case, America was robbed of their tremendous talent while they wasted their energy on anger, not creativity. This problem is very much alive in our present culture with the same bad outcomes, unless we choose to control it rather than let it control us.

Step by step you can eradicate problematic behavior with self-awareness, knowledge, problem solving and communication, and a few other decisions along the way. If you've experienced passive-aggression or hidden anger, start reading this book knowing that it's an all-important first step to leading a happier, healthier, more expressive life.

—Dr. Tim Murphy

◆

I FIRST MET Dr. Tim Murphy in the early 1990s when a colleague said he was in the beginning stages of a project that would become *The Angry Child*. I knew then that his high energy and passion for his work would take him far. In western Pennsylvania, his expertise garnered him the guest psychologist post on talk radio, "Ask Dr. Tim" segments on television, and print contributions in parenting publications. He was the first knowledgeable source that news reporters, lawyers, judges, educators, and parents would call when they had a question about child, family, and relationship issues. Once Dr. Murphy stepped up to the national stage as Congressman Murphy, national media began asking for his assessment of breaking news and human behavior.

This book is rooted in Dr. Murphy's clinical practice, our collective experiences, and much study. For the most part, it's written in both our voices, but occasionally it will reflect his work. Because we write about both genders, we'll alternate pronouns, sometimes using *he*, other times *she*. We think this book will help you immeasurably. Writing about anger management, I've recognized just how much bitterness exists on the periphery of some people's lives. We all have the capacity to get a little steamed at times. If you haven't experienced anger yourself, or witnessed someone else's struggle, check your pulse. Anger is common.

Unfortunately, understanding anger is terribly *un*common. The late Fred Rogers sang, "What do you do with the mad that you feel when you feel so mad you could bite?" Rogers tackled anger because he recognized what a powerful emotion it was, and how children yearned for healthy, safe ways of expressing it. Rogers was onto something. We all ought to learn better ways of managing "the mad we feel," instead of storing it or reacting to it, as is too often the case.

After you've read *Overcoming Passive-Aggression,* I think your own reactions will change. I know by writing this book and gaining more knowledge about a confusing behavior, my own reactions to people and situations have evolved. I make fewer mistakes with anger or passive-aggressive people, and for sure I've identified buttons that I may have unwittingly allowed others to push. In the pages ahead, we'll offer composite sketches of angry individuals and situations. Rest assured, if you recognize any of the material or situations, it's purely by coincidence because in many cases, your struggle is someone else's as well.

No one likes to admit that he's angry or drawn into someone else's bitter battle, but as we've said before, if you've done something that has contributed to your anger or enabled it to come your way, then you have greater power, with that insight, to become a part of the happier solution and move forward.

—LORIANN HOFF OBERLIN

What is Passive-Aggression and Why Is it So Bad?

ONE

PASSIVE-AGGRESSION AND HIDDEN ANGER

B EN COMPLAINED THAT he was passed over for promotions. His boss said, "You don't seem to be able to handle the responsibility." But Ben complained more, and the boss finally gave him a small project to work on as a chance to show his abilities.

This project, unbeknownst to Ben as the test case, sat on his desk collecting dust. When the boss complained that he didn't have it on time, Ben replied, "You didn't tell me when it was due. And besides, I had to finish my other work, too." Inside, Ben was pleased he got back at the boss by making him unprepared for a meeting. But guess who still didn't get a promotion? Well, of course, Ben, who attributed this to his boss's incompetence rather than his own. With lack of action, Ben created a problem, felt like a victim, and got back at his boss. Rejection, resentment, and revenge all stemmed from doing nothing.

Such is the case with many passive-aggressive people. You wouldn't commonly think that Ben was bitter or negative, on the surface at least. Ben's procrastination could well have resulted from a number of things. Throughout this book, we'll show you how to distinguish between people hiding their anger and those honestly making foolish mistakes.

Anger, always triggered by some other powerful emotion, resides in all of us. You have the choice to work through it, control it, and move past it. Mounting research reflecting decades of study concludes: Those who are happy live longer, enjoying productive and satisfying lives; those who don't live in a fairly miserable state. If anger is unremitting, it can be deadly.[1]

If you or someone you know harbors anger, not as a temporary state but as a permanent (even semipermanent) trait, count upon seeing not only clouds but also storms—clashes with other people, more than the ordinary challenges at work, and when it comes to romance, forget a dozen roses, except maybe for the thorns. Intimate relationships will likely become mired in ambivalence and constant struggle. Anger can precipitate the decline of one's mental health, and it surely compromises physical health as we will elaborate upon in the next chapter.

You think we're wrong? Keep reading this book. In these pages, we will unravel the differences between open anger and that which remains hidden. We will define, explain, and unravel the term passive-aggression, citing its weary hold upon people in friendships, marriages, and other family settings; within the workplace and school; and even behind the doors of therapy sessions. As we see things, hidden anger encompasses much more than passive-aggressive behavior, but by far, passive-aggression is the most familiar term, and so we provide it center stage throughout this book. Self-absorption, chronic depression, strong personality traits or disorders, and other conditions prove equally troublesome sidetracking relationships, career success, and overall contentment. We will help you to see inside the mind of a person who can't let go of such problematic behavior, and we'll show you how a bitter person inflicts such hostility upon you, often without your ever knowing it.

AGGRESSIVE ANGER VS. HIDDEN ANGER

IT'S SOMETIMES OKAY to be angry, but it's never okay to be mean. This applies to all kinds of anger. Aggressive anger is powerful, visible, and immediate. Aggressive anger takes the form of a threat, scream, or physical blow, breaking or destroying something. There is another type, however, that sneaks up on us both in our using it and in others using it against us. It can be subtle and covert, and not as easy to spot as aggressive anger. Hidden anger, because it is cloaked and disguised, may take time to effect its true damage.

In other words, the immediate consequences of hidden anger aren't often apparent. This is especially the case with passive-aggression, where anger is secretly expressed but in an outwardly docile way. Passive-aggression often manifests in *not* doing some required or helpful action. It might take the form of forgetting to pick you up on time, not putting money in the meter so that you get a fine, losing your keys so that you're inconvenienced, delaying the report to the last minute until you have no choice but to present material unrehearsed. Hidden anger may cause you to incur a finance charge that will irritate your spouse, or it might take the form of mailing a child support payment late, remaining silent when someone is waiting for your answer, or not filling the car with gas. It might also look half-right, half-wrong, like filing the report in the wrong drawer so it's as good as lost.

The tenet we cited—that anger is sometimes okay but should never be mean—was what we wrote about in *The Angry Child.* As a psychologist, I've often used it as a reminder with children and adults alike. Whether in a political campaign, in the corporate boardroom, in your cubicle, at the dinner table, or in the school cafeteria, anger and how we express it is a meaningful barometer of what's going on in our lives.

DEFINING HIDDEN ANGER

ANGER ISN'T ALWAYS the demon most of us might think it is. In *The Angry Child,* we presented our own definition to take the sting out of the topic: "Anger is a powerful response triggered by another negative emotion, which results in an attack of variable intensity that is not always appropriate."[2]

Hidden anger has some of these same components, but before we move forward, we want to share another new definition to help you truly embrace this concept, as well as offer character sketches of what we're talking about. Hidden anger is:

- Indirect, incongruent, and unproductive behavior
- Subtle, manipulative actions or inactivity
- Consciously planned, intentional, or slyly vindictive; or it can be unconscious
- Part of a dysfunctional pattern of dealing with others
- Allowing the perpetrator to deny responsibility for it and often appear as the victim
- Stalling because it doesn't move toward resolution; it blocks resolution
- Motivated by the intent to hurt, annoy, or destroy
- Triggered by needs that haven't been met or based upon irrational fears/beliefs
- Never positive because of its manipulative and indirect nature
- Toxic to relationships and groups of people, especially over time
- Self-perpetuating, powerful, and rarely, if ever, appropriate

Rest assured, if hidden anger is unleashed upon you, you will likely end up feeling like the bad character. You know there is a problem. You can sense it.

Only, it nags at you because you're not sure who is responsible, why it's happening, and what to do about it. Often, it's socially acceptable and excused for many reasons. Passive-aggressive people possess some keen skills, with manipulation at the top of the list. They have handy alibis and display a cunning charm at times. Ignorant of what's truly happening with this passive-aggressive person, others grant her many free passes for her behavior until they catch on, challenge her, or hold her accountable. A teacher, a boss, a doctor, a judge, even a loved one essentially gives the passive-aggressor the benefit of the doubt. Not until passive-aggressors slip up, forget to cover their tracks, or simply accrue too much reasonable doubt are they taken to task. Never wishing to fall from others' graces, they offer more excuses or explanations to keep socially masking their true intent with phrases like "It's not my fault I forgot" or "You should have told me."

Over the years since this phenomenon was first identified and labeled, mental health researchers have revised their theories and nomenclature to describe this maddening behavior and to explain why those on the receiving end have trouble determining whether it's intentional or not. Words like *ambivalent*, *negative*, and *oppositional* have appeared within the definition of passive-aggression as we'll explain. Actually, they all have their place and justifiably help to describe what happens. For instance, the passive-aggressor vacillates between wishing for independence and depending upon others. The person may say he'd like to take a more active role at work (or at home) but veers away from responsibility when given the opportunity for action, much like Ben at the start of this chapter. The "dirty trick" or underhanded tactics used by some passive-aggressive people account for the negativity, and playing the game of retaliatory "get back" through obstruction or resistance is most assuredly oppositional.

Passive-aggression, part of the bigger picture of hidden anger, can be associated with some or all of the following:

- Chronic irritability and chronic depression
- Self-absorption/narcissism/vanity (an entitlement personality)
- Low self-esteem
- Self-destructive behavior or acting out
- Substance abuse and addictive behavior
- Unacceptable conduct that's excused for many reasons

Something else incites or sparks anger because anger is a reaction to some other event or emotion. At times, anger can serve a useful or valuable purpose, especially if there is positive intent and outcome. If you're protecting yourself when you hide your anger, or if you're trying to focus on solving a problem, then anger may be useful. It may cause you to express yourself in healthy, honest, and direct communication (productive anger), rather than through manipulation, passivity, or avoidance (unproductive anger).

Let's stop to put human faces and circumstances to this new definition of hidden anger, looking especially at the outcome and the intent, and trying to gain insight. Watch for key words that relate to our new definition. See if these portraits describe anyone you know.

■ **CASE #1** ■

The Disconnected Couple

Imagine counting on your spouse to help you snag that dream job and top salary that might lead to the house down payment you need. Since you have to get your daughter ready for daycare, you ask your husband Jim to drop your cover letter and résumé in the morning mail as he walks down the street. You are never called for an interview because . . . Jim forgot to mail the résumé until weeks later. At least, he claims this when you're never called for an interview, and you later find that the company received it postmarked three weeks beyond the application deadline.

This might appear on the surface to be an honest mistake that anyone could make, but if Jim's own career is stagnant and unfulfilled, leaving him jealous, threatened, and unable to express these feelings, then the intent of his forgetfulness becomes questionable. See how innocent Jim's forgetfulness was on the surface, with no physical evidence of assault here, nothing outside of behavior that frustrated his wife. We'll see, as we unravel the needs, fears, and avoidances of hidden anger, why these are crucial elements to spot, and why if Jim kept thwarting his wife's success (i.e., by calling with upsetting news just before yet another interview) and denying his own torment, it might have powerful and ruinous effects on their relationship over time. It could prove to be vindictive, disguised by a seductive veneer.

■ **CASE #2** ■

The Intolerable Boss

You don't know extensive background about your boss, only that the last manager left of her own accord for a new position and new company. All you see is that your boss makes impossible demands, piling on the work, deadlines, and business travel, but never the right resources. What's more, the corporate promotion culture requires you to be visible at meetings and to serve on various workplace committees. If you're constantly off the premises, out of sight, you're literally out of mind as well when promotions draw near. Yet if you ask to hire additional staff to ease the crunch, and you request less travel in order to meet the office expectations, your boss sees you as demanding, claiming that "you can't work under pressure." Sure enough, the fellow in the next cubicle gets that coveted promotion, and your mood, not to mention motivation, plummet. It might be easy to think you *are* the problem. Is this passive-aggression or are you the victim of a disorganized, dysfunctional office?

If you've been in a similar situation, you know the risk of responding with your own anger. If you retaliate in a way that gets turned back on you, you may look like the fool, and it may hurt your reputation at work. On the other hand, if you step back and see it as an organizational problem, you might be able to improve the office system.

■ CASE #3 ■

The Self-Absorbed Family Member

Every Christmas, you, your two siblings, and a cousin of yours get together. Cousin Cassidy, a successful professional woman, makes a grand entrance with armloads of gifts, expecting just as many on her exit. She might give your sister a new kitchen appliance like a cappuccino machine, your brother and brother-in-law designer sweaters, and their children some much-hoped-for toys. When it's your turn, you open a box of chocolates (and we're *not* talking Godiva), despite the well-known fact that you're watching your weight. Your daughter, like most children, also had a Christmas wish list, but her surprise from Cousin Cassidy is a knit cap. When you realize that the cap came from Cassidy's own company, you know darn well she didn't spend a dime on it. What's worse? You live in Florida. When the little girl utters a less than enthusiastic thank you, Cassidy lays into you with a lecture about ungrateful children and poor parenting today, and tops it off by asking, "Where's my gift?"

If Cassidy has the reputation of never really giving to you but expecting different treatment for herself, you have a right to be annoyed. If she expects to stay in your guest room when breezing through town but pointed you to a Marriott down the street (that she knew you couldn't afford) the one time you were in her city, you'd be correct deeming her to be self-centered. Further, if in Cassidy's mind she has some childhood score to settle with you but takes it out on your children, then it's not merely indirect and hostile, but triggered by something much deeper. What was missing from Cassidy's childhood that causes her to act this way?

■ CASE #4 ■

The Unmotivated Student

Amy, your teenage daughter, energetically moves through high school with great gusto: National Honor Society her junior year; cheerleading captain next year. An A average. Her friend Stephanie is also quite active in marching band, honor society, the debate team and lacrosse, where she might even qualify for a scholarship.

Their friend Melissa is totally different, devoid of activities and achievements, struggling to get an occasional report-card B. Though smart and pretty, Melissa tells friends that she thinks she'll never get a date, and she doesn't have time for after-school activities. Amy and Stephanie can't figure out why Melissa is continually down on herself, can't say a kind word about the teachers, and seems like such a sad sack. After she breaks down in tears during lunch, Amy and Stephanie take time to console her and end up late for math once again. That's when they stop feeling sorry for her. Why should they pay a price for her misery? If Melissa can't help herself, why should they?

Melissa gets lots of attention for being moody. She's able to draw energy to herself, rather than generate it and embrace life as her friends do. Here, we see more depression, low self-esteem, negativity, ambivalence, and resistance, to the point that it's made Amy and Stephanie irritable, feeling exploited and generally angry.

These different scenarios—a forgetful husband, a demanding boss, a self-absorbed, subtly hostile cousin, and a sad, lethargic teenager—illustrate hidden anger, especially since there's a persistent pattern of indirect, often manipulative, behavior. Sometimes it's very intentional, and other times, it can remain hidden even from the perpetrator unaware of his own frustrations. In most of these examples, the perpetrator can escape blame or responsibility. "I just forgot," the husband could say of the résumé not mailed. "Your coworker deserved the promotion," your boss might say.

Cousin Cassidy could claim she got the winter hat because "I thought it would look nice on her." And Melissa could plead, "I didn't know you had a test that day. I'm so sorry. You were so nice, and I made you miserable. Please forgive me," even though her actions might clearly have "guilted" her girlfriends into minding her misery.

In the third example, if Cassidy's discharging her anger through her parenting lecture pushed your buttons enough to say something negative back to her, Cassidy could most likely retract it with, "I was *just* joking," "I didn't *really* mean it," or "You're *so* sensitive." That's because people who conceal their inner angry feelings say these things to save face, to be socially accepted because acceptance is a core need for them. Passive-aggressive people are slick, wise in the ways of brushing off the blame. You retaliate, and now they're the misunderstood victim. They win on two counts because now they've been so smooth as to gain attention twice for themselves, and they've dumped their anger on you, to boot. Even if they are not totally aware of how and why they're behaving, they're well rehearsed and get results.

Vacillation is also a key component. Too often a person who hides his anger does so because he can't really make up his mind. Should I depend upon this person or need him? But isn't it wonderful that I'm out on my own, independent, free at last, and better than him, too! In Jim's case, it might be hard to decide whether he minds his wife's success or feels threatened by it. Every time he buys into her getting ahead, some dependent, passive part of him wants to get back at his wife for her active, independent life. So he plays a dirty trick to obstruct her. Yet Jim needs his wife, wants her to think well of him, so no, he can't possibly tell her he's a little jealous (or a lot). Does this "I like you/I don't" feeling describe any relationship you're in?

AN UNWELCOME TARGET

ANGER NEVER EXISTS in a vacuum. There's usually a target. Victims of another person's wrath know firsthand how unsettling veiled hostility can be, how it can cause a worker to want to change jobs or careers, or incite a spouse to leave a marriage. I've counseled enough children to know the true hurt and confusion it can cause when perpetrated by parents. I truly believe that when children are old enough to gain their own insights into problems, they'll see any negative light parents may be trying to conceal. That became evident once with a teenage girl when she felt her mom had ruined her prom. With much anticipation, this girl opened her closet the day of the prom to find that her mother had not taken the dress she'd bought to be altered, as she'd promised. A good three inches of delicate material had needed to be hemmed. With tears in her eyes, this girl and her friend hastily did what they could to make the gown wearable that evening with a few stitches here and there, costing them needless time, frustration, and anxiety that afternoon. When she called her mom at work teary-eyed, her mother had a lame excuse, acting as if it weren't a big deal and offering an unworkable solution—"We can pin it up and no one will notice"—along with a guilt-trap line "I've been working so hard to make the money that paid for that dress."

"On the night of the prom!" this girl cried into the phone, and she reiterated as much in my office. She told me how self-conscious she was all through that evening about the dress. What wasn't a big deal to mom clearly was to her daughter. She had witnessed some of this classic passive-aggression before, only she had no real understanding of it except that mom infuriated her. This was not an event she'd soon forget, and moving forward, she was much less likely to trust mom with anything important. Not only, then, is the parent/child bond damaged, but when parents model hidden anger repeatedly, a child is at great risk for mismanaging her own anger.

This raises the question, how do you know when someone is being passive-aggressive or when he truly is overwhelmed and forgetful or maybe honestly miscalculated and made a mistake? There's no easy answer. Essentially, you must watch and learn over time. In this last case, the girl had conveyed the past poor behavior of her mother, who did seem to have some anger issues as a parent. Repeated behavior forms a pattern that speaks volumes about a person's motive and can help us to find some answers.

Say you have a forgetful person on your staff who not only made your airline reservation too late so that it left you with the middle seat way in the back, but also forgot to order the necessary materials for an important business meeting. A few days before the event, her mistake means wasted hours spent gathering last-minute, makeshift supplies that don't match, but they will now have to suffice. Is this person really incompetent? Forgetful? Well, if you know she's got proven talents on the job, excellent references, and received the memo with your request for this order four months ago, then you have reason to believe she might silently be exerting power and/or discharging some hidden anger.

As you read further, you'll learn about different actions and behaviors that, all told, might help you to draw a conclusion a lot faster. But be careful. Psychology is not a coherent, linear science. We're all learning how to be effective. Too often pop psychology says here's the cause of something, so therefore, here's the conclusion. It's simply not so smooth of a transition because one's own temperament, personality, and environment play a big role in shaping us. That said, a few incidents of forgetfulness, for instance, might mean something entirely different. In the classroom, if a teacher spots this, as well as impulsivity, blurting out answers, and falling off task, it might mean attention deficit hyperactivity disorder (ADHD), not passive-aggression at all. Forgetfulness in older adults frequently raises suspicions of Alzheimer's disease, another form of dementia, or a stress-filled lifestyle.

In the workplace, low morale indicates that there could be some hidden hostility. Take the case of the disgruntled worker who needs a job, yet isn't happy with his current position. He might be afraid of conducting a job search, and so remaining passive and staying with what is known versus what is unknown is easier—a way out of taking any risks.

You don't have to look too hard to see the ambivalence. Because the worker is stuck, and doesn't feel he can openly express his anger about it, he might intentionally do a lousy job, misfile items, or let errors slide until he infuriates or trips up his boss or coworkers. The cost of some errors or withholding can be terribly expensive, even deadly. Imagine important safety measures left off products or hazards created by consciously careless employees with a "get back" attitude toward their employer. When employees stage a work stoppage by calling in sick in droves, it's a rather passive-aggressive way of making a point, and could well backfire against their intentions.

Very often, inciting anger in another is the conscious or unconscious goal of people disguising their anger. Why? Because anger is so uncomfortable to them that they cast it onto another person, thereby getting to experience it vicariously, without having to take any responsibility. With no direct expression of anger, they can live comfortably without risking any consequences. Their fear is held in check. They try to have it both ways. They can remain passive and feel a sense of power at the same time by doing something slick. That's the aggressive part of the behavior.

We can apply this same premise to any anger concealer who is caught red-handed. She might use the common retort "I'm *not* angry!" Yet you've determined mean-spirited intent and have seen (and maybe felt) the poor outcome. Sure she was angry, but she feels compelled to deny it. To do otherwise stirs too many fears and forces her to confront what she puts great energy toward avoiding. If she admits openly to her true feelings, she might risk the relationship, and well . . . she can't do that because she's dependent upon this person.

When a person doesn't deny, he sometimes tries to retract an angry response with fence-mending words, by being contrite, or both. Occasionally, it's too late to repair the damage, for hidden anger can injure those he loves and works with, and ultimately, it destroys him in a vicious cycle as his life's plans and dreams go astray. Here, hidden anger is often the root cause of life's disappointments that may lie shrouded in excuses and blame the rest of someone's life, unless, of course, he gains new insight and a commitment to change. Sad but true, hidden anger becomes a commonly recurring theme or self-perpetuating prophecy.

WHOSE PROBLEM IS IT?

TRY TO REMEMBER a time when you had an ordinary discussion. You offered an opinion or broached a topic only to meet suddenly with fierce resistance or defensiveness—way out of proportion to your remark. Maybe you spoke of how someone hurt you, but your retelling the story takes this person back to a time in her own life, when perhaps she caused a similar problem for someone else. It hits a little close to home, triggering something powerful such as embarrassment, guilt, or another uncomfortable feeling as it did for the two women below.

Marianne was talking with Barbara, who lived the next street over, about life and people they knew. As the conversation shifted, as chatting often does, Marianne mentioned how hurtful her ex-husband's infidelity had been to live through. A passing remark—nothing more. Barbara suddenly became defensive and curt. Why did she turn on Marianne?

Without either woman realizing it, Barbara identified with Marianne because Barbara was once "the other woman" causing similar sorrow (to some other woman). She simply could not stand listening to Marianne because she wanted to squelch the discomfort. Barbara's options—since she felt she couldn't be honest without risking further embarrassment—were to become defensive, change the topic, or become standoffish so as to mask her feelings.

Situations like this occur all the time. When they do, it's helpful to remember, it's not about you (or in this case, not about Marianne); it's about the other person (Barbara). But whoever is on the receiving end of any icy tension feels a little annoyed because the reason remains hidden—the proverbial elephant in the room that no one dares to notice.

Determining some other root cause is the first piece of awareness. Don't take it personally. Second, you don't have to remain a target. Even if the angry person never becomes willing to change, if you gain insight into the problem, you can change *your* approach. So often victims of anger try diligently to fix a problem and make it go away. Yet some problems simply aren't within your grasp to solve. If you can't make any difference, then focus on what you can control: your reaction to anyone else's anger. Stay tuned for those strategies in chapters to follow. Meantime, never lose sight of how valuable your own insight is in extricating yourself from someone's angry battle. It's important to understand what others are doing so that you don't blame yourself for things you never did! This is particularly helpful if you realize that someone's anger problem runs pretty deep, as do many mental health conditions.

To summarize, you might discover someone has hidden anger or passive-aggression when he or she exhibits:

- Low frustration tolerance
- Impulsivity
- Markedly different character traits or a personality disorder
- Emotional or verbal abuse
- Physical signs of "losing it" or blowing the top off of the hostility canister
- A locked-step, dysfunctional dance with someone else
- Chronic irritability
- Low energy, passivity, and resentment of those who don't exhibit these things
- Low self-esteem
- Lifelong struggles and unhappiness

In fact, hidden anger may seem so normal to some that they'll resist any attempts to change. Healthy functioning remains a foreign concept, and they'd rather stick with what they know because, sadly enough, it often works for them. Their anger may qualify as a deeper disorder.

ANTICIPATED, APPROPRIATE ANGER

EARLIER WE EXPLAINED that the true indicator of whether hidden anger serves a purpose rests in its intent or whether it's developmentally expected. Here are a few scenarios where seeing some hidden anger wouldn't be too surprising or out of the ordinary:

- Self-protection or problem solving could justify concealing anger. Sometimes it's best to keep your feelings to yourself since no one cares that you've been inconvenienced, because it's polite or productive, or maybe you were wrong about the reasons you were angry in the first place. In a civil society, you don't always show your emotions to a clerk, coworker, or even a confidante. Self-control makes you a more pleasant person to be around. Feeling entitled to say or do whatever you feel is often just plain rude.

- Sarcastic comments as part of standup comedy might at first appear angry, but consider the source. The same applies if the talk-show host's shtick includes lobbing remarks at the celebrity *du jour* for the sake of entertainment. Sometimes sarcasm contains a hidden message that adults especially are intended to understand on a deeper level. Sometimes sarcasm crosses the line of good taste, though. When we use language or behavior to tear others down out of meanness, it's not appropriate at all.

- Unrelenting positions due to political debate or advocacy might appear as a stubborn stance, but refusal to back down in this case doesn't reflect a personality deficit but a commitment to lively debate. It could represent what's important in the current election or what constituents truly care about. On the other hand, if the person acts to destroy another, even if she knows what she's advocating is wrong, then it's angry, it's mean, and it's wrong. Again, you must account for motive and purpose, among other key factors.

- For teenagers, a certain level of rebellion comes with the territory, including procrastination, withholding, and avoidance. A child's covert antagonism is often a passing phase. Teenagers notoriously exhibit that push-pull that exemplifies the passive-aggressive person's dilemma. No longer a child yet a not quite a man or woman, the teen sends a host of mixed messages, among them "take care of me" but "leave me alone" or "I need money for a CD" but "I don't want to spend my time earning that money." It's as if they're saying, "I demand you give me responsibility! But not too much, please." It's a classic struggle between wanting to play an active role and enjoying the comforts of passivity.

We realize that this last mention isn't welcome news to some parents, but it's not typically an enduring part of childhood. Most teens develop a better repertoire of skills, becoming more confident and proactive. Only when a continued pattern of passivity, ambivalence, or obstructionism carries into adulthood does it point to a real problem.

PRODUCTIVE ANGER

BACK WHEN YOU were a student, how did you handle displeasure with your grades or a teacher? Anger's presence could have served as a catalyst for positive change and growth. It could have inspired you to get to know your teacher in a different way, so that you forged better relations and ultimately achieved a better outcome—better grades, in this case. If you discussed your grades, asked for guidance or tutoring, this could have had a more positive effect than lobbing an angry comment.

Now, replace *student* with *worker*. Then replace *teacher* with *boss*, and *grades* with *job performance* and quite possibly a raise or promotion. Or for that matter, replace *student* and *teacher* with Democratic or Republican party members, yielding a better outcome of effective legislation. One can get caught up in negative, pessimistic conspiracy theories and which party is right or wrong, or look for solutions that are best for the nation and constituents.

In any circumstances, the key ingredients are productive, honest expression and problem solving to avoid the consequences of an angry agenda, though often anger motivates us to begin this hard work. Think it's not hard? Tune into C-SPAN. Watch a tired parent and an even more exhausted child in the grocery checkout lane. Enter a corporate board room. Watch your office planning meeting. It's sure not easy, but working through anger sparks self-reflection as we clarify who we are, how we feel about something, what we will or will not tolerate, and how we will change things. Keep reading as we unravel how to do all of this.

HOW ARE THINGS IN YOUR LIFE?

TAKE A MINUTE to assess how you're doing. To complete this brief questionnaire, write down on a separate sheet of paper either "yes" or "no," regarding your own behavior. If you're tempted to write "sometimes," determine the frequency involved so that you can give each question a "yes" or a "no."

Of course, if you know a person well enough, you might be tempted to try answering from his or her viewpoint. Only that person knows the true answers, but if you're really troubled in a relationship with a friend, family member, colleague, boss, teacher, or someone else, attempting their perspective might help you to gauge the degree of difficulty you're having.

1. Was anger prohibited in your home as a child?
2. Did you (or do you) struggle to please your parents?
3. Would you describe your parents as having a negative attitude when you were growing up?
4. Do you take actions to protect the status quo?
5. Do you use brief answers or short phrases to express yourself?
6. Do you smile when you're actually frustrated?

7. Do others tell you about an interpersonal problem they think you have that you don't see?
8. Are you ever intentionally slow performing a request?
9. Do you tell others that you don't understand their requests or concerns so that they'll leave you alone?
10. When you disagree, do you feel less anxiety by silencing your frustration?
11. Do you see things mostly in black and white, with very little falling into the gray area in between?
12. If you see a coworker make a big mistake, do you keep quiet?
13. When afraid to share your opinion, do you later resent things not going your way?
14. Do you bristle when others criticize your work?
15. Do you soothe uncomfortable feelings with food, alcohol, drugs, sex, or gambling?
16. Do you often feel that problems you encounter are someone else's fault?
17. Do you continue an argument past its logical end?
18. Does the fear of rejection prevent you from taking action?
19. Do you feel that others can make better decisions than you can?
20. Have you ever turned in projects that contained errors or omissions that would cause problems for someone?
21. Do you yearn for more freedom in a relationship but at the same time wish to be close?
22. Have you had a hard time following the wishes of those in authority?
23. Do you resent someone telling you how to do a better job?
24. Do you experience a secret glee in maintaining an advantage over others?
25. Do you keep your feelings inside for so long that you eventually explode in unexpected outbursts?
26. When a person is too demanding of you, do you look for ways for him to fail?
27. Have you put your foot in someone's path because you resented that person's good fortune?

The purpose here is not to give you a definitive "score" as some quizzes do. Rather, it's to alert you to the presence of your own hidden anger, needs, fears, and things you might be avoiding. The more "yes" answers you have tallied, the more likely it is that you're concealing emotions, including anger. Concealing anger makes anyone much more apt to react inappropriately or in a passive-aggressive manner.

■

THOUGHTS, FEELINGS, AND ACTIONS MUST MATCH

CONGRUENCE—being consistent between how you feel and the way you act—is an important goal fostering honesty and communication. In other words, your thoughts, feelings, and actions should match and send the same messages. People who are incongruent may claim one thing and act in an altogether different manner. Essentially, they are hiding their true selves from others and sometimes from themselves. Feelings and actions need to resemble one another, but they also need to be appropriate (i.e., polite, mannerly) and within society's norms. The hungry screams of a young child are congruent (age linked with behavior), but the same behavior is terribly incongruent in a thirty-year-old man. Sending off mixed messages harms just about any relationship. It's like living a lie. So, make sure that you "walk your talk." This also goes a long way toward helping you become more expressive and assertive, in a positive way.

UNMASKING THE ANGER

ONE PROBLEM WITH understanding hidden anger is the vast territory we're covering. It's not a one-size-fits-all problem; at times, it's very complex. First, as long as anger remains hidden, we can't change it. Second, our goal is to acknowledge what a lot of angry people go to great lengths to conceal—that is, the core needs of angry people, what they fear or avoid, and what behavior comes out into the open. In order to shed light on a complex pattern of behavior, we've devised a visual block approach.

When we speak of an angry person's needs, we mean a deep-seated need that is almost obsessive in nature. With pervasively angry people, it borders on (or just plain is) pathological need. For instance, angry people who really need to control things may act differently than those who are depressed or those whose core need is to show off. After much thought, we outline five basic needs in various chapters:

- Control
- Manipulation
- Childlike/immature

- Self-absorption
- Depression

Yet, it's important to remember at the outset that you'll frequently find some overlap in the characteristics we outline. Passive-aggressive behavior is often born of the similar fears of being controlled or caught in confrontation, and the need to work around others more than with others. That same obsessive component applies to an angry person's fear and avoidance. We all have fears. Avoiding something uncomfortable doesn't necessarily mean you're an angry person. But here, we're talking about the extremes of fear and avoidance, to the point that you'll do just about anything to avoid expressing yourself because your faulty thinking leads you to believe that even a minor disagreement is akin to great conflict.

The third category we've blocked is what behavior you might commonly see in an anger-concealing person. As the sidebar "Thoughts, Feelings, and Actions Must Match" indicates, what you see isn't always what the angry person intends. Reading our descriptions won't be easy at times, but our unmasking hidden anger will provide a better chance to resolve, control, and change that anger. You've likely heard the sage advice that the first step toward change begins with insight. Well, it sure does. That said, not all of what we outline applies to every passive-aggressive, secretly angry person.

We hope readers have a few "aha" moments, when something suddenly fits with theory. We'll also try to be sensitive with the wording because we know that labels don't help matters, yet we do need language to describe the problem. That's why we prefer the term *anger concealer* or *anger-concealing person* because not all hidden anger comes forth in passive-aggressive behavior. We'll try to make tough material as palatable as possible, too, allowing those who want more technical information to peruse the appendix and chapter notes.

■

HOPE AHEAD

PEOPLE can change. We honestly believe this. But they usually change when it's become too difficult to remain as they are—in this case, secretly angry—and when there is a benefit to change. We'll nudge you to see those benefits, and if you're reading this book because someone's behavior has bothered you, then we'll help you to see how you may have, even unwittingly, contributed to some of the misery that comes your way. Don't worry if it seems hard to remember everything we unravel at once. You won't master this in one reading, but true to the complex nature of hidden anger, everything takes time to reveal itself!

THE NEED TO CONTROL

DOUGLAS IS A manager in the regional chapter of a nonprofit organization. As much as he'd like to have the top-performing chapter, Douglas hasn't made much happen during his tenure. With donations down and a higher-than-normal employee turnover, the national office has sent a team of consultants to recommend improvements. Since he's afraid of being blamed for the problems, yet yearns to be successful, what do you think Douglas's response will be to an outside team conducting this audit?

It's *not* going to go so well! Douglas, like others who resist change they cannot control, may even undermine attempts to improve the workplace. The motto: "I can do it better my way."

CONTROL

WHEN PEOPLE YEARN to control a situation, they rarely reflect upon what's really going on. Here, we've outlined the needs, fears, and things people avoid when you see controlling-type behavior.

NEEDS	FEARS/AVOIDS	WHAT YOU SEE
■ To have upper hand	■ Taking chances, risks	■ Black-and-white thinking
■ To be in control	■ Being hurt or blamed	■ Stalwart refusal, sees requests as demands, shuts down
■ Success	■ Failure and competition	■ No progress, no promotions at work (sometimes but not always)
	■ Dependence	■ Maintains safe status quo
	■ Losing control	■ Eating disorders

Nothing is wrong with success, but here Douglas has a much deeper need to succeed that drives him to operate in rather counterproductive ways. His own personal need to succeed above all else causes faulty thinking. He forgets that the organization must succeed in order for him to advance his own agenda. Collectively, Douglas's needs and fears cause him to shut down instead of cooperate. It's happened throughout his life, actually, and sure enough, it's likely to happen again with these auditors.

We might commonly think that a person like Douglas, who needs control over his life, would be a proactive person, taking on new challenges and climbing the corporate ladder with a glint in his eye. But if he doesn't feel able to express himself and has learned to suppress his own needs, he may very well stick with the status quo. When there's also an underlying fear of failure or not measuring up, this person takes few risks. Why? The more risks he takes, the more chances of being disappointed or hurt.

People like Douglas are stuck, and remaining stuck for any length of time often fosters anger. These folks function best in jobs that require sticking to the rules. These aren't the go-getters or the movers and shakers. They function well in steady jobs where you can rely upon them to always do the same things, but they don't do well in management taking risks, stepping up if some crisis occurs, or being open to new approaches (instead thinking rigidly).

THE NEED TO MANIPULATE

IMAGINE THAT YOU'RE at an important company meeting for which you and your coworkers have prepared for months. Ready to begin your PowerPoint presentation, you find that Mark, one of your colleagues, never updated it as you requested. If you blow this speech, you risk ridicule and bad press. In front of the others, Mark comes across as innocent, apologetic even, as if you'd never conveyed the urgency of the updates. You know what it's been like working with Mark, however. He's never very direct and seems to have a lot of insecurities. It's just like him to make you look bad to boost his own weak self-esteem. Mark's need to win isn't about ordinary success; it's about causing enough trouble that he looks better than anyone else in the office. His error has your blood boiling and leaves you floundering to regroup. You can't help but suspect that this was far more than an oversight. He's so sly, though, that you just can't prove it. People like Mark cop an excuse quite easily, and the sad part is that others actually believe them!

MANIPULATION

WHEN PEOPLE TRY to effect a certain outcome, others begin to feel swayed or pressured. It's easy to get angry in such a situation unless you can unravel what's behind the behavior—what the person needs, what she fears, or what she avoids.

NEEDS	FEARS/AVOIDS	WHAT YOU SEE
▪ To manipulate or control the outcome or the process	▪ Uncertainty	▪ Sets up situations for selfish gain, engages in sabotage
▪ To win, to have fun through fighting/hurting	▪ Having to cooperate, give and take; having to deal with others' expectations, needs, or concerns	▪ Plots, schemes to win, demands
▪ To push people's buttons, to exact revenge	▪ Authority, perceived or real	▪ Litigates not mediates
▪ To set agenda	▪ Confrontation	▪ Fights for sport of it, to win or to hurt
▪ To hide true emotions	▪ Being found out	▪ Crafts others' responses
▪ To blame, to find fault	▪ Intimacy, dependency	▪ Vengeance, often plays "get back"
▪ To be intentionally ineffective, independence	▪ Guilt, self-blame	▪ Lacks internal brakes, impulsive
▪ To keep responsibility at bay	▪ Admission of the problem or any anger	▪ Defies authority, resists, purposely stalls, thwarts preset plans, obstructs
	▪ Responsibility	▪ Lack of cooperation, problem solving
		▪ Denies, criticizes, harasses, "guilts" into
		▪ Much incongruence (thoughts, feelings, words, actions do not match)
		▪ "My way or the highway," not a big-picture person or team player
		▪ Evokes guilt or reactive anger in others

The worker who sabotages a product, "forgets" to grease the machinery, or allows a mistake to slip through the assembly line is the worker who knowingly understood that the error would result in the machine's malfunction. If this machine is a piece of farm equipment, lawnmower, or automobile, imagine the ramifications. To the angry worker, it doesn't matter if someone else might get hurt. What matters is getting even.

Here, the worker aims to take revenge (his need) because he fears authority figures (namely his boss) and usually has trouble confronting and/or cooperating (the fear). The results of this worker's fear and avoidance are plotting, scheming, vengeance, defying authority, obstructing safe manufacturing, poor problem solving, and very much an attitude of "I'll show them," a get-back behavior. When angry, he's riled up with no internal mechanism to slow down the force of his fury. We colloquially call this lacking internal brakes or being impulsive.

What's the motive behind "blue flu," the Monday-morning migraine, or a massive employee sickout? Why do people try to beat the system, like abusing the Family Medical Leave Act or finding ways to get worker's compensation? Why does someone taint their own food, report it to the media, and sue the company? Why do people become intentionally ineffective?

Revenge? Anger? If it costs them their jobs, brings bad press, or plummets the company into Chapter 11 bankruptcy, you can see how sabotaging and counterproductive the actions are. Others might witness the "seriously injured" worker lifting her children into the car some evening when by day she claims a back injury and collects worker's compensation. To the manipulative person, getting a free ride prevails. A hidden surveillance camera could capture her playing volleyball at the beach, and this worker might still deny faking it.

The college student who literally shuts down, pushing his parents' financial worry buttons is another saboteur. He may have needed to set a different agenda (overlapping here with the desire to control), but because of his fear of confronting authority (perceived or actual), he has discharged his anger to avoid responsibility and used plausible excuses ("Oh, I slept in . . . ," "The class was too hard," or "I took too full of a course load"). Maybe this student is trying to be effective, but doing it his way, which seems ineffective to everyone else. Direct, honest communication could have solved this student's problems.

Think about possible manipulative acts in everyday life. The restaurant waiter delays bringing your order; the bank teller closes her window for lunch as soon as you reach the front of the line; the clerk tells you an item is out of stock when he's simply too lazy to look in the back room; or a family member leaves your leftovers in clear view of the dog, knowing you were returning to finish your meal. Of course, recognizing poor behavior is one thing. Just be careful, as we'll remind throughout this book, not to see everything in a negative light. There could be other reasons for what you see. But if after you read various accounts, you can match up the behaviors with what you know about a person's needs or fears, then it just could be that you're dealing with a passive-aggressive person or someone else who hides her anger.

In our next chapter, we'll focus on the impact of anger on our health, career progression, academic achievement, and interpersonal happiness.

TWO

UNDERSTANDING THE PROBLEMS ASSOCIATED WITH CONCEALED EMOTIONS

I ONCE HAD a client who spoke in our sessions of her struggles with being overweight. She told me how it impacted her marriage, how she tried to please her husband by dutifully attending Weight Watchers and dieting religiously, but she cried that she just couldn't lose weight no matter how hard she tried. Then one day, she brought in a bag from the convenience store, which slid off the chair, and out dropped half a dozen candy bars. After tearfully acknowledging that she ate in between her restricted meals, she tried to run from her own responsibility in the matter by blaming a society that didn't accept overweight people. But it was clear to me that her poor self-image and self-anger came long before her weight gain. In her case, overeating gave her a passive excuse for victimization and self-pity.

Some people explode. Others seethe inside. Many do both. Some talk their problems through, while the person next to them harbors grudges. My client tried to use food to achieve happiness and cited rejection as the cause of her overindulgence. How do you express your anger?

We need only to look at news headlines and into our own daily journeys to see that in whatever form, anger is the number one interpersonal threat to our leading happy, healthy lives. The despicable acts we see on the evening news or splashed in full color on the newspaper's front page grab our attention. We're talking about terror attacks, hostages taken and killed, school violence, assaults, murder, or the shocking details of intimate violence committed against a spouse or child. Our consciousness is so steeped in them that our memory recall makes these tragedies as easily remembered as a brand name: 9/11, Columbine, the murders of Nicole Brown Simpson or Laci Peterson.

But what do these much-publicized acts of anger have to do with concealed emotions? Simple. In many cases of physical harm or aggression, there have been elements of manipulation, the quest for power and control over others, a score to settle, and at the very core, unsettled minds and heavy hearts (whether you agree with the cause or not, the emotions mattered to the attackers). This brings each terrible tragedy down to the most basic individual level.

In addition to highly publicized, very visible attacks, there are millions of hidden-anger acts each day, which destroy health and relationships, reduce worker productivity, and likely cost us billions in the workplace, courtrooms, and medical facilities.

THE TIME BOMB PROBLEM

CONTINUALLY BURIED, EMOTIONS are like time bombs, ticking louder with each day, month, and year they accumulate. Very few people can keep up the façade of normalcy when they seethe inside. When the authorities have thwarted a planned attack, it was because someone, somewhere spotted behavior or circumstances that didn't seem right. They had awareness as if positioned as a sentry to their emotional gates as well as their physical being.

In this age of heightened vigilance, everyone is more on guard against premeditated attacks. We're more skeptical of motives, and we should be skeptical as a safety and sanity measure. We know from research into domestic violence and other abusive behaviors that physical violence is often the next step after months or years of concealed psychological attack. If people don't wise up fast to someone's hidden-rage agenda, they might perpetuate their own victimization. Let there be no mistake, people who hide their anger can be very dangerous, especially over time.

ORDINARY ANGST AND ANXIETY

THESE ARE SOME individual extreme cases, and since we have a greater chance of being involved in a traffic accident than a terror attack, we don't wish to raise unnecessarily your anxiety that you will meet with such a radical example. We're far more likely—at work or school, in the shopping mall or grocery store, at home and with those we care for—to encounter ordinary, garden-variety hidden rage that doesn't make the nightly news but leaves us feeling powerless nonetheless. In the January 2004 issue, *Health* editors reported that *45 percent* of Americans said they lived in households where anger and stress were problematic.[1]

In my work as a state legislator and now as a member of Congress, I encounter many individuals who are distraught. Let's face it, if life was going swimmingly, I'd never hear from them. When it doesn't, when life has dealt them a blow, or when they perceive an injustice, they look to me to solve their dilemma. Sometimes they are just mad at the world, seeing those in public service as punching bags. Often by the time they reach my office, they're at wit's end. I guess you could say I'm accustomed to it because for more than twenty-five years I spent my days (and many evenings) as a psychologist listening to confused, sometimes raw emotion, trampled feelings, couples on the verge of divorce, parents exhausted by their obstinate kids, and children upset at authority figures in their world at large. In that sense, my career hasn't changed all that much. When people are unhappy, I see it and work to help them solve the problem. That background in learning to listen to and reflect on people's problems has helped me immeasurably as a public servant.

Consider this: The left sees conservative talk-show hosts as focusing on narrow principles. The right sees the liberals as distorting the truth to serve their ends. Each blames the other for conspiracies and manipulation. But when people distort the truth, rewrite history, or impose an agenda, they deny themselves an honest view of the facts.

My coauthor Loriann has written about the awareness she's gained in *Surviving Separation and Divorce,* chronicling the power that separation and divorce has to shape one's future. Statistics tell us that divorce occurs in half of all first marriages and in even more remarriages.[2] There is a lot of frustration, and sometimes much deeper anger, affecting many personal lives.

A cover story in *Newsweek* (September 13, 2004) dealt with the twenty-first century's age of excess,[3] particularly how parents are overindulging their children, setting them up for anxiety and possible depression in adulthood when they fail to exhibit any coping skills to deal with life's daily disappointments. Just as a childhood vaccine adds to a child's immunity, so does stress inoculation build up an ability to handle tough times.

In the age of "I want," children aren't able to sit with their anxiety, so they ever-increasingly stew over how to get more "stuff," how to be perceived as more "cool," and how to manipulate mom, dad, or even teachers into meeting their every whim. They lack limits and firm boundaries telling them where their needs and wants stop and other people's begin, and that self-sacrifice (namely, giving something back to this world) holds far more promise for their futures. Self-absorption is momentary, fleeting, and as we note in the appendix, plenty of passive-aggressive people conceal their true motives or angst and fall into this self-centered category.

So, what we're seeing today are fractured, frivolous, and certainly frantic families, just trying to tread water so that they can meet their desires as well as survive in a work culture that sometimes demands more of and promises less to the individual. It's now commonly accepted that most workers will experience approximately five to seven job changes within their careers. It's ever more rare to receive the gold watch after forty or fifty years of service to one employer. The workplace has changed. Sometimes it means working sixty hours a week at forty-hour pay. It's a 24/7 commitment with perhaps less certainty than our parents had. More and more, it's working and dealing with kids, carpools, and our jobs all at the same time.

At home, families enroll Johnny or Jane in private lessons, this team, that practice. Parenting is meted out in small doses, and when children respond by getting back at their moms and dads through poor behavior, everyone feels like the walking wounded. Children and adults cope with anger, struggling to express it, often denying it because it's uncomfortable to have.

One might argue that children, lacking maturity, have it toughest. A child's ability to impact the family doesn't end at eighteen, that's for sure. Taking the opposite stance, others might conclude that adults have a harder time because the patterns of their responses and thinking are so ingrained that they become more difficult to change or correct with each passing year.

■

TWELVE WAYS ANGER CAN HARM YOUR HEALTH —EVEN KILL YOU

PHYSICIANS and anger management researchers have found the following links between hot temper and harboring anger, and physical and emotional health:

1. Increased risk of high blood pressure
2. Higher levels of homeocysteine (amino acid), leading to arterial damage and an increased risk of coronary heart disease
3. Higher levels of C-reactive protein associated with heart disease and stroke risk
4. Increased levels of cortisol and adrenaline (the body's fight-or-flight hormones)
5. Weakened immune function (resulting from overactive hormones that stress immune system)

6. Increased body weight (from higher cortisol levels)
7. Enhanced vulnerability to pathogens, everyday germs, viruses, or familial predisposition to cancer or heart disease
8. Increased risk of periodontitis (gum disease)
9. Increased vulnerability to eating disorders
10. Higher rates of anxiety, depression, somatic complaints (aches and pains)
11. Cellular deterioration, premature aging, and shortened life span
12. Greater likelihood that angry patients will not comply with medical or psychological treatment, thereby putting their health at risk

THE UNHEALTHY ANGER PROBLEM

LINGERING ANGER, VEILED or not, leads to lasting physical health complications, including high blood pressure, coronary heart disease, weakened immune function, increased hormone levels, weight gain, and vulnerability to germs and pathogens. The outlook is no better for one's mental state, since perpetually angry individuals often lapse into various forms of depression. Eating disorders are more common in those with anger management problems. Those with heart disease, diabetes, constant stress, and/or depression are at higher risk for developing more severe health problems, not to mention that their medical costs are substantially higher than average.

HOW THE ANGRY MIND WORKS

THINK ABOUT A time when you've been angry. One or several negative emotions lay beneath your anger, triggering that anger as you acted upon it openly or stuffed it inside. If your mind feels as if it's filled with negative thoughts, faulty assumptions, and what psychologists call irrational beliefs, then you can easily work your way into a circular anger cycle as we depict below:

PRECIPITATING EVENT

Irrational Beliefs

Consequences Occur

Emotion Anxiety, Depression . . .

Anger: Leads to lashing out, acting out . . .

When people become angry, something occurs that typically sparks faulty thinking or irrational beliefs. For example, we might think "if only this could happen . . . ," or "I should . . . ," or "This must. . . ." Therapists hear "shoulda, coulda, woulda" thinking all the time. Having such beliefs, rarely based upon fact and often compounded when others around us think the same way, leads to emotions that vary within the individual and circumstance. It could be anxiety or depression, among other emotions, that triggers our becoming angry, because anger never exists alone. When these emotions build over time, that's when we're likely to feel most angry, lash or act out.

When consequences occur as a result of anger, they can be either positive or negative. Positive consequences often fuel anger because there's a payoff or "win" serving as a reward. Perhaps negative consequences result, and an angry person interprets them in some way to make them rewarding, such as the faulty thought "This would have been good if it weren't for so and so." Here, negative feelings or thoughts merely cement faulty assumptions in place. The angry person confirms to himself, "See . . . I knew this would happen." or "Others are to blame for my problems." This circular process can easily become self-sustaining.

Anyone who is on the receiving end of these negative events can also become emotional, maybe anxious or depressed, over time. The receiver never quite knows what to expect next. Chronic activation of the fight-or-flight response (anxiety in large measure) puts a person's physical health at risk as well.

Finally, we often see characterological/personality disorders diagnosed in those who cannot come to grips with their inner hostility. Anger kills and it costs us plenty. It's terribly counterproductive and frequently lands the person in a self-perpetuating snare that can only be untangled with awareness, assertiveness, and often, therapy.

Dr. Redford Williams, Director of the Behavioral Medicine Research Center at the Duke University School of Medicine, has devoted much of his work to the link between anger and poor physical health. He told *Men's Health* that chronically angry men are five to seven times more likely to be dead by age fifty than their easy-going counterparts.[4] In 2004, *Psychosomatic Medicine* cited other research at Duke University in which scientists found links between emotions of anger, hostility, and depression, testing blood for the substance called C-reactive protein (CRP). Study subjects who scored high for these three emotions had CRP blood levels two to three times higher than subjects who scored low; thus, the angry, hostile, and depressed people were thought to be more prone to heart disease.[5]

While at the University of North Carolina, epidemiologist Janice Williams, led a study of nearly thirteen thousand adults. Her findings: Anger-prone men and women, especially in middle age and with normal blood pressure, were nearly three times more likely to suffer a heart attack. The results were published in *Circulation,* a journal of the American Heart Association.[6] In 2003, the *American Journal of Cardiology* reported that men with negative emotions (anxiety, pessimism, hostility) had a higher risk of heart disease compared to peers who possessed more positive outlooks.[7]

THE ANGRY WEIGHT-GAIN PROBLEM

ALL RISK FACTORS on our "Twelve ways . . ." sidebar list are important reminders of why anger should be managed. One of the most revealing findings in recent years is the link between hostility and unhealthy weight gain. Sue Ellen Browder, author of *The Power: 11 Ways Women Gain Unhealthy Weight and How You Can Take Charge of Them,* calls this phenomenon "anger fat."[8] In her book, Browder cites a study conducted jointly by researchers at the University of Helsinki and at the University of Pittsburgh. Middle-aged women who frequently felt intensely angry and openly expressed their anger at other people gained more unhealthy fat over a thirteen-year period than less hostile women. They also had higher insulin levels.[9]

Don't think that if you're a male you're exempt from angry weight-gain. Another study found that men with angry feelings, outbursts, and claims of a lack of emotional support from others were more likely to have upper-body fat than their less angry peers. Biologically, weight gain occurs when adrenaline stimulates fat cells to empty their contents into the bloodstream. Your liver also converts fat into cholesterol, which is then absorbed into your arteries, attaching onto artery walls, thus clogging your circulatory system. Your risk of heart attack, as well as weight gain, rises.

After reading about this emotion/weight gain connection, you might still deny any connection to yourself. But think about everyday occurrences. Remember the client whose candy bars fell out in my office after she tearfully tried to convince me she just couldn't lose weight. I honestly thought that even had she dropped ninety pounds, she would still feel the same way because of her low self-esteem and internalized anger. The choice was hers to remain centered and change, but then she might have to part with her societal beliefs. This seemed too difficult for her.

It's not just caloric intake that can increase when stress levels rise. Studies show that smoking and alcohol consumption increase. Even if you don't eat, smoke, or drink more, anger can redistribute your fat, storing more of it in the visceral danger zone, internally, around the body's vital organs (heart, liver, and others) where it's been linked to other serious medical problems.

NATURE OR NURTURE

IF YOUR ANGER is out of control, your body descends on a downward spiral because one problem triggers another. Being too angry too much of the time *can* kill you. Dr. Redford Williams has also studied the genetic link with anger, finding a tiny molecular variation of a gene that we all carry that may predict those more prone to anger.[10] Science is getting closer to identifying, on the basis of genetic characteristics, those people at higher risk of intense anger and rage. But note that this doesn't take an individual off the hook. In fact, it increases the importance of taking an active role in controlling anger.

In 1996, David Lykken, a researcher at the University of Minnesota, published a paper looking at the role of genes in determining people's overall sense of satisfaction or happiness in life.[11] Studying four thousand sets of twins born in Minnesota between 1936 and 1955, comparing the data from identical and fraternal twins, he concluded that about 50 percent of a person's satisfaction with life came from genetic influence, including whether a person had a pleasant, sunny disposition, how he dealt with stress, and how anxious or depressed he was. Genetic anger research is still in its early stages, and it's certainly worth exploring.

Our concern is that some out-of-sorts people might use any research link to genetics as an excuse for a poor disposition or outlook. When some believe that people can't control anger, they're essentially saying, "They are who they are." Even if genetics, upbringing, or environment contribute to our misery, we all have a responsibility to manage our anger, channel it into something positive, or eradicate it completely. Anger, therefore, is very much a choice. Most in the field would wholeheartedly agree that, inherited or not, anger can and should be managed for one's heightened mental peace, physical health, and longevity.

USING POPULAR EXCUSES

ANOTHER REASON THAT we've become accustomed to anger as a way of life is society's conditioning us with various experts having urged angry people to vent their emotions. Go ahead, blow off steam, break some dishes, punch a pillow, and visualize the one you're most angry toward. Wrong! More recent studies have backed the prevailing theory that venting anger only reinforces the connection between anger and violence. Buying into the "I have to let it out" syndrome can make things worse because you're then more likely to respond through attack or aggression the next time you struggle with anger.

Dr. Brad J. Bushman, an associate professor of psychology at Iowa State University, led a study in 1999 on letting out aggression.[12] He and his colleagues found that study subjects who were given the message of displaced aggression (that hitting objects was an effective release) did indeed appear later to be more aggressive toward rivals or innocent third parties. Venting anger—by hitting a pillow, throwing something, or kicking a punching bag—is more likely to keep anger alive than to erase it, making it counterproductive.

Even exercise has been called into question. Bushman's study found that exercise actually kept angry people at a heightened arousal level. "The arousal from the exercise could be misattributed as anger if the person is provoked after exercising," Bushman told us. Doing something incompatible to aggression or venting, like reading, watching a funny movie, or listening to music might help to alleviate a person's anger. Others have long felt that physical exercise dissipates anger and improves mood.

OTHER WAYS HIDDEN ANGER AFFECTS US

RESEARCHERS ANWAR T. MERCHANT, DMD, ScD and his colleagues at Harvard School of Dental Medicine reported in the *Journal of the American Dental Association* (JADA) that men who were angry on a daily basis had a 43 percent higher risk of developing periodontitis (gum disease) compared with men who reported seldom being angry.[13] In their study, they asked questions regarding whether the men argued with others, slammed doors, said nasty things, and lost their tempers, and found that such anger expression was positively associated with gum disease risk.

Additionally, chronic pain patients who are angry sometimes do not recover as quickly as happier patients might, and increasingly physicians are finding a link between some chronic pain and mood.

It's not surprising that angry folks sometimes battle low self-esteem and sexual or intellectual inhibitions, and have low energy levels. Often, they feel their creativity has been zapped as well. Ben Franklin was once quoted as saying, "Whatever is begun in anger ends in shame." Hundreds of years later, how true that is. Sometimes that remorse eats away at self-esteem, evokes anger, or manifests in helplessness or depression. Sustained depression, we know, can become chronic and much harder to overcome.

However, the psychological study of positive emotions has received much press coverage. *Time* editors ran "The Science of Happiness" as their January 17, 2005 cover story, describing the work of researchers like Martin Selgiman, PhD, who brought a new theme to the American Psychological Association during his tenure as president in 1998.[14] The magazine called this newfound focus "an explosion of research on happiness, optimism, positive emotions, and healthy character traits." Seligman wrote *Authentic Happiness* among other titles.[15]

We know from these researchers and authors that a positive, optimistic outlook can speed the healing process when a bone has been fractured, slow the progression of certain infections, and protect us against culprits like cardiovascular disease and stroke.

According to research published in the Proceedings of the National Academy of Sciences (December 2004), chronic care-giving stress was associated with cell aging (thereby impacting health and possible longevity). Elissa Epel, a psychiatrist at the University of California at San Francisco, conducted research involving mothers who raised chronically ill children and were subjected to greater-than-average environmental stress. The findings linked psychological stress to a cellular indicator of aging in those otherwise healthy women.[16]

A 2001 study in the *Journal of Applied Psychology* found that people who report high levels of career control, yet lack self-confidence, blame themselves for negative consequences and succumb more readily to infectious diseases.[17] Research out of Carnegie Mellon University found that people suffering from chronic stress (at work or home) were twice as likely to catch a cold or the flu.[18] The greater the stress, the greater the risk of getting sick.

Finally, the last health implication we'll highlight is the noncompliant patient. One's own problematic behaviors—stalling, forgetting to take medication or adhere to treatment plans, and arguing with medical or mental health professionals—stand in the way of good health. In cases like this, patients could conceal their frustration out of anger at themselves. If they possess the irrational belief that the physician holds the miracle cure, they may even harbor anger toward the medical team. Sometimes patients wish for health-care practitioners to do all the work, eradicate their pain completely, or make things 100 percent perfect, but we know that living life requires much tolerance (sometimes in pain), certainly when recovering from illness or injury. So, too, the patients may just bristle at the doctor's every suggestion or move.

In my practice, I once treated a boy whose mom usually brought him to sessions. One time, the dad came instead and was a bit nasty, as I remember him. His attitude: "Well, I guess you aren't as good as I thought. My son still isn't better and we've been coming here a whole month!" Trouble was, there was no "we." With his first visit, dad was determined to prove mom and me wrong.

Healthcare providers may need to pay extra-close attention to the behaviors we detail because they need to change their approaches with patients who react negatively to authority figures. They must adjust because their stalled patients sure as heck won't budge. This applies to angry patients who refuse to give up smoking, take their medicine as prescribed, exercise, or make other lifestyle changes. To comply with treatment means giving up power and admitting that the healthcare provider is right. I once met a guy who complained *ad infinitum* about his doctor, saying he didn't know what he was talking about. I said, "Why not go to a different doctor?"

He replied, "Because he's the best supposedly, but if he doesn't know what he's doing, then everyone else is a bigger waste of my time." Do you see this man's faulty thinking?

It takes a lot of patience and persistence to work with such patients. When healthcare providers gently educate and coach their patients rather than dictate to them, they back out of the authority figure role, giving their patients much more of a personal stake in their own care. This is how you turn a difficult patient into one much less likely to whine, resist, and hand you back a load of excuses. Everyone, including the doctor, should feel tremendously better.

MORE EFFECTS:
ACADEMIC STRUGGLES AND THREATENED CAREERS

ACADEMIC ACHIEVEMENT AND/or career progression is often stymied or sabotaged altogether when anger lurks in the background. Research has pegged passive-aggressive individuals as more apt to be underachievers inside the classroom and in the workplace. Many adopt a "why bother?" attitude, never fully committing to a job they both love and loathe. So, too, a passive-aggressive manager may unwittingly avoid hiring the best person for the job because deep down she fears that she'll be eclipsed by someone else with talent, drive, or determination—qualities this manager may desperately want herself. Now, reminded of her own deficits by a stellar résumé, the manager obstructs (or so she thinks) the applicant's career progression by refusing to interview or hire someone who might compete.

Others concealing their anger react to situations at home or irrational beliefs that we discussed earlier. Some of these children are mislabeled as having ADHD when actually their behavior is a deliberate choice not to pay attention in order to manipulate others. Sure, they're hurting their own grades and their own futures, but their anger prevents them from expressing their emotions in constructive ways.

Selective attention is a means of avoiding responsibility as well. When Johnny refuses to work, it may require more time and energy to get him on track or to deal with any misbehavior. Therefore, it becomes everyone's problem, affecting not only the teacher, but also other classmates, Johnny's parents, and even the other kids' parents if they're upset.

We see outright passive-aggression in higher education when parents send their offspring to college or graduate school, and their son or daughter simply shuts down. The student would rather study another major, or perhaps do something entirely different with his or her life. Wasting hard-earned tuition dollars may seem like the way to "get back" at mom or dad for their control because too frequently these students can't openly express their true wishes. Maybe there is justifiable anger because if they did express themselves, it wouldn't do much good. Here, the parents may exert too much influence, and the son or daughter needs to disengage and learn how to be appropriately assertive.

Never underestimate how an angry student might take out his anger in the classroom. When students interrupt the professor or argue the theory of her every lecture, we see the symptom of acting out against authority figures (which may have its roots in childhood).

In the workplace, hidden anger is not merely annoying; it can have long-lasting, even deadly, consequences. It can cost millions—sometimes billions—of dollars in lost contracts, reduced efficiency, and even worker safety in some settings. Planned mistakes equal sabotage. Faulty workmanship brings on lawsuits. Worker anxiety can lead to depression, and untreated, the cost of mental illness rises—for the worker's health and expense, the employer in lost productivity and premiums, and anyone interacting with that employee who is not himself, at least for a while. In monetary terms alone, untreated depression costs an extra $2,000 per year per employee, but if these employees get help, everything can be fine. Not all depressed workers are bad workers. Many want to do a good job but are overwhelmed by this temporary setback. Anger can be a part of depression, but the two don't always go hand in hand.

All of this gives good reason for managers, human resource departments, and others to offer stress reduction seminars and anger management classes. The results of bottled-up anger certainly provide the impetus for superiors to listen to their employees. I have found in all my years as a practicing psychologist and now as a congressman that when clients or constituents feel heard and listened to, it calms them a great deal, enough to often enough allow them to let go of emotional reactivity and begin the real work of finding solutions to problems.

WHY HIDDEN ANGER PREVAILS

JUST AS THE depressed employee likely wants to be a good worker (caring spouse, good student), the person who hides his anger is rarely the evil villain we might think. An anger-concealing person is frequently conflicted, unable to follow through with much action, cooperation, or problem solving. Just when he's on the verge of negotiating a compromise or helping out, he finds a reason not to. Staying the same is easier, much as in the popular notion that the devil we know is better than the one we do not. Changing behavior that has worked in the past makes a person anxious. So, the person stays in role.

This often means that if you're on the receiving end of button-pushing, stalling, excuses, and passive withholding, you may come off looking demanding, overbearing, or controlling if you react (sometimes, even if you don't respond). That's what is so disconcerting.

Other people's sour moods also have the potential to make you feel guilty or intimidated, or to cause you to question things. You might think, "Maybe it really is *my* problem."

Of course, if the person who conceals his anger has a substantial ego, it's easy to pass himself off in a positive light. No "bad guy" profile here, for he does a convincing job getting others to buy into and accept his ruse. Problem is: You come across as the fall guy when you shouldn't. If you've ever been ensnared like this, you know how difficult it is to deal with manipulative and hostile people. You want everyone else to "get it." Unfortunately, angry people mask such behavior and generate a lot of attention.

WHY PEOPLE DON'T CHANGE

ANGRY PEOPLE OFTEN push aside change, and we'll show how this plays out at work, in school, and at home. In the last chapter, we'll discuss the process of change in more detail, but for now, angry people may:

1. Not see their problems (lack insight) so they do not change.
2. See their problems but still have a payoff so they don't change.
3. Try to change but don't know how, so they lapse back.

4. Have an environment (or enablers) who push them back to their old ways.
5. Enjoy even the negative attention over no attention at all.

Hidden anger continues because it works. It works in the family, workplace, classroom, even at times in the legal system. People buy into the negative, subtly angry behaviors because they don't know enough about the signs, symptoms, triggers, secondary gains (payoffs), or other ramifications of hidden anger. It might even look normal to others who don't have a happy worldview of human behavior and lack optimism.

Just as others cannot "make" us angry, they cannot "cure" our burdens. We see this often in troubled marriages where one spouse's expectations aren't met. The marriage turned out to be more of an evolving process than a panacea. Because adult behaviors and patterns have taken a long time to develop, it may take a long time to eradicate them, as well. If the anger-concealing person does seek treatment, it's not uncommon to see starts and stops because the individual's core conflicts arise with the therapists as he recreates situations that keep him from changing. By *transference*, a clinical term, we make others what they aren't by projecting our feelings onto them. So, just as a passive-aggressive person may self-sabotage his chances for success elsewhere, he may stand in the way of his own counseling, rationalizing that the therapist doesn't understand him. He may prolong therapy or select the least competent helper to avoid taking responsibility, to get back at whoever thought of counseling in the first place, or to run up copayments for whomever pays—with the intent of hurting the person in the pocketbook. In a school setting, a child might keep an angry battle brewing, making little headway with the school counseling office, just to embarrass or embroil the teacher, classmates, or the school personnel.

Angry thoughts and behaviors that aren't managed may cripple relationships, stall decisions, and end opportunities. They may leave a destructive path, but it doesn't have to be that way

■

ANGRY/HAPPY PEOPLE COMPARISON

EVER wondered what anger looks like when contrasted with its more cheerful opposite? Life is not bleak, and we want to emphasize how your thoughts and behaviors can help to overcome low mood, frustration, self-centeredness, and embedded anger. This chart depicts what runs contrary to the negative traits we're discussing.

ANGRY PEOPLE	HAPPY PEOPLE
Irritated	Compassionate and empathic
Impulsive	Patient
Seek immediate gratification	Can delay gratification, require more of self
Demand	Ask
Blast or maintain silence	Openly and calmly discusses
Need to control or obstruct	Want to negotiate, cooperate, resolve problems
Criticize	Respect
Dig in heels	Accept change or differences
Immature, childish	Mature and possessing perspective
Tense, frowns, sighs	Relaxed, smiles, laughter
Blame	Take responsibility
Threaten, punish	Reward/praise
Put down	Inspire
Rely upon rage talk, swearing	Choose more inspiring vocabulary
Closed-minded, solitary	Open minded, request help, reach out
Surrounded by negative people	Prefer positive people
Unhealthy habits and weight	Fit, trim, and healthy lifestyle
Harm or destroy relationships	Cultivate and build relationships
Focus on pessimism	Work at optimism
Sedentary, passive	Active, energetic
Destructive (sometimes actively so)	Constructive
Give up too easily	Persevere, push forward

LEARNING AND GROWING FROM ANGER

THE FACE OF anger wears many expressions, not all bad. We encourage you to use anger as a tool and to see its potential for positive change and bringing people closer instead of separating them. Our memories of bad experiences greatly affect our lives. They can hold us back or thrust us forward. We can learn to deal with them and survive, or we can use bad experiences to transform us—not just to help us survive, but thrive!

This reminds us of a tale about the man looking for a shortcut on his way home. He sees a sign, "Beware of Dog," but ignores it. This man climbs over a fence and gets chased, but outruns Fang, the dog. Next time, he hopes the dog isn't there, so he cuts across again. This time, Fang nips at him, but again he gets away fast enough. Third time, he thinks he can again outrun the dog, but . . . he gets bitten. He complains to a friend about this "mean" dog, and the friend says, "Stay out of the yard and you won't get bitten!" If he goes again, what does it mean? If he stays away, what does it mean? That's what it's like with our memories. We can learn from them or keep ruminating about them. Our past experiences won't change. What we do with them—now that can change!

In the next chapter, we explore how hidden anger often forms early in life. Angry children may feel, much as psychologist Abraham Maslow said that if their only tool is a hammer, throughout life, every problem looks like a nail.

THREE

CHILDHOOD ROOTS
OF PASSIVE-AGGRESSION

ARLOS, AT TWENTY-NINE, complains. According to his wife Rosa, he complains a lot. His whining, fishing for her compliments, and inability to make decisions not only grate on Rosa's nerves, but trouble her because she'd like to start a family of their own. Problem is, she feels a lot more like Carlos's mom than his wife. Rosa's sister-in-law dubbed her own older brother a little resentful and passive-aggressive, but is he? Working through this chapter, we'll find out why Carlos acts as he docs.

As we indicated, if you haven't experienced anger, then essentially you haven't lived. Everyone gets angry from time to time, and it's precisely because we are all prone to feel occasional anger that we must keep an eye on it. It's the intensity of that anger, the persistence or frequency of it, and the choices we make in how to use angry feelings that matter more than merely having them. When the symptoms of hidden anger endure over many years, thcn it truly poses a problem.

Who exactly is at risk? If you've had an angry childhood and these past issues aren't resolved, you may be more susceptible to acting passive-aggressively or concealing bitterness. A family history of anger, addiction, or particular mental health problems may put you at higher risk because some of this is heritable or learned behavior. Very often, victims of abuse (physical, sexual, or psychological) become increasingly angry over time when these earlier wounds or traumas continue to fester. A very angry person may remember every slight, barb, humiliation, and physical blow, often laying the burden where it doesn't belong—upon someone else.

Whenever he experiences a setback—death, divorce, or other loss, job complications, prolonged stress and anxiety—hidden anger can erupt so strongly that others may wonder why there's so much of it. Sure, the circumstances may be a problem, but the level of anger just doesn't fit. Where else could it come from? Quite possibly from experiences long ago in childhood.

YOUR OWN CHILDHOOD

WHAT DO YOU remember from your childhood? Happiness? Sad times? Problems that you overcame or ones that overwhelmed you?

If you felt your body tense at the mere thought of remembering your youth, perhaps the remembrances aren't so spectacular. For some, childhood wasn't a carefree time. In fact, it might have been anything but carefree, reflecting sadness or pain.

Our memories are a two-way street. Who we are now influences what we recall, and what we recall influences how and exactly what we remember. The happy adult may recall pleasant memories and see them as more influential than the negative ones. The sad person, on the other hand, may give more weight to the negative life experiences and allow these to cast a pall over what comes after. Every one of us has some unpleasant memories that shape us. Once we realize that, these memories keep shaping us only if we allow them to; in other words, we can halt the transfer of old experiences into the present because this clouds our ability to think clearly in the here and now. If you experienced failure or success as a child after taking risks or trying incredibly hard, your efforts may have been met with acceptance and love, or with rejection and anger.

Maybe the memories are wrapped up in so much misery that even though they are ten, twenty, or thirty years old, you still get upset. Thus, you try to hide from them.

Those who conceal anger often cannot express themselves freely because of childhood memories (often called childhood wounds). They are stuck, unable to break with the past, see the present, or move forward without tainted memories. Sometimes you may be aware of the influence—"my boss reminds me of my stepfather, whom I hated!"—or sometimes you may not be aware why you get so worked up over nothing.

TOUCHING YOUR CHILDHOOD MEMORIES OF ANGER

To AID YOU as you remember how you handled anger as a child, here is a short list of questions. Try to answer them all. On a sheet of paper, jot your answers to the following:

1. What were the times/circumstances where anger typically erupted in your family?
2. How did your parents, siblings, or others in your home express their anger? Specifically, what did they say? How did they act? How did they react to anger in others?
3. If there was one button any of these people pushed on you most frequently, what was it?
4. What was the result when family members showed anger? Did it solve problems or make them worse?
5. Give examples of when you remember feeling most angry. How did you express that anger?
6. How is that expression of anger in your youth different from how you express anger today?
7. How different is your expression of anger from that of your family?
8. What would you most like to change about your way of surfacing anger now?

THE ROOTS OF CHILDHOOD ANGER

THIS EIGHT-POINT quiz was designed to provoke thought about your own childhood roots of anger. In the last chapter, we explored why people get angry and listed environment, parenting, a family history of frustration, stress, addictions, and other problems as possible risk factors for developing anger management problems. But wait a minute! Before you experience any guilt or sadness about that, realize that every family has its struggles. In more than twenty-five years of clinical practice and in all my years in public service, I've yet to meet one family who has lived what we'd colloquially call a charmed life. I'm always intrigued when people claim: "My parents were never angry." I'll make the educated guess that anger was there all right. But whereas some could express it and move on, some kept it hidden.

Where was it lurking? How did it surface? Remember, the fact that anger surfaced is not, in and of itself, a terrible thing. It might be quite good, especially if it were expressed in a healthy manner that solved problems. The answer depends upon the intent of that anger, what it looked like, what people's reactions were, and how it was dealt with after the fact. Did your family harbor resentment or take care of anger quickly so that it would not (or could not) linger and later be concealed?

To better understand how your family dealt with anger, let's look at its stages. In our first book, *The Angry Child: Regaining Control When Your Child Is Out of Control,* we detailed Dr. Murphy's four stages of anger.[1] That took an entire chapter, and we won't go into much detail here, but at least knowing these stages is helpful. Anger starts with a *buildup* that sets the foundation of a situation. It might stem from recalling old, unresolved conflicts, developmental stressors, or poor problem-solving skills. Hidden anger very often contributes to the buildup. When a person is "quick-tempered," his buildup doesn't take long. For others, the buildup amasses over many days, months, or even years. To prevent anger from becoming a problem, it's always best to prevent any buildup from ever happening.

A *spark,* big or small, sets off the conflict. We all respond differently to a spark, which could be a situation or a thought. Some swallow it as if it had only a small impact, while others fly into an immediate rage. The spark could be stubbing your toes, getting cut off in traffic, losing your keys, or remembering something your ex-friend said to you. It can be a feeling of jealousy, hurt, or disappointment that sparks anger. If you can learn to recognize a hidden spark, you might defuse the problem enough to prevent its smoldering, because as we defined hidden anger, a smoldering spark (anger) will become powerful, especially over time.

Stage three—the *explosion*—is the unforgettable one, at least in *The Angry Child.* You'll recognize it from the yelling, fighting, thrown dish, threat, and so on. It can be the volcanic eruption, or when hidden, the slow rumbling that remains underground. The explosion may well occur, but why it occurs may remain a mystery.

How can that be? How can something explode without the angry person or anyone around her noticing? If people conceal anger, they may use indirect methods such as sarcasm, unwarranted criticism, resisting, stalling, procrastinating, sabotaging, sending incongruent signals, or becoming sad, anxious, or hypersensitive. When indirect anger takes a negative form we see sneak attacks like vandalism, theft, computer viruses, and more.

And sometimes even if people feel justified in being silently angry, they can deny it's there in ways that are terribly unhealthy: smoking, drinking, using drugs, having eating disorders, injuring themselves, or cheating on a spouse for revenge.

Mind you, this explosion *can* be visible and recognized by all, even with a pattern of anger concealment, because most people can only hide their anger successfully for so long. The best thing to do during an explosion (if you recognize the moment) is to contain it, control it, so it doesn't cause harm to anyone. But just because it is curtailed doesn't mean it's over.

The final and fourth stage of anger is the *aftermath,* the most overlooked yet most important stage because if you fail to address the incident and resolve what went wrong, it will contribute to the buildup next time. Solving the problem is the goal, for prevention's sake, warding off a cycle of hidden anger based upon trampled feelings, unspoken grievances, and anything else that isn't shared but needs to be put on the table between the parties.

CHARACTERISTICS OF ANGRY CHILDREN . . . AND ADULTS!

READERS OFTEN ASK us after reading *The Angry Child* if the ten traits we outlined apply not only to children but also to adults, and our answer is yes. The angst doesn't end at eighteen. The sidebar "Ten Traits of the Angry Child" briefly lists a few ways that these traits show up in children and adults who display indirect anger.

■

TEN TRAITS OF THE ANGRY CHILD

1. Makes his own misery
2. Can't analyze problems
3. Blames others for his misfortune
4. Turns bad feelings into mad feelings
5. Lacks empathy
6. Attacks people rather than solves problems
7. Uses anger to gain power
8. Indulges in destructive self-talk
9. Confuses anger with self-esteem
10. Can be nice when he wants to be

Excerpted from *The Angry Child: Regaining Control When Your Child Is Out of Control,* © 2001 by Dr. Tim Murphy.

The self-perpetuating cycle of triggering emotions, acting out that leads to consequences, convincing an angry person just how correct his (usually false) beliefs really were is an example of a person *creating one's own misery.* When he relies on underhanded comments or tactics, and insulates himself from the very factors of change, guess what? He's making his own misery.

In the thought process, the *inability to analyze a problem* contributes to the faulty thinking. When an angry person operates from a worldview anticipating loss, she might hide her anger by acting out indirectly to minimize this loss—a preemptive strike. Doing so enables her to feel she's in control and often that helps soothe her anxieties or other feelings.

The silent refusal to discuss what's bothering her while preferring to wallow in self-pity is a classic example of this second trait. "I'm angry so I don't need to talk about it anymore" is also what I commonly saw in my practice and what I call *feelthink,* or confusing feelings with fact. In other words, "I feel; therefore it is so." If her emotions are all the data she relies upon to draw a conclusion, she's operating under the faulty analysis, feelthink. This gets the angry person in trouble when she impulsively acts on her anger, believing it's justified when it's clearly not.

Trait three. One of the most common defenses people use when they want to disown anger is *blaming others* for their misfortune, and researchers concur that passive-aggressive people often resent others, thinking that everyone else has a sweeter deal, the easier life, and that they themselves have it toughest.

When something triggers or sparks negative emotions that characteristically turn into anger, *bad feelings become mad feelings,* with such a limited range of expression. People concealing anger haven't mastered honest, open expression. Often, they can't even get to voicing, "I'm mad," as general and nondescript as that is; they just opt for a silent attack.

Lacking empathy is the fifth trait, and certainly children or adults who engage in "get back" behaviors, those who obstruct others' wishes, create no-win situations, and feign innocence so that others are left bewildered or embarrassed do not possess much empathy. Chronically depressed people are short of empathy because they're too busy feeling sorry for themselves. Imagine Eeyore in *Winnie the Pooh,* and you'll see what we mean. Such people don't see that someone may be trying to be helpful, for instance. They see that person's behavior as meddling.

Indirect anger is all about the sneak attack, the sniping remarks, extacting revenge, or mastering the next setup to control a situation one can't otherwise handle successfully—*attacking people rather than solving problems.* Problem solving requires respect for the other side, a belief that "I may not agree with you, but we can solve this anyway." Problem solving requires a belief that a future with a solution is worth more than hurting someone in the present. Those who disguise their anger have little interest in compromise or resolution, and if there is narcissism or self-centered thinking, it's usually a fight for any other reason than to solve a problem. It's to win, destroy, or maybe even for the sport of being disagreeable and negative. All of these methods, and many others, help the angry person to indirectly *gain power,* trait seven. As we'll see throughout this book, passive-aggressive people seek control and power.

The eighth trait—*destructive self-talk*—is similar to those irrational beliefs we mentioned in the self-perpetuating cycle of anger. It's the complete opposite of the positive-psychology movement, for sure! We see this all the time when indirect anger manifests as a not-too-subtle dig, or in complaining, whining, blaming, denial, projecting or displacing emotion, feigning innocence, or letting oneself off the hook by rationalizing away responsibility. Often, the angry person skillfully crafts (silently, in her own mind, that is) other people's responses, such as "I just know my boss will tell me that's no excuse to miss work, so I'm going to come in late anyway."

Confusing anger with self-esteem is another trait. Poor self-esteem undermines a person's well-being enough to impact school or work performance, interpersonal relationships, and future success. In severe cases, it can lead to anxiety disorders and depression. Healthy self-esteem drives our ability to navigate daily hassles while we respect other people. Because the one concealing anger shuns the risk of rejection or failure, he refuses to speak up, fails to be acknowledged, and obstructs his own chances of success. He pushes opportunities away, keeping them (and people) at a distance because he has trouble committing to anything or anyone. Never or rarely assuming responsibility for his actions makes him feel less competent, and then he often resents those who *can* use their talents to get ahead.

In fact, this person's self-esteem gets confused because of the ambivalence inherent in the indirect anger style. The child or adult simply can't decide how he feels about himself. No matter what appraisal he arrives at, there's a problem. "I appear good if I keep quiet, but being silent I feel incompetent."

Furthermore, the person with extremely high self-esteem comes across as so self-indulgent, so caught up in her own world that others find it difficult to get close. Self-centered people frustrate us over time, because they're not accustomed to hearing "no" as a viable answer and because their behaviors and automatic thoughts frustrate them, leading to a substantial reservoir of untapped anger. Having self-esteem is not the same as being psychologically healthy. Our prisons are filled with people who feel too good about themselves.

Finally, angry children and adults *can be quite charming, quite nice, when they want to be.* For instance, the angry smile is indeed the epitome of incongruent behavior, and this is the tenth trait. What one communicates is not one's true intent. If you're visibly okay, but seethe inside, you're hiding anger. If you claim, "Oh sure . . . that's fine," when you mean "Hell no, that won't stand," you're cloaking, swallowing, stuffing those negative feelings.

This trait illustrates that angry people are not 100 percent evil, but that they are capable of being wonderful. That's what seduces women into marriages with abusive men and employers into hiring what turns out to be the wrong employee. That's also what provides hope that angry people can get better.

Think here about the classic manipulator intent upon revenge. Think about the child who tells his teacher he'll help his classmate or stay after school to set up tomorrow's assembly. Sometimes these kids really want to be good, but if a child has no intention of assisting and purposely "forgets" to show up later, he's manipulating the teacher, coming off as the good student when it matters, and perhaps thwarting another's satisfaction or plan. Especially if the teacher has no way of knowing the outcome, the child may very well succeed because his actions remain hidden from all but himself. Of course, people do this even unwittingly. Men tell women they'll call after the first date. They don't feel that they can be honest, and yes, they've seduced the woman, raising her hopes. The behavior and outcome would be a lot worse if he strung her along, getting more out of the relationship than he gave, building her hopes for a future when he only wanted a few fun times. This example is far from pathological and is innocent enough, but it still illustrates how people get hurt when others are incongruent.

HOW HIDDEN ANGER TAKES UP RESIDENCE

Now that we know a little bit about how anger cycles through us, we'll address how anger got to be concealed in the first place, including those parents, children, and families who didn't encourage honest expression in their homes—families where anger was or still is emotionally on the run, not just occasionally, but as a problematic pattern. Kids who sugarcoat their hostility don't grow beyond it. Never developing better coping strategies or skill sets for self-expression, they can become adults who, beneath the seductive veneer, harbor vindictive intent. The buildup can be *that* long . . . and enduring. Or, it can be adults who were mean as children, but learned to cloak that meanness with passive-aggression.

But as we've indicated, for anger to work, it must serve a purpose—not always a good purpose, mind you, but a purpose nonetheless. We've identified seven functions.

HIDDEN ANGER THAT PROTECTS

WHEN PEOPLE ARE stuck, it's usually because what worked so well for them in the past isn't working so well any longer.

Connie, for instance, developed the habit of concealing her true thoughts and feelings as a kid because in the shadow of her older brother, who could do no wrong, nothing measured up. Keeping quiet got her through college, but now as a married woman, she expects her husband George to read her mind. The same strategy just doesn't work so well in adulthood. Connie needs to say what she thinks, tell George what she needs or expects, instead of hoping he'll guess correctly. She might need help learning such new skills because habits or defenses designed to protect one in childhood have limited usefulness later in life. Passive-aggression was once thought to be an "immature defense" because it was indirect, but also self-defeating. [2]

Sometimes there are other reasons for defenses. Adults are supposed to do the protecting and defending. Sadly enough, some children aren't protected, and when children feel emotionally unsafe, they resort to:

- Blaming ("He did it, not me!")
- Denial ("No, I didn't.")
- Projection ("I'm not bad, *you're* bad," when a child is appropriately disciplined)
- Repression ("I don't want to talk about it.")
- Displacement ("Well, Nana said I could have it.")
- Rationalization ("I can't help it because . . .")
- Undoing (child asks a question in class using a provocative word then softens it by claiming "I was only asking a question," or "Just kidding . . . can't you take a joke?")
- Isolation of affect ("I didn't mind being beaten up . . . really." When the child speaks nonchalantly of a traumatic event, thereby isolating himself from his emotions)
- Reaction formation (boy has crush on a little girl but denies the fact to his friends and claims to hate her, even taunting her because it's uncomfortable for him to have a crush on her—this shows the masking of one feeling by displaying its opposite behavior.)

Sometimes using defenses like these might have nothing to do with being safe and everything to do with negotiating childhood. It's important to distinguish the difference between a child's developing expression skills and a child stuck in a negative rut.

When a child is overprotected, this poses other problems as the teenager, then young adult, feels stuck. Parents who never allow roots and wings to grow foster ambivalence when their son or daughter wants to be independent, yet knows no other place as safe as dependence. Take Sam, whose harsh mom and dad squashed his desire to become a photographer and study art in high school. Most of Sam's opinions ran contrary to his parents' views, and when he tried to pull away to establish his own identity their rejection stung enough to keep him in their grasp. Sam kept to himself to protect himself from the diatribes, but in the long run, his parents harmed the relationship. After years of living at home with what he later acknowledged was his "smother mother," Sam moved across country and put himself through art school.

According to Scott Wetzler, PhD, one pattern that seems to appear with many secretly angry men was an overly close mother and a more distant father who relegated most of the parenting to mom.[3] Perhaps this could apply to women as well because it can have implications later in life if someone like Sam encounters others in authority and sees them as being as intrusive as his parent.

HIDDEN ANGER AS A REACTION

IF A CHILD's home was not a secure, nurturing place but rather one of physical, emotional, or sexual abuse, where anger got significant attention and showed its force, a child's need to hide anger is the voice of stress—not only protective but also a reaction to such events. As odd as it might be, children often learn to identify with a hostile parent or caregiver. They accept what comes their way and remain convinced that if they do tell someone what's going on, more abuse will be heaped upon them. Of course, not all abuse victims end up passive-aggressive. Troubling times hold some people back, while others use such incidents as a source of strength to move beyond them.

Growing from challenge might also occur with a disability or something that makes a child feel different. If we took to heart the messages that Fred Rogers taught children, we'd realize that everybody is special, everybody is fine, and as Rogers sang "your body's special and so is mine."[4] Understandably, children who live with a learning disability; speech, hearing, or visual impairment; developmental delay; or other problem may begin to resent their lot in life unless they are taught well how to cope and use their strengths. Teachers without proper perspective may chalk up a child's anger as just another behavior problem. Understanding the trigger is pivotal to improving the situation, for the child, the teacher, classmates, even parents.

"Disabilities prevent some students from attaining the developmental goals of each stage within the expected time frame. This is especially true for children with learning disabilities and emotional disorders whose disabilities are not apparent to others," write Nicholas J. Long and Jody E. Long in *Managing Passive-Aggressive Behavior of Children and Youth at School and Home*.[5] As a practicing child psychologist, I saw numerous children whose frustration grew from their classroom performance (or even athletic inabilities), and sometimes, these children's self-esteem plummeted. Their peer relations and home life also suffered. Anyone facing a disability goes through a normal grieving process similar to what the late Elisabeth Kubler-Ross chronicled in her pivotal book *On Death and Dying*.[6] The stages she outlined: denial, anger, bargaining, depression, and acceptance. Coming to terms with a disability is very similar. Larry B. Silver MD, who practices psychiatry in Maryland and Washington, D.C., writes in *The Misunderstood Child* that parents need to work through their own reactions to a learning disability, and that the three most prevalent emotions are denial (as in "No, it can't be true"), anger ("Why me?" "Why my child?"), and guilt ("It must be my fault").[7] Parents also go through stages of anger as school personnel try to help parents who aren't ready to accept their child's problem. They may also experience tremendous frustration when trying to advocate for better accommodations or special education, meeting resistance and/or ignorance.

HIDDEN ANGER AS A STAGE

GIVEN THE BEHAVIORS outlined in this book—laziness, forgetfulness, procrastination, constant irritability—does a teenager come to mind? Physical growth during the adolescent years often catapults well beyond emotional maturity. Not a child, yet unable to psychologically or financially provide for themselves, teens yearn for freedom, but appreciate limits as well. One day they are Mr. or Ms. Independent, and the next it's "Dad, can you help me?" or "Mom, can you take me to the mall?" Get to that mall and you'd better keep out of sight because most teens want to be as far away from their parents as possible.

It's this push-pull between those two extremes that causes teenagers to test authority (parents, teachers, principals), give in to occasional peer pressure to conform, or become moody while undergoing a physical, psychological, social, not to mention neurological upheaval.

Vacillating between these extremes is entirely normal. A certain amount of passive-aggressive behavior has always been a part of pushing the envelope into adulthood. When kids reach independence, this silent rebellion usually ceases and much of the time children embrace parental notions that they previously resisted. Yes . . . it's true. They may well appreciate all you did by age thirty, or once they have children of their own. However, if you're concerned about continued oppositional behavior, blocking, simmering anger, or another troublesome behavior in your teen, it's always good to check this out with your child's school counselor or your pediatrician. We'll also discuss this later in the book.

HIDDEN ANGER SEARCHING FOR ATTACHMENT

TYPICALLY, BABIES AND their caregivers form a secure attachment by the time the infant turns nine months old, but the writings of Mary Ainsworth, Mary Main, and Jude Cassidy distinguish three types of insecure attachments: babies who turn away or ignore their caregivers (avoidant attachment), angry, inconsolable children (resistant or ambivalent attachment), and confused infants not knowing what's happened with their caregivers (disorganized or disoriented attachment).[8] Of course, attachment problems could result from a caregiver's behavior or from the child's problems (e.g., autism).

Numerous studies back the notion that the more secure the attachment, the more successful one's social interactions throughout life, as evidenced by increased empathy and trust, improved self-confidence, higher-quality relationships, and fewer conflicts as well as fewer behavioral problems. Thus, if home is hostile or the child doesn't bond properly with his parents, the only way to retaliate is silently, sneaking anger out in small doses, sometimes without knowing he's even doing it. Chronically depressed children, who have lost the zest for life, have developed a bleak worldview, with everything out of their control, and besides . . . why bother? Pay attention if a child sees the world's cup as half-empty and dark instead of half-full of hope and promise.

HIDDEN ANGER WHEN COPING WITH CHANGE

CHANGING FAMILY DYNAMICS can cause hidden anger as well. How often do you find yourself slipping back into a role when you're with your extended family? If a younger sibling grows up, but the older ones try to restore their comfortable pecking order, you've got some problems. Why is it that some families can move with one another through the life span and others cannot?

Theodore Millon writing with Roger D. Davis offered insight into such negative behavior in their 1996 book (see appendix and chapter notes). "Many negativists felt that they had been 'replaced' by a younger sibling and that their parents' affections were withdrawn and redirected to a newborn child," they wrote, acknowledging that there were typically strong feelings of jealousy and resentment.[9]

Perhaps some kids want so badly to be the "good children" that they can't risk being honest. No one asked them if they wanted a baby brother or sister, who now steals all their thunder and gets presents, while they might get less attention and more chores. Wait until mom or dad leaves the room, and they might taunt their younger sibling. If caught, then what? Remembering that list of defenses, they'll cop a few, such as undoing ("I didn't mean to hit her") or rationalizing ("I couldn't help it, my toy just hit him"). Millon and Davis suggest that displaced resentment might *not* be intended for the younger sibling but actually for the parents themselves.[10] Once again, the risk of dealing with mom and dad directly is too great, and the younger sibling is an easier target for such anger.

HIDDEN ANGER AS A LEARNED BEHAVIOR

WE'RE ALL PRODUCTS of our environment. Within the United States, regions differ in their attitudes and norms. Certain corporate cultures and certainly southern hospitality give us the message of social graces, service with a smile. "My pleasure" became a motto at the Ritz Carlton chain, where clearly employees learned the message to serve happily even if they were having a horrendous day. The client is always right, as the professional cliché goes. Or is he? If you're a service worker and you ingest a steady diet of whatever the public dishes out, you may find that it gives way to discontent on the job, feeling slighted, or harboring hostile feelings toward those who have treated you poorly. Talk about being a product of a negative environment!

It's so important, however, not to assume that behavior is passive-aggressive until you've tested out other reasons for it. Culture is one. Certain cultures instill a sense of respect for one's elders that goes beyond Western cultural standards. For instance, in Asian cultures children are taught not to question their elders or to test authority, because it's a sign of great disrespect if you do. Can you see how harmful an inaccurate assumption could be if you were a teacher with an unusually silent student? The child might feel frustrated by this learned pattern of holding back while other kids raise their hands and offer debate.

Culture also can cause anger in children when they leave an isolated community where they felt emotionally safe and understood. If they encounter prejudice against their culture, faith, or other differences, they might be tempted to hide intrinsic aspects of themselves in order to fit in. At the same time, they might become ambivalent over that choice and angry about their own anxiety and others' inability to accept them for who they are.

Parents, of course, have the greatest influence over learned behavior. If a child never observes you work a problem through to resolution, but instead sees you storm off, sulk, smooth over difficulty, slam doors, or say "nothing's wrong" (through an angry smile), then you externally reinforce the message that anger is bad. If a child continues indirect, inappropriate behavior long past its being a stage, then the child lacks skills that could elicit positive attention. Chances are good that she's been reinforced in the wrong behaviors.

HIDDEN ANGER DUE TO OTHER FACTORS

CHILDREN WHO LACK adequate opportunity to develop social skills are also at higher risk of concealing their anger. Isolated by geography, the lack of same-age playmates, or other circumstances, the child's play takes a solitary form rather than one with give and take, subtle cues, and developing empathy. Sure, a child can be creative and imaginative on her own, or sometimes find ways around it, adapting to older or younger playmates. Interpersonal play helps a child to develop competent social skills.

Consistency between parents, teachers, and other caregivers is also paramount. Think about trying to serve two different bosses. No one wins. It's much the same for the child who receives one message from mom, another from dad, maybe even a third from the nanny or childcare worker. The child legitimately feels confused and ambivalent. These kids must have their antennae up because they might get the opposite of what one would typically expect. Just when they think they've done a job well, dad will come down hard on them. Whenever they expect a class sticker, they get a demerit, all because the teacher (or parent at home) is inconsistent. This inconsistency drives a child's frustration.

It's a parent's job to help a child resolve feelings, not run from them because they're so complex to figure out. "I have long believed that whatever is mentionable is manageable," said the late Fred Rogers writing in *The Journal of Family Communication*.[11] This is so true. Family Communications, the company that Rogers founded, offers many anger management resources for children, which are listed in the back of this book.[12]

TRANSFORMING AN ANGRY CHILDHOOD

IF YOU GREW up sloughing anger off as if it wasn't worthy of your energy or expressing it in subtle, sugarcoated, or even sarcastic ways, it's never too late to change your anger management style. Keep reading because we offer practical tips about strengthening your family, becoming less reactive, and encouraging open expression in later chapters.

As we close our discussion of childhood, remember Carlos from the start of this chapter? He complains a lot according to his wife Rosa, and she is concerned about his somewhat childlike behavior because he's rarely decisive, often acting needy. Even his younger sister calls him passive-aggressive. Carlos says that's just the way he is. He likes Rosa's attention. Big deal. Do you think there might be a childhood root to Carlos's problems here? So as not to be sexist, do you think that Rosa is picking on her poor husband?

Sometimes it's hard to tell. Cultural expectations might play a role in their marriage, but past problems with his younger sister or parents might also. His seeking approval or attention could stem from feeling replaced by his younger sister. Many older brothers or sisters feel robbed of their due; thus, they try in a host of ways (too often negative) to get attention. When a person complains of aches and pains, he might also return to that childlike state where a caregiver attended to every scrape or fall. Even with inconsistent parenting, mom or dad would usually rally around with a little comfort. The automatic thought is: if saying I was hurt got me attention as a little boy, maybe it will work again!

CHILDLIKE NEEDS

CHILDREN OFTEN ACT out because of unmet needs or things they're afraid of, and if these conflicts aren't resolved by adulthood, the angry adult may appear immature, avoiding the same things based upon those age-old fears. They may keep searching, even without knowing they're doing it, for what they never achieved as a child. In the table that follows, we list what you might commonly see and where it originates.

NEEDS	FEARS/AVOIDS	WHAT YOU SEE
■ To recreate earlier experience from childhood	■ Being loved conditionally	■ Wants to be cared for
■ To be seen as the "good boy" or "good girl"	■ Losing rank in family	■ Transfers issues to others
■ Independence yet feels dependent	■ Powerlessness	■ Seeks approval
	■ Never getting it right	■ Body aches and pains, whines, anxiety
	■ Responsibility	■ Ambivalence, waffling, resistance
		■ Unwilling to make decisions

Given the small bits that we know about Carlos's family, he could be recreating earlier experiences to get the nurturance he perhaps lost when his sister came along. Sometimes he might like being dependent upon Rosa, allowing her to make decisions, but at other times he likes making them for himself. If this is a continued pattern, lasting a few years, then it might well look a bit immature to Rosa, who needs him to assume greater responsibility, especially if they are to create their own family. Still, the situation is not beyond hope. In fact, understanding one's childhood and the troubles that may have stemmed from it can come as a tremendous relief to many people.

Where you've been doesn't define where you are going. No one escapes his or her youth without a few scars. Refuse to be held back by events beyond your control. If you've confused or walled off your emotions so that your own negative circumstances prevent you from connecting with your spouse or children, from empathizing with what it's like to walk in their shoes, then counseling could help.

Passive-Aggression
in Different
Settings

FOUR

COPING WITH
HIDDEN ANGER
AT WORK AND SCHOOL

PICTURE YOURSELF A busy bank vice president overseeing several departments and traveling to give numerous presentations. You rely upon your staff, including Kyle who manages your schedule. When you're on the road you email him with various requests, but Kyle isn't very quick on the uptake. He lets these messages pile up until you have to ask two and three times whether he received your instructions or material. Then, his terse "got it" leaves you wondering which message he's replying to, and when you ask him to be more precise, he summarily leaves out the details in future replies.

During an important meeting to review the next week, you ask him about "potential apt. with Mr. Y." appearing on your schedule. "Who is Mr. Y? What company is he with?"

"I'm not sure," Kyle replies matter-of-factly, ignoring your look of disdain.

"Tell me more about the event on the twenty-sixth?" you ask, moving on.

"I don't know," Kyle answers. This goes on for half of your thirty-minute meeting.

"Kyle, it's clear you haven't prepared for this meeting. What's more, your failure to follow my requests and stay on top of things is interfering with your job . . . and mine. Don't come in here again without the concrete details of my schedule and these events," you tell him, squarely.

"I'm sorry. Honestly, I'm sorry. Can't you be patient with me?" Kyle asks.

"Patient? I've been patient the last three times I've asked you to improve this and get organized. You're wasting my time when you aren't doing your job."

"Well, maybe if you would give me less to do, I could get it all done."

You give Kyle another stern look. Dejected, he walks out of your office, never apologizing for his shoddy performance. Days later, you have to reconstruct the details of the meeting that never were discussed. In the meantime, your secretary receives complaints at least every other day about unreturned phone calls and presentations where the materials never arrived. Soon, you hear that Kyle has filed a complaint with Human Resources that you're giving him work beyond his job description and he's so stressed out from all the pressure. These types of headaches you just don't need!

MANY PEOPLE SPEND easily eight to twelve hours a day at work or in school, sometimes more. Beyond the hours, if you must deal with an irascible boss, a disagreeable student, or a backstabbing coworker, you're ready to walk out the door. Problem is, you need the money, or the education. You must stick it out and cope with these personalities while trying to keep your own demeanor from plummeting.

In this chapter, we'll explore the best strategies for coping with the anger lurking in the nearest cubicle or desk. We'll also steer you clear of emotional reactions that creep into your own behavior if you're not careful.

QUIZ: WHAT'S YOUR PERFORMANCE STYLE?

TAKE THIS QUIZ to become more aware of your own on-the-job or in-the-classroom style, using the key below:

> 1 not like me
> 2 only slightly like me
> 3 somewhat like me
> 4 very much like me

1. _____ It bothers me when requests are made of me at work or school.
2. _____ I prefer to work my own way to get the job accomplished, even if it takes longer.
3. _____ I'd rather keep my feelings to myself.
4. _____ I'm comfortable with my job duties and don't look to increase them.

5. ____ Most people seem to tolerate conflict better than I do.

6. ____ Criticism bothers me.

7. ____ When asked to do things I dislike, it's not a big deal because the request may be forgotten.

8. ____ Appearing successful is what counts.

9. ____ I wish I could change things but can live with the way things are.

10. ____ I shouldn't make my frustration or anger obvious.

11. ____ Talking things over creates more problems than solutions.

12. ____ I'm skeptical of new assignments and plans unless I had a hand in creating them.

13. ____ I've felt the same concerns/disappointments before in similar situations.

14. ____ If I know I'll be getting feedback I might not like, I'd rather be absent that day.

15. ____ I can do the job better if allowed to do it myself.

16. ____ People at work/school are not to be trusted.

17. ____ I feel pretty good knowing things that others don't and having an advantage over them.

18. ____ When I disagree, sarcasm works better than being direct.

19. ____ I wish I felt more confident about my skills, my talents, and myself.

20. ____ It's tough to tell others about my decisions most of the time.

21. ____ When something requires quick action, I feel uneasy and pressured.

22. ____ When new supervisors/teachers are hired, I feel extra cautious.

23. ____ If someone isn't doing his job right, I'll keep quiet; let them find out the hard way.

24. ____ If I make a mistake, I definitely do not want to discuss it with my supervisor/teacher.

25. ____ I'm uncomfortable when someone talks to me about how to do my job better.

Tally the total number of points and compare with the key below.

A score of 25–43: Your style is fairly direct and open to self-expression, adaptability, and new challenges. It's unlikely that you hide much, and are not afraid to deal productively with problems.

A score of 34–62: Your style is somewhat direct, but in some cases, you might shy away from or feel uncomfortable with confrontation. Be aware of this because remaining open and willing to adapt yields great things.

A score of 63–81: Your style is somewhat indirect. Confrontation makes you uneasy. If this sounds like you, it might be wise to talk this over with someone you trust and who can offer you honest feedback.

A score of 82–100: Your style is pretty much indirect. While it may work for you, it's likely that you've hidden some frustrations along the way because you sidestep people, situations, even challenges that might actually benefit you. Be open to assistance to boost your assertiveness and self-confidence.

WHAT GOT US SO ANGRY?

WHEN SOMEONE ASKS impressionable youngsters what they want to be when they grow up, they rarely say a stressed-out doctor, disgruntled employee, laid-off dot-comer, or cynical civil servant. Mix and match. Add other positions. It all spells an undercurrent of anxiety and stress that feeds people's anger. In the academic setting, there's been a dramatic increase in college students with mental health problems over the last ten to fifteen years, according to the American Psychological Association.[1] While incidents of anxiety, depression, and sexual assault made up this picture, so did stress and anger.

The off-the-cuff remark someone made to disparage your presentation, the backhanded compliment that was really a thinly-veiled dig, even the subtle snub when your parking space is taken away or you fail to receive a much-coveted invitation to lunch—these acts discharge anger for some and provoke it in others. Stress might manifest with the evasive boss who won't give you a needed answer or the student who assumes the victim position with "You're always on me." Your own perceptions may be a significant stressor. If you take offense and feel a level of injustice has been served, you're frustrated all right, but is it out of proportion to what triggered it? It's important to understand that even inertia is a reaction. It halts goals. When the lunchroom is filled with sad sacks or the executive dining room exudes egotism, it doesn't exactly incite others to jump onboard and achieve greatness either.

THE TENOR OF TODAY'S WORKPLACE

TODAY, RATHER THAN having a lifetime, guaranteed job, the typical worker will change positions five to seven times, maybe more. Every career has its stressors.

In professional services, millions of healthcare workers, teachers, and others start each day fearful of grievances and angry lawsuits. Much-needed physicians stop delivering babies or abandon their practices because they can't afford the steep malpractice premiums. Do you think these professionals accustomed to giving care don't react with a little anger, in need of care themselves? The angst filters down to the average citizen who pays literally and figuratively in less obvious ways.

In the wake of 9/11, the anxiety of working in a high-rise office complex in certain cities as well as the fears about a cyclical economy predispose many workers to job insecurity and aggravation. Beyond health, safety, and finances, office gossip and inexperienced and poorly-trained workers annoy us. Management might institute ill-conceived changes, and later, when productivity or morale suffers, they dodge any responsibility to cover their ruinous decisions. Living from paycheck to paycheck, drawing on savings to pay bills and child-care expenses—all of these stressors mean that people may take out their frustrations on those who had nothing to do with the underlying circumstances.

Conversely, enjoying your work, feeling self-assured, safe, that you make a difference, and have input yields a tremendous emotional lift. Ditto for those who feel they work with a respectful, above-board group of people. Employees with adequate work-life balance also show higher rates of self-esteem and overall satisfaction, according to a 2002 study released in the *Academy of Management Journal.*[2]

DOLLARS & SENSE OF ON-THE-JOB STRESS

As INDICATED BY the National Institute of Mental Health, depression costs American business $44 billion each year.[3] The Health Enhancement Research Organization, a nonprofit coalition of employers and healthcare providers, found that stress factored into 25 percent of all healthcare costs.[4] In many high-pressure work climates, stress-related medical conditions such as migraine headaches, gastrointestinal ailments, anxiety and depression, obesity, high blood pressure, and heart disease caused health-insurance premiums to jump 30 to 40 percent from previous years. Absenteeism is costly. In 2004, the American Psychological Association found that one in four respondents took a "mental health day" off the job due to stress.[5] In a study led by Kathryn Rost, PhD of the University of Colorado Health System, researchers found that when specially trained health-care providers offered "enhanced" treatment (antidepressant medication and/or counseling) for depression, depressed workers were more productive at work and missed fewer workdays than those with standard treatment. That additional productivity added up to an estimated value of $2,601 per each depressed, full-time employee.[6]

Having a preexisting condition certainly exacerbates job stress and burnout. Having heart disease means that you're twice as likely to be depressed, and those healthcare costs rise as well. Not surprisingly, when employers recognize the effects of unrealistic demands and undue stress placed upon their workers, morale improves, productivity climbs, healthcare costs decrease, employee retention rates increase, and the company benefits in various other ways—not to mention how home life and individual mental health improve, thereby making workers more creative and relaxed, and better able to tend to their duties.

WORKAHOLICS AND JOB-RELATED STRESS

WE CALL ADDICTION to a job workaholism, and it's caused by anxious thoughts that no performance level is good enough (therefore, constant work relieves the anxiety), or it's imposed upon workers by an organizational culture that demands more than most can bear. Regardless, it makes workers seethe inside. When difficult personalities enter the picture, burnout sets in. Job anxiety/stress = burnout = increased risk of anger and negativity.

Workaholics will tell you that while they might thoroughly enjoy their jobs, they'd rather not put in fifty to seventy hour weeks—the ability to focus upon anything outside of work seems to be stolen. So is any semblance of normality for your family when members report much tension, feelings of loss, and hidden anger stemming from your absence. There are high personal demands placed upon others because of the workaholic's constant "driven" path without the satisfaction that goes along with it. If you're never satisfied, then working becomes an end in itself.

The lyrics to Harry Chapin's "Cats in the Cradle" describe a child with a workaholic father: "There were planes to catch and bills to pay; he learned to walk while I was away." When intense jobs drive even the family agenda, parents may be physically, yet not emotionally, present.

How do you know you're a workaholic?

1. Do you feel married to your job, at work early in the morning, during the lunch break, late into the night, and on weekends when you could be relaxing?
2. Are you highly competitive? Prone to anger if you can't assume your driven schedule?
3. Does work always come before important relationships, parenting, or household responsibilities?
4. Do you feel disorganized? Unable to accomplish your work in the time allotted?
5. Are you the type that can't utter the word "no" when presented with more work?
6. Do you thrive on the constant pressure of deadlines? The escape that work affords from other areas of your life?
7. Do you read only work-related literature?
8. Is there a payoff beyond income, such as getting in good with the boss, boosting your own sense of self-worth, or the ability to brag about how many hours you put in at the office?

Working occasional overtime due to a personnel shortage, seasonal work (e.g., the CPA at tax time), or new, unexpected demands is understandable, but over time, the stress of working too many hours adds up. De-stress by:

- Becoming self-aware of your workaholism. Pick up on "hints" dropped by family, friends, or even your coworkers.
- Make daily goals and to-do lists. Completed tasks provide a sense of accomplishment. Focus on these accomplishments and not just the climb before you.
- Watch your diet. Avoid the vending machine's refined sugars, flours, and fats. Snack on fruits and vegetables, and sip water to stay hydrated. High-protein lunches stave off hunger and keep you energized.
- Cut back on caffeine. Some coffee can perk you up, too much, and you're ready for a fatigue-fall later. The same applies to caffeinated soft drinks and tea.
- Exercise at least twenty to thirty minutes each day, more if you can. Schedule workout time. Walking during lunch or your commute burns off stress and calories. Grabbing sunshine lightens your mood as well.

- Sleep at least eight hours each night or determine the right amount of sleep for you. Don't work right up until bedtime either. Too little shut-eye gives way to irritability, anger, and . . . you guessed it . . . acting on that anger.
- Take a daily respite from cell phones, BlackBerries, pagers, email, and other devices, especially during meals and family times.
- Take regular vacations from routine demands. Feel a sense of accomplishment doing something out of the ordinary. Schedule the time and stick to it. Use your driven nature on the job to be as perfect at home with your family. Recharge your batteries.
- Find what positive-psychology guru Martin Seligman, PhD calls your signature strength, or what you do well that sets you apart. Your current job should play to those strengths.

■

CREATING A BETTER WORKPLACE CULTURE

TODAY, workers have been let go in corporate downsizing, yet the workload has been delegated to a dwindling group of employees. According to the National Institute for Occupational Safety and Health (NIOSH), directed by Congress to study the psychological aspects of job safety and health, stressful work conditions include: Heavy workload; infrequent breaks; long hours; routine tasks with no real meaning; under-utilizing workers' skills; lack of participation in decision making; few family-friendly policies; lack of support; conflicting or uncertain job expectations; too much responsibility; job insecurity; lack of advancement, growth, and opportunity; rapid changes for which workers are unprepared; and unpleasant or dangerous conditions.[7]

You build a pleasant workplace based upon a desire to do well, taking pride in your work, supporting each other, and sharing in successes. Employers can create an atmosphere where the stressors that feed hidden anger decline if they:

- ◆ Involve employees. Honor their experience. Enlist them in decisions, especially if they will be the ones to implement changes you decide upon or inherit the new technology you acquire for on-the-job use.
- ◆ Listen and pay active attention. Ego and entitlement wall off good ideas. Managers who are poor listeners often feel *their*

opinions haven't mattered. So they repeat patterns modeled in their own careers. Stop and listen. In Congress, we call this reaching across the aisle. Everyone can do it.

◆ Choose problem solving over power-oriented conflict resolution. Brainstorm for ideas, evaluate your options, think through any obstacles, and make your decisions accordingly. Commit your solution to paper, implement it, and review it regularly. Fine-tune it if necessary, admitting your mistakes.

◆ Offer outlets for frustration—from the suggestion box to teaching employees how to communicate more effectively, assert themselves, and make better decisions.

EIGHT ANGER TYPES AT WORK OR IN SCHOOL

Scott Adams outlined workplace anxieties through *Dilbert,* making us laugh. No one aims to become comic-strip fodder, but indeed you meet all personalities at work. We've selected our own eight personality types to discuss: Backstabbers, Avengers, Controllers, Cynics, Eeyores, Blamers, Mutes, and Stars. Someone you know may even fit more than one category.

THE BACKSTABBER	
HOW THEY BEHAVE	**HOW YOU SHOULD RESPOND**
▪ Betrays	▪ Remember, he/she crave attention and need a bully pulpit; don't provide one.
▪ Takes credit for your work	▪ Hand deliver your work to the boss to lessen chance of the backstabber taking credit for it; leave a paper trail; document your work.
▪ Breaks confidences	▪ Deal directly but gently with offender; use empathy to prevent repeat offenses and be prepared with facts.
▪ Plays up to those in authority, treats suborinates poorly	▪ Kill him/her with kindness and keep to yourself; smile—so they'll have nothing to use against you.
▪ Sabotages others' work directly or through gossip	▪ Don't gossip.

The barber who sells his business to another barber, agrees to a noncompete clause in the agreement, takes the money, but whispers to customers that his scissors are ready again six miles up the street is a backstabber. Forget being grateful that he found a buyer, this guy bites the hand that feeds him. That he's in violation of a restrictive covenant means nothing because he feels entitled to customers that legally convey to the new shop owner. The backstabber often resembles the avenger described next, but the distinction between the two is the motive—one is motivated by his own promotion, the other by revenge.

THE AVENGER

HOW THEY BEHAVE	HOW YOU SHOULD RESPOND
▪ Acts on anger when provoked and feeling increasingly hopeless	▪ Since revenge is often about views of injustice, resist laying into the person.
▪ Obstructs goals, violates norms and promises, withholds	▪ Ask what seems fair and unfair.
▪ Sabotages, pulls the wool over people's eyes, embarrasses	▪ Promote honest communication without the anger.
▪ Assails power or status, "disses" or criticizes, covert and overt actions	▪ Hold the person accountable for her actions but without your own anger.
▪ Rationalizes own behavior as self-defense	

Workers with their sights set on vengeance operate from an "I don't get mad, I get even" approach. Examples of revenge include overbilling a client because you're annoyed with him, cutting a customer's hair too short because you're annoyed that she doesn't tip better, waiting until a team meeting to disclose embarrassing information, sabotaging equipment, or purposely excluding someone from an important event in order to cause intentional hurt and/or embarrassment. In 2002, *The Washington Post* featured an article titled "Capital Offenses: Snubbery in the First Degree" in which it described snubs as anything but "overt whacks"—more as "passive-aggressive power plays, slights of omission like the 'overlooked' invitation, missed mention or neglected courtesy call."[8]

In *Counterproductive Work Behavior,* Suzy Fox and Paul E. Spector discuss revenge, concluding that it's provoked with certain goals behind it, including goal obstruction and violation of rules, norms, or promises, as well as attempts to derogate a person's status or power. However, the vengeful person may rationalize his actions as self-defense based upon irrational beliefs or feelings, not facts. There's often a perception of perceived injustice.[9]

According to Richard Driscoll, PhD, who practices psychology and researches interpersonal conflict in Knoxville, Tennessee, the person claiming "I'm not angry" can have a real yen for vengeance from feeling mistreated. Thus, he owes the world revenge. His motto: anything not for me is against me. "In an angry state they're more likely to see things as provocation and attack back," Driscoll says, likening this to a true catfight where if you separate the players, you'll likely be scratched by even your own animal in attack mode. If you're the angry worker, the key, he says, is learning to say what makes you angry, only omitting the anger.

THE CONTROLLER

HOW THEY BEHAVE	HOW YOU SHOULD RESPOND
■ Manipulates for control	■ Resist sharing heartfelt thoughts even when he/she turns on the charm because it could be used in a self-serving way to manipulate.
■ Demands his/her way, threatens and wields power	
■ Wrestles with anxiety, may be overwhelmed by demanding organizational culture or job	■ Find common ground; agree with the person occasionally.
■ Vents frustrations	■ Get the person to back your idea by pointing out how it serves his/her interest.
■ Lacks confidence when not in charge	

When the supervisor selects the Friday after Thanksgiving for a mandatory meeting, knowing it will pull countless people away from a long weekend and holiday season kickoff, we see a controller. This is akin to the hastily-called meeting at 4:45 on a Friday before the start of a long summer weekend—an example that could be considered manipulative, demanding, power-wielding, and possibly threatening (if you bucked the system, you'd certainly encounter risk). Causing such inconvenience and doing something that deliberately annoys others indirectly discharges frustrations, placing them on other people.

The worker who calls in "sick" regularly, does the minimal amount of work necessary to keep her job until she's eligible for her pension, and couldn't care less that her absences force you to stay late is also a controller. If it's always about her needs, there's some ego and "star" qualities mixed in here as well. Some people work just hard enough to keep their job, but never cross the line, remaining merely marginal workers, not bad enough to be fired, but barely good enough to stay hired. Being underemployed is very common among passive-aggressive people.

THE CYNIC

HOW THEY BEHAVE	HOW YOU SHOULD RESPOND
■ Acts suspicious and paranoid, especially of authority	■ Use humor to distract him/her; smile.
■ Uses sarcasm	■ Steer clear when in a low ebb yourself so as not to fall under the person's influence.
■ Sees things negatively	
■ Criticizes	■ Work hard to stay positive; be polite.
■ Rationalizes away criticisms as just and appropriate	■ Arm yourself with stats, quotes, and facts to counter his/her cynicism.
■ Uses cynicism as a superficial pseudointellectual to seem as if he/she is knowledgeable and acts as if further analysis isn't worthy of his/her time.	■ Question your own sense of dread; is it his/her suspicion, rather than yours?
	■ Don't play the same game of sarcasm and cynicism.
	■ Seek out positive people at work.

Lobbyists set lofty goals to persuade others and must maintain positive relationships. Even if they "lose" today, they have to be ready for tomorrow. But if anyone championing a particular cause aims for 100 percent goal-attainment and accepts nothing less, she sets herself up for a letdown. Such is the case of the woman who achieved 80 percent of her agenda. You'd think she'd brim with delight, but instead she makes sarcastic remarks around her office, attributing negative motives to those who set the goal. She becomes paranoid and critical. Creating a downbeat atmosphere sure won't help on the next set of goals. What's more, it spills over onto those around her, and in any workplace, the one making cynical comments stands to lose a lot when the remarks get back to those who likely won't rally around the person or the cause next time.

A musician, secretly anxious about his own failed recording attempts, is steamed while reviewing a CD for the music review column he writes, feeling "I could have done a better job with this!" Instead of networking, maybe learning a few strategies, he becomes cynical, using his column to pan the local artist's music while lobbing low blows at his reputation, all under the guise of "opinion" and "free press," when truly it's cynical and vindictive (the avenger).

A business person who allows her critical commentary to multiply enters the office with not only a briefcase dangling from her shoulder but also a large chip of suspicion. Nothing is good enough for the cynical worker. To her, the company is going nowhere, so she undermines others' attempts to succeed, even using her cynicism to appear intellectually superior, acting as if she's trying to help, all the while pointing out the weaknesses in your work.

Unable to adapt to change, cynical workers feel unnecessary competition or suspicion when newcomers join the team. They feel spied upon, vulnerable. The fear may be about wanting to make good impressions or about being found incompetent. Fear triggers avoidance through sarcastic comments and other behavior that pushes people away before they can do the rejecting.

THE EEYORE

HOW THEY BEHAVE	HOW YOU SHOULD RESPOND
■ Plays victim, whimpers, moans	■ Ignore this because you don't want to positively reinforce the person's whining.
■ Sees things as "glass half-empty" rather than "half-full"	
■ Feels sorry for him/herself	■ Remind the person he/she's got a chance to leave and direct his/her own destiny.
■ Pessimistic; complains a lot	
■ Self-sabotages	■ Refuse to do the work for the person or accept his/her responsibility.
■ Passive; often underemployed; may have chronic low moods and/or addictions	■ Offer assertiveness training if you're the supervisor.
■ Does nothing beyond job description	■ Offer an alternative to the front-desk position because first impressions aren't likely this person's strong suit.
■ Exhibits some mute traits also	

"I'm really trying," Eeyore, the popular character in *Winnie the Pooh*, might say. It could be just as well the sad-sack worker in your office. "I just forgot. I'm not doing it on purpose." Eeyore views the world from "a glass half-empty" perspective. These folks greet you with a long face and offer a host of excuses why things don't get accomplished. There's a bit of the blamer in them because they are perpetual victims—martyrs to their own cause.

A worker who lets the tragic loss of a loved one define every facet of her life, including her failures at work, operates with the motto: "You don't understand." If her boss, who has put up with inertia and incomplete work, finally confronts her, no matter how compassionately, she may still perpetuate her victim status. When, predictably, she falls back on her motto, her boss might agree saying, "You're right, I've never lost someone so close but after six years, you need to move forward with your life, and you can't reasonably blame your performance here on that loss." He might even go the extra mile suggesting that she see a counselor for her grieving and engage the employee assistance program, but shirking responsibility for her behavior, she labels her boss a tyrant in front of coworkers. This woman's victim mentality successfully splits staff loyalty, embarrasses the boss, and creates an undercurrent of gossip. She remains the injured party instead of hearing the advice and moving forward because she can always look down upon those who "don't understand."

These people can continually search for the secondary gain of their sadness, scoping out a new employee to tell their tale of woe and reap more sympathy. What might happen if the woman in the example gave up her sadness? In cases of loss, a worker like this might falsely equate feeling better to not having loved the departed enough, as odd as that may sound.

Eeyore and his sad comrades might also become a little down in the dumps when they don't get what they want. You'll see some tantrums or emotional meltdowns. The whiz kid, the most popular girl, or the jock accustomed to much admiration K–12, becomes depressed when faced with equal or better talent beyond high school.

Remember that the passive-aggressive person sometimes needs attention, love, admiration, but at the same time exhibits behavior that literally pushes others away. When others have had enough and exit the relationship, you may also see depression. It might stem from ambivalence because the passive-aggressor can't decide whether he wants in or out of a particular relationship, job, or academic program. Those whose world concept is half-empty rather than full of life are often hypersensitive, prone to addictions, and may self-medicate their hurt. This could take the form of alcohol or substance abuse, overeating, gambling, acting out sexually—anything that numbs the feelings of emptiness, even momentarily.

Self-esteem is a problem for depressed passive-aggressive workers because they often lack the self-confidence to be competitive. As Scott Wetzler and Leslie Morey pointed out in a journal article, "They doubt they can win, and should they win they expect success to make them even more vulnerable," they wrote. "Consequently, they inhibit their competitive drive and ambition (tying their own hands), making the competition covert."[10]

If you see a coworker or employee procrastinating with a task, being intentionally inefficient, or displaying a "woe is me" victim mentality, it might just be lagging self-esteem, or it could also be more serious underlying anxiety in addition to a mood disorder.

■

COPING WITH DISAPPOINTMENT

NEGATIVE workers or students cope poorly when disappointment sets in. A dream dies. A tragic loss occurs. Something long sought after isn't within their grasp. Holding onto the pessimism can start in youth when you don't make the team or the cheerleading squad, or don't get accepted by your first choice of college. Youth and adults both understand the heartbreak of unrequited love, and the stakes are no less meaningful in youth.

How is it that some people can be disappointed by a lack of acceptance, relationship, sports medal, job opportunity, or even political election but rise the next day, and begin erasing the loss with fulfillment until they brim with pride and success? Yet others wake with a negative attitude that, left unchecked, leads to hidden hostility, and possibly depression. In a trying circumstance, some people fail because of it, others survive despite it, and still others succeed because of it, becoming stronger over the long run.

Think of Donald Trump's line "You're fired!" How would you cope? Stay unemployed? Find another job but never really correct what caused the problem in the first place? Or, without obsessing, learn from what went wrong, hone your skills, build a better image, and land in an even better position?

We can shape some adversities into happiness. Having control over our own thoughts grants us the chance to change a situation and see it in a new light. In all too many cases, the crisis isn't truly the problem—the response is. In a work world that applauds position, status, money, and achievement, try these steps if disappointment shakes your moorings:

◆ Give yourself time to grieve. A major life setback resembles a death—bringing about denial, anger, bargaining, depression, and acceptance.

◆ Adjust your expectations. Take a step back. Analyze where you were, where you are now, and where you wish to be. Did you feel a sense of entitlement? Are you asking too much? Does the stigma of "failure" or "loss" wear you down? If so, lighten up, ease up on your expectations, or jettison them all together.

◆ Learn from your loss. A certain amount of "shoulda, coulda, woulda" thinking is normal. Regret is usually about a step we didn't take or a second guess as to what "might" have happened. If you don't *learn* from what you didn't have, you'll never *earn* what you wish to have. Put closure on this step and move onto the next ones.

◆ Reframe the disappointment. Some better fit for your abilities could steer you along a path that you'll look upon as a blessing someday. If you've lost a job, might this be the time to find a truly better position? Become self-employed? Switch careers? Go back for more education? Spend time with family and friends (even briefly)? If you didn't get the 4.0 average, will it truly make a difference in one year, five, or ten? Examine new feelings about your loss. What opportunities does it open up? What strengths do you have to build upon?

◆ Rehearse new behavior. Take your new expectations and feelings and match up new actions. Think you can't? Resistance will most assuredly keep you in the same spot. Even minor changes build momentum for future change.

◆ Practice positive self-talk. Eliminate words like "maybe" or "can't" from your daily vocabulary. Replace "I'll hope to" with "I will." Ask yourself "why not?" every time you're tempted to think "It won't work."

◆ List your successes. Commit your goals to print. Writing these down and posting them is very conscious and powerfully prescriptive. Write down steps toward each goal so that you can check off your successes.

◆ Act "as if" you can. When you want something, try to behave "as if" you already have it, "as if" you can. It's similar to dressing for the job you aspire to rather than the one you have, helping management to picture you in that promoted role.

◆ If you haven't been let go yet, prepare. Always save money. Focus on doing your job well. Build your skills and résumé so that you don't feel trapped in a job.

◆ Surround yourself with the right resources—positive, encouraging people. Limit your time around naysayers. Read books and articles about successful people. Learn to think like a believer and achiever!

◆ Keep at it. Did the Wright Brothers give up on their invention? No! Did Martin Luther King let threats and violence alter his dream? No! Did Hayden Smith stop along the way? Of course, you don't recognize Hayden. He gave up! Underachievers feel little control in life, whereas achievers embrace a work ethic and keep their motivation alive.

Disappointment can define you. Choose to move beyond bitterness, to claim new and exciting opportunities that will illuminate the path before you.

THE BLAMER

HOW THEY BEHAVE	HOW YOU SHOULD RESPOND
▪ Can't argue fairly	▪ Have a clear grasp of facts and point these out.
▪ Avoids responsibility	▪ Don't do his/her job or work.
▪ Dumps on everyone else	▪ Limit time for his/her dumping; walk away.
▪ Minimizes or exaggerates	▪ Argue fairly yourself.
▪ Rationalizes	▪ Avoid emotional, knee-jerk reaction.

In healthcare, it's not uncommon to see a patient who fails to take responsibility for getting better—the noncompliant patient—otherwise known as the help-rejecting complainer. These people are angry that they're afflicted or in pain. Of course, there's a certain amount of justifiable anger, since no one wishes to be unhealthy. But when a patient points the finger at others (even filing unnecessary malpractice suits) or self-sabotages recovery by refusing to follow advice and treatment, you wonder what secondary gain she obtains.

Though Helen has some back pain, it presents far worse than doctors might expect from the x rays taken. If a physician has referred Helen, a perpetual complainer, to see a counselor and has given Helen the name of a psychiatrist to consider antidepressant or anxiety medication, sparks fly from Helen's hidden anger. There is an increased co-occurrence of depression, stress, and back pain. Thus, it's reasonable for a doctor to screen for it and refer patients like Helen for consultations if there are signs of depression or anxiety.

"I don't need a shrink," she might say. "This doctor can't fix me. He thinks it's all in my head." Here, Helen is twisting the truth to fit her avoidance and remain safe. As long as she can refuse to accept a mind/body connection, she can blame her doctor(s). Helen might be a bit self-centered, too, because calling attention to her ailments does yield a secondary gain of attention. By projecting negativity, she receives sympathy. This can easily become a self-perpetuating, circular pattern. It keeps the doctor on edge to the point where he may refer Helen to another doctor. Then, she'll complain about being "abandoned," or maybe she abandons doctors by jumping from one to another in search of the miracle cure, and of course, gets a steady stream of sympathy, at least initially, from new healthcare providers. She's got the secondary gain maintaining her pain, all the while avoiding the real treatment that she needs. Additionally, the sympathy cycle drives the complainer's family and friends nuts.

In a business setting, employees that blame use the same "jumping around" pattern. Or you might experience the following scenario: You've sent a colleague needed spreadsheets and attached files multiple times. He's always got an excuse why he hasn't gotten back to you. "Can you send those files again?" he might ask right before your joint deadline. One more problem, one more delay. You feel like screaming, "Lack of planning on your part does not warrant an emergency on mine!"

What if this colleague honestly has a legitimate excuse? Perhaps his wife walked out, and he's suddenly taken on single-parent responsibilities. Bills are piling up, maybe his daughter was diagnosed with an illness, and he's juggling way too much. Then his behavior may merely *appear* to be passive-aggressive when honest, open communication would have cleared away any misunderstandings. Compassion and support will help him regain strength and solve problems. Remember: If it's about secondary gain, any compassion and support will feed the problem.

THE MUTE

HOW THEY BEHAVE	HOW YOU SHOULD RESPOND
■ Ignores, avoids, denies	■ Don't feel invalidated.
■ Uses silence	■ Maintain your self-esteem.
■ Swallows everything	■ Expect him/her to deny problems.
■ Has no follow-through	■ Offer warmth to his/her icy demeanor.
■ Procrastinates, indecisive	■ Refuse to match his/her mute behavior.
■ Purposely excludes you from information or meetings	■ Be very clear in your communications.
■ When the going gets tough, he/she gets quiet	■ Clarify your expectations of him/her.
	■ Don't assume that silence means agreement (or disagreement).

Imagine the child whose parents enroll her in a private school because she's unhappy, only once she's got the uniform, she refuses to attend classes. This exemplifies using silence to make powerful points. This girl might miss the bus one day, have a migraine another, and claim the teacher is picking on her. Each time, she denies what's really going on, sometimes to herself. If she masks her true intent (to drop out of school), she succeeds at manipulating everyone and most likely self-sabotages her future.

Adults use silence a lot, too. Imagine teaching a class, especially if it's online with only written communication, and while you ask your students at various times for feedback of how they're coming along with the work, and how you might help them, they remain mum. You interpret their silence as "no problem," and you're astounded when one offers formal feedback at the end of the semester telling the dean that they expected much more of your assistance.

Picture parishioners sitting through a long-winded sermon, annoyed when it's commonplace. If this minister keeps his audience captive because he feels overwhelmed by a grueling schedule, and resentful that he has no sounding board, it's socially well masked because it's silent. If this man felt entitled to take others' time, then there's a bit of star quality or ego here. Those who speak in public must have some; too much spells trouble.

You might hear silence when your coworker chooses not to pass along important information that might save others hassle, inconvenience, or worry. Maybe it's the boss who makes a decision that impacts you, and he doesn't fully disclose why. If you're working for a one-man operation and get fired, you might never know the reason. In a larger company, if the boss moves your office or takes away your parking space to get back at you, this "cold shoulder" or silent approach sends powerful negative messages, though very indirectly.

THE STAR

HOW THEY BEHAVE	HOW YOU SHOULD RESPOND
■ Concerned with his/her own agenda, preoccupied with self	■ Realize you may feel positive about him/her, but over time, see problems
■ Ingratiates self successfully	■ Realize that he/she rejects mentoring.
■ Thinks he/she is a superstar	■ Include the star on the team using the person's strengths; help the person to feel that his/her ideas are vital.
■ Requires special treatment	■ Ignore his/her know-it-all nature.
■ Showcases own achievements	■ Don't argue over who is right because this person thinks that . he/she always is.
■ Snubs others, above the rules	
■ Sees you as competition	
■ Displays little or no empathy	
■ "Legend in his/her own mind"	
■ Forms triangle	

We saved the star for last because it coexists with other worker-type styles. Certainly in your own work life you will run up against many who believe that they are stars. This behavior also fits with the overlap between the narcissist and other passive-aggressive traits (see the appendix).

Stars might think that they deserve superstar status. They are indeed legends in their own minds. The star is adept at getting the credit, grabbing all the publicity, or gaining the notoriety by being in the right place at the right time. The typical star pushes his agenda, not yours, like a lawyer you hire to represent the educational interests of your special-needs child. You'd expect a little compassion, some empathy, right? He touts his abilities making you buy into his hot-shot lawyer status, yet as soon as he deposits your retainer he disregards anyone's input but his own. Countless mistakes crop up. On documents, he doesn't even get the child's name, school, or disability straight. He bills you for revisions but becomes indignant when you ask for a credit. How could you be so darn ungrateful when you have one of the best attorneys? So he tells you. This can apply to many who provide a service—the car salesman, the stockbroker, anyone.

THE STAR HAS DEFINITE POTENTIAL

CHANNELED CONSTRUCTIVELY, MANY stars can use their ego for constructive outcomes. It does take a little chutzpah to get up in front of a crowd to speak, act in a play, or take on leadership. According to Nina Brown, EdD, a licensed professional counselor who wrote *Working with the Self-Absorbed: How to Handle Narcissistic People on the Job,* healthy adult narcissism means having empathy, creativity, the ability to delay gratification while accepting personal responsibility and others' personal space and boundaries.[11] It also encompasses the ability to laugh (even at oneself) and form satisfying relationships. Plenty of people in the government or military, actors/actresses, athletes, and business leaders have achieved superstar status in their fields. Many have a right to be proud, a need to delegate responsibilities, and have earned their perks in life, but true class, of course, means never stepping over or on people to get your way, achieve, or maintain your status.

WHEN THE STAR BECOMES A PROBLEM

SO ON ONE end of the spectrum, star qualities can be channeled into productivity, strategy, and vision; on the other hand, too much narcissism becomes pathological, controlling, and harmful. Nina Brown feels that self-centered people have considerable anger—both expressed and hidden. "Anger is one emotion that they seem to be able to access easily, therefore it does not remain hidden for very long," she says.

When self-absorption crosses the line, Brown calls it a destructive narcissistic pattern. Here, our star might give you mixed messages, provoking anger and pushing your buttons. Remember our lawyer—the guy who feels he's done such stellar work that he's entitled to overbill for his services. When you ask for an adjustment, his telling you that you've employed "the best" might push your guilt button. Stars are good at sending these mixed messages because they disguise their words and actions to project a good image. Many need to become what we call a "false social hero" because they need to impress others with their great deeds. Often, they need to impress themselves. While they project self-esteem, it's often inaccurate self-esteem, not a healthy self-concept. They fear rejection and embarrassment, and they don't want to feel that they've caused their own problems because they avoid guilt and self-blame at all costs. Think of the clichéd used car salesman, the home remodeling contractor, or dare I say, some public officials (though after writing this book, all eyes will be on me, I'm sure!). Let's be honest: Those in some professions need to talk a good game, but do they deliver? If they're genuine and congruent they do. If the home contractor gives off mixed messages, however, he'll likely cost you more money and hassle. Your three-week kitchen replacement might take six months and ten grand extra!

The star's indirect style can cause a sudden behavioral shift, with him becoming obsequious or contrite, but still not truly empathic. Those who remain stubborn often form triangles, taking issues to third parties (in order to make someone look bad and themselves look powerful) rather than negotiate a dispute directly. Apparently, they never learned in geometry that the shortest distance between two points is a straight line. Forming such triangles perpetuates everyone's anger. Triangulation is a troublesome tactic if a team member (or classmate in school) bypasses you with a problem and goes above your head or around you to the boss (or professor). That's forming a triangle. It spreads the problem three ways. It *can* work as a last resort if there is an impasse, but as we know, direct communication is always optimal, certainly as a first-step measure. Otherwise, forming triangles has the payoff of provoking someone's anger by embarrassing them or causing other difficulty.

■

HOW TO COPE WITH THE STAR AT WORK

IF **your boss is the star,** you won't feel you can have a life beyond the office, but you must. Otherwise, stress may show up in somatic complaints such as tension headaches or stomach ailments. When working with the star, remember, it's not about you. Don't take his clipped conversations as personal put-offs and don't internalize the attitudes and criticisms. Don't hitch your wagon to this boss's cart, either, as mentoring you likely isn't top priority because his career matters most. You are there only to serve.

If there are too many stars in your organization, you may need to consider a new job. Those in authority think way too highly of themselves, and likely, they make self-centered decisions far from what helps the customer, consumer, or employees. Keep your résumé current and keep networking. You deserve to feel self-confident. When authority figures remain silent and scarce, rarely venturing from corner offices, you'll see the style filter down so that department directors and project managers act in the same self-centered manner. Managers model behavior to the organization.[12] Then, you know you must make the decision of how to tolerate this or leave, lest you fall under the spell and buy into the negative behavior, too. Be clear about your goals and your work. Document it. Do the best you can to solve problems and stay out of office gossip.

When the star is your coworker, you may not have to worry about being fired, but you'll watch your coworker climb up the ladder ingratiating his way, doing whatever it takes, because as Alan A. Cavaiola, PhD and Neil J. Lavender, PhD, authors of *Toxic Coworkers: How to Deal with Dysfunctional People on the Job,* point out, "This is the individual who likes to sit in the boss's chair after everyone has left for the day, just to try it out for size."[13] Don't expect change without much awareness and effort on that person's part—certainly not on yours. Pick your battles wisely as arguing gets you nowhere. Don't anticipate empathy and keep anything heartfelt to yourself. Sure enough, you might make yourself vulnerable, sharing something personal, but you won't likely get a response that makes you feel listened to or cared about. Worse, self-absorbed people can tear apart your confidence because boundary confusion means that certain rules (such as keeping a secret) work only for them, not you.

When your employee is the star, ambivalence reigns with loyalty on the surface (the charm), as they simultaneously search for ways to take you down. Rules meant for the staff at large don't apply to that person, at least according to his distorted thinking. The star has a poor sense of personal boundaries (barges into your office, interrupts you a lot, invades your personal space), misses important cues, and often fails to follow the chain of command (going above or around your authority).

This isn't your ideal front-desk candidate because arrogance makes a poor first impression. If you try to bring along self-centered employees, they'll likely reject your mentoring. Forget it; they'll find fault with your constructive criticism, making you feel guilty for offering feedback in the first place.

But since plenty of outstanding performers exhibit ego, channel it to reap the benefits. Play to their need to be superior. Cavaiola and Lavender write that narcissistic employees react better to words like *admire*, *best*, *outstanding*, and *superior*.[14] To positively reinforce what you wish to see more of, we offer our suggested phrases taking a cue from these words:

"I'd like for you to achieve more because everyone *admires* your drive and determination to close a deal. Let's set a new goal with that in mind."

"You're simply the *best* at figuring these things out. Do you think you could have an answer for me by close of the day tomorrow?"

"I'm looking for an *outstanding* person to take on this task. I need just the right employee."

"You've got such *superior* strengths in this one area, Jane. That's why we're taking you off of this other project so that you can focus on this for us."

Once you've gotten your star onboard with a project or request, provide ample opportunity for that person to hear others' feedback because this forces the star—even momentarily—off his pedestal. Remind him about team effort to downplay competitive instincts and help everyone toward a common mission.

DEALING WITH HIDDEN ANGER AT WORK

TAKE FROM THIS chapter new awareness about how to cope better, work harder, and avoid becoming like any of these eight angry types. Whenever you deal with hidden anger on the job or in the classroom, we suggest that you:

- Allow the passive-aggressive person a little freedom, yet set boundaries.
- Use caution when responding. Give yourself distance and time to think.
- Resist the urge to retaliate. Guard against knee-jerk reactions.
- Refuse to own their anger. Misery might enjoy company, but you will not be miserable.

- Remain aware of your emotions, frustration, and confusion. Separate feelings from the facts. Understand that others may try to manipulate your emotions.
- Avoid trying to "fix" the angry person or hoping for miraculous change.
- Use "I" statements as well as clear, consistent messages.
- Document problem behaviors in performance appraisals if you're the supervisor or teacher; exposing a superior's hidden anger is a tough call.
- Talk to your coworkers first, document, and then go to your manager. Don't respond to hidden anger or passive-aggression with gossip or anger yourself.
- Distance yourself. The worst-case scenario may demand that you end relationships, change work environments, or switch into another class. Best case: those concealing (and projecting) their anger quit, leaving you and your comrades in peace.

FIVE

RECOGNIZING HIDDEN ANGER IN COUPLES AND MARRIAGES

O NE DAY AT work, Tom got a call from his wife Sarah.

"It's been a tough day. What do you say we go out to dinner tonight? Sarah asked.

"I'm not sure when I'm going to get home," Tom said. "You go on without me."

"But I'm a little tired of eating alone. Can't we do something together?"

"Look," Tom said. "I'm in the middle of something and you interrupted me again. I have to go. I'll see you later." And at that, Tom hung up.

Sarah called back right away. At the implication that her calling was a regular habit (which it was not), she was now even more annoyed, but Tom just let the call go straight to voicemail.

In this chapter, we'll reveal hidden anger and negative undercurrents between couples and within marriages, building upon what we've learned thus far. Those in any kind of committed relationship can benefit, but we direct much of the material toward husbands and wives.

When two people form a couple, each person's individual process—that is, their style and the way they navigate life in general—either complements the other person's process or clashes with it. You could also substitute personal default for one's process because it's the mode we slip into most commonly. What's your process or personal default mode? Do you ever shirk responsibility, cop an excuse, and put the blame on your partner? Keep silent and maintain your distance? Become critical? Must others walk on eggshells because of your conflict style? No one is perfect, but if you slip into these styles quite quickly, your partner can likely identify your process faster than you can.

Traits, habits, communication and problem-solving skills, optimistic or pessimistic worldviews, as well as anger management styles, all merge into the complex dynamics of partnership and marriage. The Biblical theme of "two becoming one" serves as an important guide in many aspects of the couple relationship, but let's never forget that we're dealing with two distinct individuals, each with a past and a present, each with a set of needs, fears, and issues that the parties deal with in either a straightforward or indirect manner. When needs go unfulfilled, fear or anxiety interferes with goals and happiness, or individuals get stuck trying to move themselves or their marriages forward, negativity and/or ambivalence can easily tempt them to conceal emotions, hide annoyances, and deal circuitously with problems and with one another. We'll show you how to keep this from happening.

THE COUPLE FORMS AN IMPORTANT FOUNDATION

NOT ONLY IS a strong marriage the foundation of the larger family unit, but it also has tremendous influence upon your overall health. According to sociologist Linda J. Waite and researcher Maggie Gallagher in *The Case for Marriage,* "The evidence from four decades of research is surprisingly clear: A good marriage is both men's and women's best bet for living a long and healthy life."[1] Many scientific studies record the links between marital status and one's well-being.[2]

But, findings presented at the annual meeting of the American Psychological Association in 2004 revealed that a lousy marriage can make you feel . . . well, sick. Negative spousal behaviors such as excessive demands or criticism seems to increase the likelihood of developing ongoing health problems, according to Jamila Bookwala, a psychology professor at Lafayette College in Pennsylvania.[3] So while there are plenty of positive effects to be gained from marriage, being in one that's troubled can do more harm than good.

If we carry resentment, buried emotion, and unresolved issues with us, it's sure to cost a hefty price, bankrupting our spirits, our loved one's spirits, maybe even our bank accounts. When one gets caught up in the cycle of rejection, resentment, and revenge, sometimes people's anger wells up to the point where they experience visceral reactions—noticeable signs of stress such as the anxiety-induced fight-or-flight response, rapid heartbeat or other somatic symptoms—when they must deal with a manipulative or self-absorbed spouse, significant other, or family member. If the situation gets bad enough, it can become emotionally abusive.

WHERE IS THE LOVE?

WOULDN'T IT BE wonderful if during the courting stage, there could be some sign from the heavens declaring that danger lies ahead. But there's no skywriting that displays "Speed bumps with mother issues!" or "Dangerous curve: disengaged partner!"

Premarital counseling can be so very useful as you identify issues that trigger arguments and learn about a partner's background. Be sure that the counseling or education program you choose is effective. Many faith-based programs address these areas, but also consider a few visits to a licensed counselor or therapist. Rid yourself of any negative connotation that this raises, and view it instead as a wise investment in your relationship, even after you've marched back up the aisle.

It's always amazing the tens of thousands of dollars people spend on a couple's wedding—essentially one day in their lives—while little, if any, investment goes toward premarital counseling, education, or relationship skills. We applaud groups like Smart Marriages that encourage the giving of gift certificates that couples can use for premarital counseling or education seminars.[4] If you spot an opportunity, sometimes through your church, synagogue, or house of worship to participate in relationship-building seminars, sign up. This goes for those in new or established relationships. Increasingly, insurance providers recognize the benefit to their members of covering marriage and family therapy as well as individual counseling.

A lack of education and poor preparation for marriage then are certainly factors in why hidden anger can seep into a relationship even when the two parties anticipate a bright future. Hidden anger isn't always easy to recognize. Mix in the excitement of new love, optimism that runs wild, and endorphins—those feel-good hormones—and you can see how blinded people become to patterns in a potential mate's personality or family of origin. Even when a person we're attracted to has one foot in and one foot out of the relationship, we're unlikely to detect any ambivalence as we gloss over what we don't wish to see.

Finally, hidden anger can set into a marriage because of unrealistic expectations, marrying in the hopes of changing the other person, to be rescued from a bad plight, or for any other shallow reason. Some men and women concern themselves more with the fantasy or image of being that happy couple than with the true, hard work becoming that happy couple requires.

HOW HIDDEN ANGER SURFACES

TRACY AND JOE, both in their late twenties, have been married about a year. Like many couples who planned large nuptials while holding down two full-time jobs, Tracy and Joe didn't take time out for marriage education. They felt they knew each other pretty well, but as time went by, little issues and the individual way they each processed daily annoyances crept between them. Wisely, they decided to check in with a marriage counselor.

In one of their sessions, Tracy shared how she didn't feel they were on the same page. While they both established the goal of saving for a house down payment and agreed to live frugally, she felt Joe disparaged her by making light of mutual decisions or correcting her, especially in front of his family. When Joe's mother mentioned her more-expensive hair salon, Tracy said how satisfied they were at the local discount place. Joe immediately made a crack about this even though he was the one who suggested the discount salon, clipped their coupons, and never expressed dissatisfaction until now. To Tracy, Joe always became the obedient little boy near his family. Joe, when he first heard Tracy's hurt over this, felt she was too sensitive. Besides, he told the therapist, Tracy was too bossy, wanting them to establish different traditions at the holidays.

If Tracy's right that Joe sides with family instead of her, sets his wife up to feel left out, and adheres to *his* family's traditions—a lot—then Joe displays undifferentiated behavior, a concept brought to the forefront in couples and family therapy (see the sidebar "Family Influences Us"). In other words, he's a little too emotionally drawn to his original family at the expense of the new family he's creating with Tracy.

Complaints like these sound trivial, but little incidents add up, provoking ire. Once hidden anger or passive-aggressive patterns become ingrained in a couple's relationship, husbands or wives rely upon poor excuses ("she's too sensitive") or rigid behavior ("I've always done it this way"). If neatly tucking away true feelings keeps the peace, the anger concealer keeps hiding them and refuses to cut the apron strings at the expense of adult independence, and here at the cost of a warm, connected marriage. If, over time, these faulty patterns are left unchecked, Joe and Tracy will forget about using a better, more open range of expression, leaving them with a rather dishonest relationship.

■

FAMILY INFLUENCES US

MURRAY Bowen, MD, worked with families at the Menninger Clinic in Kansas and at the National Institute of Mental Health in the 1950s, and continued his research with families at Georgetown University. Bowen embraced a radically different view of emotional functioning, seeing the family as the pivotal influence, with behaviors passing down through the generations. All families, he found, traveled along a continuum with emotional fusion (more closeness than normal) on one end of the spectrum and differentiation (independence) at the other end.

Most of us leave our families at a time in our lives (late adolescence) in which we're gaining the outward appearance of independence and learning to exist emotionally on our own. Young adults transform their parental relationships. Too often that's not a *fait accompli* by the time they pack their bags and set up their first apartment. An undifferentiated person hasn't accomplished some of this independence. Consequently, when situations arise, he responds with more emotion and less self-control, especially around issues that raise anxiety. Quite simply, our original family installs our emotional buttons, and if we don't free ourselves of that intense influence, they remain in possession of the remote control. We may react when they or others push our buttons with the same level of adolescent anger. This fits with the research of passive-aggression being an immature reaction.[5] Even grown, well-established people can react this way.

Bowen posited that people tend to choose mates who are similarly undifferentiated or emotionally reactive. When we talk about keeping hidden anger at bay, this means that if two people who have not gained a fair degree of emotional independence marry, there may be problems, or at least some work, transforming important relationships.

FINDING THE LOVE AND SUPPORT YOU NEED

WHAT IF JOE had some valid points as they continued counseling? To Joe, Tracy seemed to be bossy. Maybe she was, and maybe she wasn't, but in relationships, appearance is everything. If Tracy came from a family lacking in warmth, she might have had high hopes for establishing both a new family and a successful in-law relationship—new starts for her. Joe certainly shouldn't embarrass his wife but smooth the way with his family (rather than make her acceptance more difficult). This would show Tracy how important she is to him. Their marriage would also be stronger if he could look at Tracy's intent and see what comes across as negative (her wanting them to adopt new traditions) as positive.

Earlier we mentioned that each of us has an individual process or style that's generally apparent. For instance, Tracy might be a very direct and linear person with a plan in mind to get from one point to another, evident in the way she thinks as well as in conversations. Joe's process might be more indirect as seen by his making wisecracks rather than directly communicating a point. Tracy may need to lighten up a bit, or it could be that Joe makes jokes to avoid discussing certain topics and to steer clear of anything unpleasant. The problem is that marriage and partnership require a bit of surrender, allowing yourself to become more vulnerable to the other person. Their styles are clashing here, and that's gotten Joe and Tracy stuck.

In *Getting the Love You Want,* Harville Hendrix, PhD explores the theory that while you might think that men and women would look for the opposite of what they had in an unhappy childhood, most people are attracted to mates with a mixture of their caretakers' positive *and* negative traits.[6] Of course, the negative ones grab our attention far more readily. As Hendrix found, there is a close correlation between traits in your partners and the traits of your parents. You gravitate toward the old order or conditions similar to those of your upbringing so that you have that second chance to make things right. Anger can set in when one partner places undue expectations for "getting it right" or sometimes believes that a spouse will satisfy all emotional needs. That's setting the bar just too high. If one person's expectations are left unfulfilled, that person gets annoyed, and sooner or later it seeps out through overt or covert means. This is particularly the case when the partners can't admit the error of their expectations or dependency, or when they can't take responsibility for being even a little bit off base. Instead, passive-aggressive behavior becomes a more civil way of dealing with one another, however misguidedly. Remember, passive-aggressive people vacillate between wanting to be dependent and independent. During those dependent times, partners surely don't want to risk "offending" a spouse. So, they conceal their feelings.

HOW TO SPOT WHEN YOU'RE OUT OF SYNC

IF YOU'RE STILL a little unsure of where you stand in your relationship—that is, if your style conflicts with that of your partner—answer these questions:

1. Do you criticize that which first attracted you to your partner?
2. Does it feel as if competition or rivalry has set in?

3. Do you have trouble committing your angry feelings to "not so angry" words?
4. Do you know what emotional buttons you shouldn't push on your spouse, but sometimes do anyway?
5. Have you felt that your needs regularly take a back seat to your partner's?
6. Do you ever feel as if your spouse had a blow or revelation coming; therefore, you don't quite wince when incidents occur, as you mentally think he or she deserved to be uncomfortable, even, knowing how stabbed he or she must feel?
7. Are there fewer meaningful conversations and is there little room left for laughter?
8. Have simple courtesies seemingly vanished?
9. Does much less affection fill the space between you?
10. Has a sense of dread taken over where once anticipation filled any time spent apart?

The more times you answered "yes" to these ten questions, the more concerned you should be. Let this not alarm you but raise your awareness of the importance of building communication skills and strategies.

KEEPING HIDDEN ANGER OUT OF YOUR MARRIAGE

JOHN GOTTMAN, PHD is a professor of psychology at the University of Washington, founder of the Seattle Marital and Family Institute (dubbed the "Love Lab"). He's also a noted author and relationship researcher. Through years of tape recording and analyzing the interactions of married couples, Gottman applies hard science to the understanding of loving relationships. He and his colleagues have developed a mathematical model that predicts a couple's potential for divorce within four years. While couples discussed money or annoying habits, he recorded data such as heart rate and perspiration, and observed their language, mannerisms, and responses. Within minutes, Gottman's team found that if the ratio of positive to negative behavior and communication stayed at five to one, the couple was likely to have a happy future. They called this "positive sentiment override." Displays of contempt, defensiveness, criticism, withdrawal, or the use of diminishing language or behavior predicted less longevity of the union.[7]

Thus, the prescription for steering your relationship to happier interaction rests in a few frequently forgotten tips. Happy couples:

- Appreciate opportunities to communicate. They don't shy away from conflict, stuff emotions, or hide matters, hoping they'll mysteriously vanish.
- Listen without comment avoiding knee-jerk reactions made out of a defensive posture. They quell the desire to interrupt, realizing they'll each get a turn.
- Express appreciation for a spouse's honesty and willingness to share. Partners reflect what the other has said to demonstrate true understanding—that they "got it."
- Show interest in the other's feelings and consider new opinions. No black-and-white, all-or-nothing thinking here. To solve a problem, happy couples see shades of gray and develop a middle ground. They accept differences for what they are—differences in thought, not an attack upon the person.
- Express empathy through words, body language, and behavior.
- Hold foolish words and cross behavior in check. They express matters openly using "I" statements, engaging the other party, not withdrawing nor isolating nor venting frustration to show displeasure (i.e., slamming doors or using sarcasm).
- Respect individual boundaries, physical as well as emotional.
- Watch out for unresolved issues. Red flags: When your partner becomes silent, harsh, or defensive in response to a fairly benign remark. Give-up lines like "It's no use talking to you" or "Oh, never mind" are also tip-offs.
- Convey pride for each other's achievements and concern for hardships. Honor boundaries such as knowing when to gently tease and when teasing is hurtful.
- Find time for one another, including unscheduled time to read the Sunday paper, enjoy recreation, or take care of household errands or chores together.
- Enjoy sharing their lives but don't rely upon a spouse as the key to each one's fulfillment. Each finds satisfaction independent of the marriage.

Obviously, these points are easier to accomplish in some weeks than in others. A marriage under job stress, illness, or the strain of lingering issues, or during the parenting initiative (from birth to teen and beyond) has less stamina to endure frustrating moments. Here come into play the words "over time" from our description of hidden anger. Months and years of smoothing over what's wrong in a relationship won't automatically make it right.

■

IRRATIONAL BELIEFS ABOUT CONFLICT

As we have unveiled, people who hide their anger often fear and avoid conflict. In a successful marriage, conflict indeed has its place.

In a 1989 study published in the *Journal of Consulting and Clinical Psychology,* John Gottman and Lowell Krokoff found that disagreement over the long term of a relationship is not harmful. Quite the contrary, it's a withdrawal from conflict as well as continued defensiveness and inflexibility that lead to the demise of many marriages.[8] Expressing one's heartfelt feelings may be uncomfortable, maybe even painful, but if they are honestly expressed so that the partner can tolerate it (or at least not expressed inappropriately), this adds to the strength and health of the marriage. Research conducted by Donald H. Baucom at the University of North Carolina, Norman Epstein at the University of Maryland, and their colleagues found that partners who both avoided contact may protect each other directly, but the act of avoidance had other negative effects upon their intimacy and marital satisfaction.[9]

COMMON ANGER PROBLEMS AND HOW TO SOLVE THEM

CONFLICT HAPPENS. IF one partner shies away from it, while the other faces situations head on, you can see the inherent struggle from the start. Too often it leaves real indecision, loneliness, jealousy, or another uncomfortable feeling. Powerful emotions leak out, without our even knowing it, causing tremendous hurt in those we love and care for.

EMOTIONAL DISTANCE

THIS HAPPENS COMMONLY when one partner, typically the wife, craves closeness, more conversation, and couple time. When she can't get her husband out from behind the newspaper or his desk at work, she becomes more vocal in her requests. Not surprisingly, he bristles or, wishing to keep her happy, attempts to please her. Sometimes genuine gender differences just plain get in the way, and scenarios like these end miserably with hurt on both sides. Why?

News flash: Men and women are different! Not better. Not worse. Different. Women tend to think in a linear fashion and include more emotional input into their thinking. They have at times an innate ability to access many more words, far faster, than most men. Men don't think with as much emotional content. When pushed to discuss problems that they haven't fully thought through, men may shut down, back away, or wait it out until they're ready to deal with the request or demand. This can sometimes look passive-aggressive when it's really a matter of timing and process. Give the same man some time to gather his thoughts, and he'll likely be more open, less cranky, and a far better communicator next time around. There might not be the chasm of distance between the two.

Here too, women should realize that their girlfriends serve an important function. They need to check and recheck their unrealistic expectations of men. Women validate each other through conversation, sharing an interest in similar subjects, browsing, shopping, having a glass of wine, or exchanging kind gestures. So often when a man and woman are caught in some sort of pursuer-distancer dynamic, the key to turning this struggle around is counterintuitive. A lot of people think if she keeps after him, he'll get the message. He might go grab his fishing pole and tackle instead!

Realizing her need for companionship, a woman is better off showing her husband that she has a fulfilling life and rewarding work. Better yet, she could go off with a good novel or on a weekend getaway with gal pals, for this sends a stronger message, allowing him to ultimately come to her instead of her requesting closeness of him. Ladies: Make him think togetherness is *his* idea!

Will this paradoxical tactic always work? Of course not; nothing is foolproof. This is only one way that will work with one type of couple. In other cases, the man needs to be the one to reach out. In most cases, *both* need to do some work. There could be a more profound struggle underlying any spouse's nagging or distancing.

One partner might be terribly self-centered or negative. She might be down in the dumps. Or, his wife could remind him of his mother. That's why counselors working with such couples frequently hear complaints about unavailability or the fear of intimacy. Partners of self-absorbed or anger-concealing people spend inordinate amounts of time trying to clear up confusion and understand what's happening. It's doubly difficult when one or both partners struggles with poor self-image. People with a real self-esteem deficit don't feel 100 percent safe sharing their true selves. They can get trapped in a cycle of addiction to approval that drives them to seek and reject intimacy at the same time. It's as if they are saying, "What can I do to make you love someone as unlovable as me?" Intimacy requires sharing as well as the ability to receive 100 percent of a loved one's true self, the rose-colored images as well as the murkier ones. Many passive-aggressive people struggle with their own self-concept.

Marriage or any intimate relationship often equates to the final surrender for a person harboring hidden anger. In their journal article, Wetzler and Morey expressed it best: "The passive-aggressive individual is caught between dependency, which they resent, and autonomy, which they fear. They want others to think that they are not dependent, but such people bind themselves closer to others than they care to admit. They foster dependency and then struggle against it because they feel controlled and vulnerable, feeling trapped when they are expected to express intimate feelings."[10]

In their 1996 book, Theodore Millon and Roger Davis write that being unpredictable and discontented—another form of distancing—produces certain secondary gains for the negative person. "A negativistic man, who is unwilling or unable to decide whether to 'grow up' or remain a 'child,' explodes emotionally whenever his wife expects 'too much' of him. Afterward, he expresses guilt, becomes contrite, and pleads forbearance on her part," they write.[11] If you see this type of behavior, it's manipulative because it essentially halts any additional requests (seen as demands) and effects the ultimate need as the outcome—to be left alone.

Of course, to be fair to both genders, women can also contribute to the unpleasant and passive-aggressive dynamics. Once some men show their softer, more emotional sides some women may resent them for no longer being the alpha males that protect and defend them. A woman may have set up a scenario, resenting the man for a situation she helped place him in, with the attitude of "If you can't stand up to me, how will you protect me in the big, bad world?" The man, who dared to become vulnerable and surrender a bit of himself, now doubts his ability to get the role she expected him to play quite right. Though typically more verbal, women can also show their disdain quite indirectly through the hostile sigh or nonverbal cue that leaves men feeling frustrated.

FINANCIAL STRESS

Money, the way it validates us and influences our daily decisions, affects all too many couples in a negative way. Quite simply, it often equates to power, and therein lies the proverbial struggle. When secretly annoyed, money becomes a weapon to wage war upon partners, to "one up" them, or prove a point. The wife who has never honestly acknowledged that she has ADHD may finally relent and go into therapy. Not of her choice, mind you, but off she goes nonetheless. Ten sessions later she's not really committing to better organization, improved communication, or more control over her anger, but she's still attending. Twenty sessions later, and still nothing's happening. It's not that she tolerates the therapist as much as she is running up a hefty tab that ultimately her husband will have to pay out of pocket. In this sense, the wife's intent is malevolent or all about the secondary gain (getting back at her husband, the frugal one).

Women (or men) may accrue much debt on shopping sprees their spouses know nothing about. When the bills come and the credit-card collectors start calling, the spender feigns ignorance, not understanding how things got so bad. "I thought we had a credit balance on that account," she might say. Or, "It was such a good buy. . . . I just knew you wouldn't want me to miss the sale."

Money can even become the sword that never directly touches one's hands. Take the couple remodeling their kitchen. They thought they had selected all the cabinet components and colors, but when the wife changed the countertop and backsplash selections (unbeknownst to her husband), she held him captive in a color and design scheme with his least favorite choices. Every morning, he'd pour his coffee surrounded by constant reminders that his wife had her way over his, and in order to fix it, he'd have to cough up another $6,000.

Since money spent or needing to be spent brings with it such powerful feelings, couples must establish mutual goals early in their marriages and routinely discuss where they are financially and what may have changed due to career changes, job layoffs, taking time off to raise the children, or some other unexpected scenario. With any change in circumstance comes a change in the couple's financial plan. These discussions should take place with much sincerity and all concerns on the table. Speak openly. If you keep from your wife that you aren't certain that you can, or even want to, bear the total financial load while she stays home with the kids, say so. With honest disclosure, you can solve the problem. Concealing the concern only allows your feelings to well up. Maybe she works a few hours a week, while you trade off for a few chores and childcare. Maybe she takes off only a limited amount of time, or finds a way to work from home to ease your concerns. Trust in your ability to work together when financial issues loom so that resentments don't set in and undermine your relationship.

■

IRRITABILITY IN MEN AND WOMEN

JED Diamond, author of *Male Menopause* and *The Irritable Male Syndrome: Managing the 4 Key Causes of Depression and Aggression*, surveyed nearly ten thousand males between the ages of ten and seventy-five, finding irritability in various forms. In three of the seven types he identified, a passive-aggressive style was present with primary behaviors such as impatience, blame, frustration, hypersensitivity, moodiness, and just plain being grumpy.[12] "These males often have a lot of anger and rage but are trying to hold it back," Diamond says. "The result is that it comes out in indirect ways . . . They can also be quite explosive, seemingly over small slights." Additionally, these men face consequences in the form of high blood pressure, diabetes, obesity, and erectile dysfunction.

Diamond believes that men need to recognize this emotional pain and anger instead of blaming it on others. "Once he recognizes that there is something going on inside him, he can begin to regain control of his life and express his feelings more directly," he told us.

Male irritability is a much newer phenomenon being discussed. Most women have self-reported for years feeling edgy due to hormonal shifts, but it's unfortunate that both genders often stereotype a woman's mood as "PMS." Maybe it is, but maybe not. Certainly both sexes now have researchers following their behavior and biochemistry.

If men and women feel short-tempered, it's best to implement self-help strategies such as relaxation techniques, getting a good night's sleep, improving diet and nutrition, having a social network, and a career that enhances their lives. Look to outside stressors that cause any sudden irritability. Couples need to work on these life balance issues together and need to rule out more biological or age-related causes with their primary care physicians.

FAMILY CRISES

WHEN SPOUSES SHUT each other out emotionally, they're ill-equipped to handle urgent situations that demand their attention, whether it's a sudden job loss, family illness, a child who gets into trouble, or merely a child who needs more of their collective attention because of social, educational, or health-related concerns. Years ago as a practicing psychologist, I worked with families in the neonatal intensive care unit at a Pittsburgh hospital. I found this work rewarding because I knew how much support these families needed. Illness or the death of a child often pulls a couple and family apart. Having a sickly baby significantly increases the chance that the father will walk out, according to a report published in *Demography* in 2004, where Nancy Reichman and her colleagues at Robert Wood Johnson Medical School in New Jersey described their study of the families of 3,000 newborns.[13]

Similar walk-offs occur when a child is diagnosed with disabilities after birth. For whatever reasons, women typically endure the strain. Men might feel that they have failed somehow, deny what's really happening, and resist being supportive because by being so requires admitting that which they can't face. Women in our society are often raised to be the nurturing parent. When men do not learn this, they may flee rather than face a situation. Some parents blame themselves or their spouse, and still others may go off on their own to start another family, trying to achieve what they didn't have or "get right" the first time. It leaves those left behind feeling sad and angry.

Children with disabilities often consume much of the couple's energy, finances, and free time. "My son's childhood was hell," claimed the mother of a now-teenage boy with an aggravated case of ADHD. "To this day, our house looks like it's been in a war zone." Parents of autistic children reveal how heartbreaking it is to forgo vacations or an evening out because no one among family or friends wants to take on the responsibility that special-needs children require. Some must make difficult choices, opting for residential placement just to save themselves from overwhelming stress. Another mom whose son had physical and behavioral problems said that her child put her at odds with her husband on almost a daily basis, and shared how she resented that her husband would not even read more than a single paragraph of material about their son's condition to educate himself though he commuted by train to the office each day. His indirect message: It's your problem.

In troubled marriages, crisis unearths further problems that have been stuffed into the closet and never resolved. Lacking problem-solving and communication skills, new burdens have the power to seize any remaining energy the couple has left so that they further attack one another rather than rally around a common cause, manage the predicament, and grow stronger from it. Those parents who do pull together tell how much the experience has taught them about themselves as individuals, their values, and their priorities in life.

Mental illness is another such crisis. Research from the University of Colorado at Boulder, appearing in the *Journal of Consulting and Clinical Psychology* (October 2004) revealed that when one spouse suffers from depression, both spouses report an unsatisfying, unhappy marriage.[14] The more intractable the condition, the more the marriage suffered. After 9/11, many first responders reported anxiety and sleep disturbance, post-traumatic stress disorder, and depression. If this sounds like you, seek the help of a qualified professional to counsel you individually or as part of couple's therapy, where both partners commit to counseling. If one partner feels coerced, awareness likely won't result, and worse yet, he or she may prolong therapy to frustrate a spouse, run up debt, or receive attention with no real motivation toward change, as we saw in one of the examples. Some less-than-willing patients may select the least competent therapist or mental health agency, further stalling progress and/or avoiding realities they'd rather keep concealed.

INFIDELITY

WHERE HIDDEN ANGER lurks in a marriage and communication has broken down, jealousy and entitlement set in. Even in what we look upon as good unions, as the late Shirley Glass, PhD noted, marriages become vulnerable to affairs. Glass, who with Jean Coppock Shaeheli wrote *Not "Just Friends,"* discussed how infidelity can sometimes reflect an ensuing power struggle. Certainly there are many reasons behind straying from one's vows, including power, neglect, or giving up on the commitment, but when there is an ensuing power struggle, the affair is attempted, however foolishly, to correct the perceived imbalance. Whereas the spouse with more financial wherewithal or personality, or the better job feels entitled to indulge him or herself, the less powerful partner, Glass writes, may also attempt to even the score.[15]

When this happens, expect that the unfaithful spouse will be filled with negative self-talk, rationalize actions, project more blame, and often feel more entitled. Not a lot of introspection takes place at this stage. Of course, work on the true problem ceases, and concealing the affair or other acting-out behavior takes priority.

Infidelity is often less about sexual satisfaction and much more a barometer of other emotions, including hidden anger built upon unrealistic expectations, beliefs, or fears. It can also be part of one's depressive or impulsive symptoms. Being intimate with someone else puts distance between the betrayer and the spouse, and the truly promiscuous partner, afraid of revealing too much in a committed relationship, shows real trust and vulnerability issues. It can also be fueled by one or both partner's inability to admit a failed and totally mismatched relationship. Rather than solve their conflicts or separate, they remain bound in their own misery. They stay together, as miserable as they are, because they cannot stand to be alone. They see the hurt they endure (and often ignore) from each other as preferable to loneliness. And they are tempted into a whole host of behaviors that hide the hurt.

Other behavior or avoidance serves as a barometer of the couple's interactions as well. When a partner spends time in Internet chat rooms or looking at pornography in a compulsive way, that partner is tuning out of the relationship, looking away from rather than to the relationship with any honest attempt to salvage it. That's meant not to equate two partners viewing erotic material together to rejuvenate their intimate life with compulsive behavior. If the intent is to "get back" at your spouse because you carry a grudge, clearly it's wrong. Rather than put energy into the marriage, this person saps energy from it through such undermining. Discuss your needs, expectations, turn-ons, and turn-offs. Together. Don't have the conversation with yourself! But passive-aggressive partners want to be both in and out of the relationship. They depend upon their partner, yet feel entitled to their own way as well. So, when the going gets difficult or the conversations are too uncomfortable to have, they make choices with steep consequences.

When any type of unfaithful, discreet behavior becomes the epicenter of punitive actions, the anger will only flourish when the truth is revealed, even becoming much more overt (i.e., in outbursts) at least for a period of time. It can also simmer as suspicions aren't discussed directly but characterized by subversive or covert acts of aggression.

Expect more strain when trust has been broken because trust needs to be earned back. For reconciliation to work, both parties must wish to strengthen their relationship and overcome their problems. In other words, a spouse discovers evidence of the cyberaffair, and now becomes more reactive, distrustful, and vigilant (with good reason given what's been lost). This, in turn, annoys the passive-aggressive partner, who further pulls away because this now "proves" the irrational beliefs at the core of this mindset. Negative self-talk takes over, and it becomes self-perpetuating until the cycle is broken. Playing victim is easier than becoming the mender or problem solver.

OTHER ESCAPES

WHEN FRUSTRATION FESTERS, spouses act out of character. Sometimes, if there is awareness and an open attitude, one party might only need to say, "That's not like you . . . What's really going on?" Other times, that concealed anger has the power to become spiraling and self-destructive with addictive behavior, alcoholism, or substance abuse, as well as produce avoidant conduct such as Internet addiction (with or without chat rooms and cyberaffairs) and workaholism, where the person finds more meaning at the office than at home.

While affairs are obvious examples of extramarital triangles, disenfranchised spouses often triangle in other substitutes. We discussed the alienating force of workaholism already, but too much time spent on the golf course or doing some other hobby is equally isolating, both for the one indulging in the pastime and the one left behind. Unhappy spouses may triangle in food or possessions, for instance, as they try, in failed attempts, to consume their way to happiness. Sometimes, the mere act of letting go of one's self-control and body image is a passive-aggressive, distancing act. The person who can't honestly communicate that she wants out of a relationship might not take care of herself, gaining significant weight and becoming less desirous of any sexual advances. It's a roundabout, indirect way of saying "Not tonight, honey" akin to "I have a headache" when there really is none. It's a silent withdrawal leaving your partner confused, searching for explanations.

When self-destructive behavior sets in—whether it manifests in drug or alcohol use, gambling, pornography, or leading some other double life—dysfunctional patterns are clearly more entrenched, and it will take much more than a self-help book to overcome them. If there isn't anger at the core driving the behavior in some way, it will be there in the clean-up stage as guilt or self-blame sets in, though you shouldn't avoid this aftermath phase. The real issues that triggered such conduct need to be addressed. Sometimes these types of preoccupations stem from an inability to love and/or be loved.

Finally, anger-concealing partners use silent escapes to make their inability to cope with ordinary life transitions. When baby makes three, some wives use the child to keep their husbands away (and then complain that he's not a family man), or the demands of parenthood overwhelm a husband so that he feels he's competing with his own child for his wife's attention. According to Scott Wetzler, these conflicts about being a parent, at least to some degree, can mirror the man's conflict with his own father.[16]

■

DIFFERENT WAYS OF DISCONNECT

PEOPLE cut themselves off from loved ones or situations demanding their attention, in a variety of unhealthy ways, because they're temporarily unable to address a problem. When people disengage or disconnect, you might see them doing any of the following:

• tuning out • turning away • overworking • being dishonest • interrupting • nagging• perpetually being late • criticizing • being sarcastic • being silent • being rude • acting out • engaging in infidelity • shaming • withholding affection or sex • coercing • judging• being paranoid • drinking or spending excessively • having persistent anxiety • foot-dragging and stalling

HEALING AN ANGRY MARRIAGE

WHEN SPOUSES ARE unhappy, they're much more likely to attribute the difficulty to some negative trait, attaching the label of "paranoid," "lazy," "irresponsible," "selfish" to whatever bothers them. Each spouse gradually projects the blame elsewhere. Instead of admitting with any awareness that they're contributing to the problem, they enhance the problem. This stymies meaningful change and their chances of growing closer.

Any relationship worth having is worth the effort of not being so angry. Healing bitter feelings and resentments takes forgiveness, learning to fight fairly, commitment to change . . . and just plain commitment. Yes, we used that "fight" word, knowing that even in the most fight-phobic union, most every husband and wife will have a few of these. Try these tips to argue fairly and resolve issues:

- Start with a commitment to problem resolution, and base your actions on love and respect.
- Understand the ways in which you disconnect (see the "Different Ways of Disconnect" sidebar). Awareness of how you behave is half the battle to overcome a bad habit. Know that your own anger style might cause the goal of resolution to jump the tracks into a blind attack. Practice, if necessary, before you speak. Be ready for the unexpected attempts by your spouse to sidetrack the discussion.
- Learn appropriate assertiveness (not being too frank or too rude). In fact, we're known for the motto: you can sometimes be angry, but should never be mean. Learn to be expressive, but without the venom. Avoid labels and exaggerations (those *always* and *never* words). Refrain from sarcasm as a means to emit hidden anger.
- Stick to one issue and be willing to reach a fair middle ground. Compromise is a true art form. Agree to disagree, even for a short while. Distance from a problem can add insight. But make the commitment to resolve it, not run from or ignore it.
- Nurture and express your affection. Keep doing kind things for one another to reflect the bond between you. Give affection a priority place. Make time for intimacy and search for creative ways to keep your love alive.
- Accept each other's differences, while trying to also seek things to share as a couple, just the two of you. Learn to tolerate occasional disappointment, plus the ebb and flow of most any close relationship.

- Laugh together. Find humor, if possible, in whatever problem you're attempting to solve. We emphasize mutually understood humor, however, because if it's not that, it's like throwing some Miracle-Gro on the issue. There is a distinct difference between laughing *with* and laughing *at* someone. Passive-aggressive people often choose the latter, whereas happy people enjoy the endorphin-releasing moment together.
- Forgive. This is the critical antidote to break the toxic cycle of rejection, resentment, and revenge. People who feel hurt end up hurting others. Somewhere along the line, someone has to stand up and say "the hurting stops with me." Forgiveness is the essential first step.

SIX

DEALING WITH

HIDDEN ANGER IN FAMILIES

Erika, who just finished her last semester of college, will be awarded her bachelor's degree in speech pathology, but in order to really achieve success in this field, she knows she'll need to continue her education. Waiting for her parents to arrive, the day is bittersweet; it's "move out" day, and she wishes she could continue her studies without interruption. But Erika had made a deal with her folks when she'd taken a summer semester abroad instead of making money to help defray school costs. Her parents paid for the credits instead of her working and banking extra money, so she felt she was upholding her part of the bargain by moving back home to find a job and save up for her master's degree.

After mom and dad got everything loaded into the family's SUV, Erika said a tearful goodbye to her roommate, who was staying on, headed straight for graduate school.

"I just couldn't convince her to stay," mom said, smiling at Erika's roommate. "It's not like she didn't have money available from her grandmother's estate."

Silence filled the space between them. Erika's tears flowed faster, disguising her hurt. To give her roommate the impression that she wanted to leave? And, at no time did mom ever mention that staying was an option, and never did she disclose that Erika had been left or had access to additional funding for graduate school. Rather mom had talked incessantly about Erika's arrival back home, where they'd store her things, the whole nine yards. At times, Erika got the impression that her mom clearly didn't understand the need for higher credentials in certain lines of work; at other times, she wondered if mom merely resented her ambitions, seeing as how she never got the opportunity to go to college.

The entire ride home Erika felt she'd been dealt an embarrassing blow, because now it was too late to process her application and register for classes. Besides, her roommate had already found another girl to share housing with as soon as Erika cleared her things. The whole course of events seemed confusing, but all Erika could feel was simmering anger.

In *The Angry Child,* we said that one's family is the single most important influence upon psychological development. Because the family is a system, if something (like a lot of anger) affects one member, it affects other family members as well. A lot of us look upon families as safe harbors, where everyone *should* get along and *ought* to understand each other and respect their opinions and feelings. Right? It's ideal, but it leads to frustration. Extended families also give us tremendous opportunity to practice becoming less reactive and understand the source of mean behavior because we carry family influences with us throughout life, into future relationships, into the families we create, even into the workplace.

FOUR ANGRY FAMILY TYPES

NO PERFECT FAMILY exists, and anger is often a part of most. We believe that there are four family styles that characterize anger in different ways and many reasons why a family may experience anger. After a while, the anger can take on a life of its own and gets entrenched into the family's expression patterns. Sometimes we are too close to it to actually see the style, but we may find it easier to spot in other families (visiting the in-laws), or we see it after we've been away for awhile (at reunions or at Thanksgiving). So too, perhaps someone more objective can readily recognize it.

If you are able to identify the anger style in your family you can do something about it. You can define the underlying emotions triggering that anger, deal directly with them, and interpret any mean habits as they come forth. Most families occasionally show a mixture of these four family styles. It's only worrisome if a family remains stuck, and particularly if they have no awareness or take no responsibility for what's happening.

The Troubled Family Where Anger Is the Voice of Pain

Troubled families are overwhelmed by hurt that stems from marital strife or divorce, financial problems, drug or alcohol abuse, some other addiction, mental illness, or the death of a family member. Parents struggling with one another might place their children smack in the middle of their conflict. In my practice, I'd often find families dropping off Johnny with the hopes that I'd restore normalcy by "fixing" their child. But knowing that the family is so pivotal, I'd ask in the parent interview, "How's your marriage?" Almost immediately, I could gain insight into the true problem, especially if defenses kicked in with a reply akin to "What do you mean— our marriage? What does *that* have to do with Johnny?" Rest assured it has a lot to do with individual family members who might act out the pain felt by that veiled strife. So, if you skipped over the couples and marriage chapter, do read it for added insight regarding the family.

When tragedy strikes, family members often are unavailable to each other, unaware of their emotions, or confused by multiple or conflicting emotions. The remedies for troubled families who hide their feelings depend upon the source of the pain.

Grief counseling would be appropriate when the pain of loss leads to one's lashing out in indirect ways or one's persistent resentment of those who have what the person feels she has lost. Where addiction triggers anger, getting proper treatment is crucial. Until then, the addict remains more committed to the next fix than to the family. It's tough to compete with potent drugs, alcohol, gambling, or other habits. If you bury the problem as well as your anger, you're merely passing it along to the next generation. Take care of it now. Where there is a mood disorder, medication can restore happiness, and counseling works effectively on thoughts. Within the medical community, we know so much more today about brain-based dysfunction and how to treat it. If the stigma bothers you, discuss this with a therapist because treatment usually is not long term, and it's rare these days to find someone who hasn't grappled with anxiety, depression, or some other problem. Recovery is achievable.

The Frantic Family Where Anger Is the Voice of Stress

Imagine a family where dad is gone on business much of the time, so mom makes Michael, her sixteen-year-old son, the "man of the house," responsible for not only his own chores but dad's as well. What's more, mom is lonely, and when Michael bolts out the door for a pickup game of basketball, mom objects. She forgets that she'd cajoled him into using dad's symphony ticket and that he hasn't seen his good buddies for the better part of a week with all he has to do. Michael is seething, yet if he expresses this to mom, she'll dwell upon her loneliness. Michael's anger is the voice of stress.

The family might be stuck with dad's travel, but mom (and dad) could realize the burden it creates for Michael. No teenage boy wants to become mom's substitute companion (not this regularly), so mom needs to call a female friend to use the extra ticket or hire outside help for the chores.

Frantic families face a host of challenges. William Doherty of the University of Minnesota's Department of Family Social Science has written about the importance of taking back your family time—pulling it away from harried schedules of scout troops, church meetings, music lessons, sports teams, and service clubs and placing the importance upon family meal time, vacations, or outings as a family unit.[1] *USA Today* featured his comments in January 2005 and cited survey research.[2] According to the University of Michigan, only one in three U.S. families dined together, whereas two in three did so in the 1970s. The average "soccer mom" spends more time behind the wheel than at the kitchen table. What's more, researchers found that children who dined with their families showed higher student achievement test scores, not to mention that a better diet contributed to their overall health because these children consumed more fruits and vegetables, and less fat, fried food, and soda.[3]

Setting aside time speaks volumes sending the nonverbal message you send regarding the importance of these relationships. The frantic family says, "We'll talk about it later," whereas the committed, expressive family finds the time for "What's going on?" or "How was your day?" A frantic family only pays attention when crisis looms, thus small, solvable problems go untouched. What do you think happens there? Anger sets in, and if it's not dealt with—you guessed it again—it gets buried.

There is really only one remedy to the frantic family: Slow down. Make family time a priority. Schedule it. Yes, even with teenagers who would much rather hang out with friends, have sacrosanct time for meals, outings, or just plain conversation. Touch base frequently to discuss issues that arise. Your budding gymnast won't lose status nor will your son jeopardize his chance of a football scholarship. When you're together, tone down the noise from televisions, music, and cell phones. Your teenager's headset comes off the ears, and you put down the newspaper long enough to listen. Remember that family time or mealtime is not the appropriate venue for assigning household jobs, chastising the kids about messy rooms, or reviewing the latest troubling report card. It's about being with one another, often without any set agenda, to see where the connections form and what is going on in everyone's individual lives. Despite a lot of psychological hype, there is indeed no substitute for time.

The Angry Family Where Anger Is the Voice of Power

Where adults are short-tempered, cynical, critical, or controlling, anger can be very open and deliberate, or it can be concealed as well. Sometimes, it's both. In either case it expresses a quest for power where no one ever really wins.

Austin is a typical teen, drawn to friends and activities far more than to chores or homework. Once spring rolls around, one of his main responsibilities is to mow the lawn, empty the grass catcher, weed-whack, and sweep up the clippings. For his effort Austin earns fifteen dollars each week. His father ran him through the routine a couple of times in mid-April. By the end of May, after six weeks, you'd think Austin would know better than to cop the excuse "I forgot" when his mother got tired of everyone tracking grass inside.

"Austin, please go out and finish your job. You know you're to sweep up."

"Dad said to mow the lawn this morning. I did," Austin replied.

Realizing a convenient way out when she heard one, his mother felt frustrated that Austin was becoming so oppositional. "Please just finish the entire job, the way you're supposed to."

"But Mom, I'm fixing my guitar. No one said anything about sweeping. Get off my back."

Doubly frustrated, feeling ignored and somewhat disrespected, mom upped the ante. "If you don't go out there right now young man, you can forget the fifteen dollars . . . all of it!"

"Sure . . . be that way. All my friends make twenty dollars. You guys can treat yourself to dinner, paying me slave wages! And now, no wages!"

"Keep it up, Austin, and you'll be not only grounded for the evening, but I'll take away your guitar, too."

Austin, knowing his mother was capable of doing just that, stormed past her to the garage, grabbing the push broom and slamming the button to raise the door. Rolling her eyes at yet another battle, *at least the sidewalk will be clean,* she thought.

That evening, she ran an errand. Sitting down into the driver's seat, she sighed. She'd just stepped into a six-inch pile of grass clippings strewn around the door of her car.

In families like Austin's, there are similar undercurrents that feed upon themselves. Just as our canine friends sense who is alpha, Austin probably didn't give his father as hard a time. Clearly, he also knew how to push mom's buttons. While mom asked Austin nicely the first time or two, this episode led her to mete out discipline with multiple threats. Docking his pay slightly may have been a more appropriate consequence than threatening to pay nothing, to ground him, *and* to take away his guitar.

Maybe mom felt tired after a day at work, resented Austin vying for the number-two position in the family, or had had it with her son's smart remarks. But when family members sense anger as the voice of power and predict how it will affect others, things escalate. Here, fueling the anger was counterproductive to Austin's getting a raise, too.

Everyday incidents like this highlight a spiteful undercurrent. Angry families use power with putdowns, sarcasm, intimidation, criticism, and withholding information. One family member might set the dinner table, and as everyone sits down, someone grumbles, "You forgot the spoons." After a sibling makes a homemade pie, one sourpuss sister might remark, "You left out the cinnamon."

In an extended family, you might tell a relative that Aunt Millie was admitted to the hospital with terrible migraines and high blood pressure only to hear, "Oh she always did get herself so worked up." Sometimes it's not the content of what's said as much as the process of how it's said, with a hostile sigh, a grumble, void of any compassion or praise. "Thanks for setting the table, but I'm not finding the spoons. Could you bring some over please?" is factually correct and better delivered at least. Other things are better left unsaid, like criticizing someone's best effort. So, what if you could make a better pie? If you passively sat back and let someone else bake one, but also serve it to you, keep quiet.

Family members also wield power when withholding information so that they can ask later, rather indignantly, "didn't you know . . . ?" This sets up a situation that's to their advantage (because they need to feel important and powerful).

I worked in my practice with families that communicated through argument with cutting remarks wedged conveniently into their conversations, so much so that I could hardly interject a word. By the time I pointed out this type of hidden anger, they were onto the next nasty note. So during one session, I videotaped a family, and we reviewed the tape. "My son acts just like I do," the father said with embarrassment that motivated him to change his ways. Here, the family had to see their patterns on a screen in order to believe them.

Change doesn't come easily when power plays have become long-standing habits. You've got to shake up the faulty routines that get you stuck. If things aren't working out with your old way of interacting, for everyone's sake, try a new way. Try various ways until something pulls you from old habits that cause new problems. Do *something* different!

Witness the mom who refuses to talk about finances though funds are tight, or the kids who leave their clothes, backpacks, and tennis shoes strewn throughout the house. Shake up these faulty patterns with mom not only discussing the family budget but also learning to use financial software, and the kids having a contest to see who could have the most well-organized room, with none of their belongings tossed anywhere but in specified spaces.

Family members are always best served by properly expressing their frustrations, needs, wants, losses, and other feelings. Put them on the table, honestly and appropriately, so that they don't seep back into your behavior. Learn to tolerate stress and use relaxation techniques to manage anger that quells inside of you. Listen to music, watch a comedy together, or if necessary, talk to a therapist to unravel where the anger originates. When we talk about shaking up bad habits, angry families need to practice other ways of communicating; for instance, no critical remark can be waged without first paying at least five compliments. Yes, this requires some effort. You shouldn't ignore problems, but don't dwell on them either.

Finally, when you become aware how anger influenced any behavior, don't forget the aftermath stage of anger management. You want to teach your child that your parenting style emanates from thoughtful action, not impulsive provocation.

The Indulging Family Where Anger Is the Voice of Desire

How many times do you hear of children today who have possessions many adults didn't claim until adulthood. Cell phones, laptops, maybe even their own automobile—just a few of the things kids own that weren't even on their parents' wish lists at their age. Try telling a teenager, who sees friends having or doing what he or she yearns for, the dreaded "no," and anger is the voice of desire, all right. Here, too, the anger can be covert, as in, the child's refusal to cooperate.

You see the indulgence of young children in the grocery store while their parent is trying to negotiate the checkout lane. "If only" they could have that candy bar? Other times, "if only" they could have a TV in their bedrooms? Other kids have one. Why can't they? Parents, too often responding out of some other emotion (like guilt for not being around), give in. Home *ought* to be peaceful, right? Thus, parents aren't always aware of when and how they feed their children's desires. Most assuredly, they don't realize how these indulgences—good things in their minds—set their children up for a life of limited coping skills and no tolerance for the words *no*, or *wait*, or *not right now*.

Distancing yourself, you can see that these words are truly called for, but in a family where anger is hidden by indulgence, it's not a demarcated boundary. Often, parental indulgence takes on three forms—surrender, confusion, and spoiling.

Parents, too, often surrender to keep the peace or maintain a connection they so desperately want with their child. They might act confused as if leaving a child's request unfulfilled is somehow harmful or unhealthy. When dad secretly aims to make mom look bad because the marriage is floundering, giving into to a child because he knows that it provokes mom—now that is passive-aggressive behavior. Spoiling equates to lavishing gifts and to being permissive. How many times have you been annoyed with your child for chores left unattended that you've just decided you might as well do yourself. What would it have taught Austin, from our earlier example, if his mom had swept the grass to complete his chore, or if she just ignored the clippings on the hardwood floors, vacuuming in anger instead of dealing with the real problem?

Regardless of your reason for indulging your child, the results remain the same. Child gets angry enough = he gets what he wants = he grows up with little to no stamina for stress and no patience. He'll take this attitude into future relationships and work experiences. Think we're wrong? Reread the chapter on workplace attitudes and dealing with difficult coworkers. Insert your child's name. Sadly enough, that's what could play out if parents allow children to manipulate with their anger instead of managing it and growing from it.

Of course, nothing replaces understanding child development and the difference between needs and wants, at any age. Realize, too, that children need limits. They'll never come right out and tell you this, however. If you can find the child who tells you "Mom, I need you to set the timer so that I only play my GameBoy for thirty minutes," please let us know. Rather, the child will later appreciate that you distracted her with a better activity, got her involved in the latest Harry Potter book, helped her develop a winning chess strategy, or helped her shoot hoops better in the driveway.

For those parents who regret prior indulgence, it's not too late. Make a concerted effort to change your parenting style, and have some supportive people for encouragement—a friend, a fellow parent, a therapist—because they can help you to distinguish your own conflicts from your child's true needs.

PREVENTING INDIRECT ANGER IN YOUR FAMILY

HONESTLY, MOST FAMILIES have been passive-aggressive, even just occasionally. It's the persistent pattern that's burdensome. Parents who use passive-aggressive tactics often raise children who do the same. By age, pay attention to the following red flags:

Young children: Especially during transitions, be alert for hidden anger. The child stressed by a separation, divorce, death, or another transition may not tell you, but may convey his upset through his actions. Prepare children for the birth of a sibling, for they like to be told important things, often feeling uncomfortable or uncertain how to ask.[4] Watch for passive-aggression after the new arrival. Don't leave children alone with the infant because they're savvy enough to whack baby sister just when you turn the corner, fail to hand the bottle back after baby drops it, or "lose" little brother's favorite blanket or pacifier. Also rein in your enthusiasm to avoid showing favoritism. Maybe after having several daughters you're overjoyed with a little boy, or maybe your second or third child comes at a time in your life that's easier or happier for you. Be sensitive to your older child's feelings of being "replaced" or the daunting step up that being the big boy or big girl requires.

Older children: Model good behavior such as fair fighting, setting goals, and working to attain them as well as identifying and solving problems in steps. Provide opportunities for active social play because this boosts not only their problem-solving repertoire but also their self-esteem. When your child's behavior shifts unexpectedly, be alert for other issues, including learning disabilities, bullying, low self-esteem, and peer pressure. Avoid shaming them when things go poorly. Berating a child for not understanding only adds to a sense of helplessness, and in turn, keeps the anger cycle going within them. Talk instead. Share the hopes, values, and skills you're trying to teach.

Teenagers: As adolescents begin their quest for independence, teach them the difference between being assertive and being aggressive. Respectfully recognize unreasonable motives and use this as a teaching moment. Set clear limits, gradually increasing freedom. Provide praise, solid feedback, and increased responsibility, especially as they reach certain milestones (e.g., once they are eligible to drive, they're also responsible for earning money to power and insure the vehicle.)

When you don't see eye-to-eye, belittling or otherwise condemning teens leads them to shut down. When communication is lost, so is any influence that you, as parent, have upon the child. Since peers and the media exert powerful influences, discuss why you disapprove of certain lyrics or how behavior displayed in certain sitcoms runs against your values. If you only tell them "No!" when they ask to have the hot new CD, without explaining why you believe it's not appropriate, you risk coming off as controlling. There too, if you say "Oh, no problem" to everything a child wants, you may come across as less than effective in your parental role and risk raising the indulged child.

Adult family members: With busy lives, adults are overwhelmed with routine obligations and become caretakers of everyone else except themselves—especially those with jobs, households, children, and older parents needing support. Resentment sets in, especially if they feel taken for granted. Recognize that you cannot be all things to all people, and that you need support. Have honest, open talks about this. If others aren't in a position to ease the load, still take the time to be good to yourself. Surround yourself with supportive people who have positive energy that boosts you up rather than pulls you down.

The elderly: Older individuals face changes in routines and finances due to retirement, and sometimes they experience the decline of their health and other capabilities. Many feel a loss of control, sadness, or regret. It's especially important for the elderly to keep mentally active because studies show that even playing cards, doing crossword puzzles, and enjoying social outings keeps the mind fit. When we engage our cognitive resources, we improve our memories and our outlook remains more open (less indirect) and optimistic. Face decisions you're tempted to put off such as downsizing housing, parting with possessions, and simplifying your lifestyle. Unfortunately, some seniors fail to be a part of their own solutions, and when problems occur (they get sick, they fall, or they cannot take care of themselves or their property) others must step in and make those choices for them. Irritability and anger sets in because of this loss of control. You can prevent silent seething with proper planning and reframing negatives into positives.

VANITY IN THE FAMILY

ENTIRE WORKS HAVE been written about the vain family (see the chapter notes and resources), but when you sense that mom or dad wants to be a pal rather than a parent or push children into their interests or careers to fulfill or relive their own hopes and dreams, or when their arrogance gets in the way of family harmony, you might have vanity in the family.

False Social Heroes as Parents

Some people grow into adulthood still sorting through much hidden anger because they have difficulty pulling away from demanding, self-absorbed families. They end up seeing one or both parents (and sometimes siblings) in an unfavorable light, and to a child in particular, there's nothing quite like discovering that a parent now does that which they took stands against before.

Yet, some parents play this vain role as if they are false social heroes, that is, they need the appearance of good deeds in the community and/or an upstanding family image to save face or make up for inadequate performance, past misdeeds, or sometimes merely lost dreams. They are wearing their "I should have, could have, would have" regrets on their sleeves, and they have such a hard time accepting any past mistakes that the self-blame or guilt comes across as arrogance—or the complete opposite of understanding.

False social heroes volunteer at the local soup kitchen, but they're too busy with their community work to come home and make a wholesome meal for their own families. You find them having cheated on their wives when they were particularly riled up against the guy down the street who did the same. Or, they're arrested for driving under the influence after years of organizing the local Mothers Against Drunk Driving campaigns.

The false social hero sends a very mismatched message in which what they ascribe to publicly isn't what they practice personally. Yet if you call them on it, they'll be contrite, apologize profusely, tell you they never meant to send whatever poor message they conveyed. And tomorrow, they're back trying to impress everyone with their good works.

How to Deal with the Vanity

First, understand the problem. In healthy families, parents meet their own and their children's needs. Things get turned around in the vain family because the responsibility for caring for the parent shifts to the child, as if parenting one's parent. Other signs of skewed roles: Children don't react to or run with their own emotions or hunches, but wait to see what others (typically parents) expect or need. Only then do they react, positively or negatively. If there's anger, it's generally tucked away, out of sight.

Self-centered parents usually can handle babies, but when these little darlings mature, their vanity gets in the way of meeting more complex needs. You'll see a heightened self-focus that in milder versions means that the child misses out on growth opportunities, educational or fun events because the parent's needs regularly supercede all others, and in its worst form develops into profound neglect as when a child's needs for safety, clothing, shelter, food, medical attention, or nurturance aren't met. You might see self-focused parents conceal physical, sexual, or emotional abuse, substance abuse and addictions, or more profound mental illness because they don't understand the impact upon the child. Meeting their own needs is primary; doing anything for a child occurs as an afterthought and only if it's easy.

When the child accustomed to this grows up, intimacy in adult relationships proves terribly difficult to attain without trust that's never been established in earlier relationships. This person has had to erect self-protective walls because in the troubled, addicted family, or in the angry family with physical or verbal battering, there's been a severe breach of trust, harder to overcome, and a dysfunctional way of life concealed over a longer span of time. There's been more to hide and process emotionally. Overcoming an angry or self-absorbed family heritage isn't impossible, but is more difficult if you don't ever recognize it. Otherwise, you fall into old habits, defenses, and dysfunction that can pollute new relationships.

Covert narcissistic families, according to Stephanie Donaldson-Pressman and Robert M. Pressman, look fine to those outside looking in, and actually they don't look too bad from the inside either. But as these authors write in *The Narcissistic Family*, "Obviously, if the children are expected to meet parental needs, then they are not getting their own needs met, or learning how to express their needs and feelings appropriately. Quite the contrary: What the children are learning is how to mask their feelings, how to pretend to feel things they do not feel, and how to keep from experiencing their real feelings."[5]

If the parent isn't psychologically able to meet the child's needs, then painfully, the child must adapt because as the Pressmans report, it's the only way for the child to gain attention, acceptance, and approval. Can you imagine the self-absorbed parent being told "No," "You can't make me," or "It's mine" by a developing child? Diapers, bottles, cuddling, and smiles were manageable at the infant stage, but not this, not to the parent feeling entitled, special, or quite large in self-proclaimed stature. The child, in fact, is viewed not as a separate and developing being, but merely as an extension of the self-absorbed parent.

Parenting the Vain Parent

As the child grows, this concept of parenting one's parent manifests in a variety of ways, including triangulation. Triangles occur when a parent uses the child or when two parties form a covert relationship that blocks out the other. It shows up as parent and child versus the other parent, or parent and child versus another child. Whenever a parent confides in a child with the intent that he or she will carry the message to the other parent, it's indirect. The triangle makes it impossible to communicate because the two block the third. Where there is perpetual aloofness or unavailability, unclear boundaries (using possessions without asking, barging in without knocking), expecting the child to read the parent's mind or attend to the parent's every whim (instantly at that), and taking great offense if the child expresses different opinions or anything that doesn't fit with the "parent line," you've got a dysfunctional dynamic.

Families wall off feelings, hiding them, often forgetting where they placed those strong emotions until something else occurs later (such as in important relationships when it all floods back). Then reactivity (the spark we learned about earlier) sets in, and the anger-concealing pattern resurfaces. What's more, maybe your parents have been emotionally absent, and you're just plain tired of putting their needs before your own. There's no magic answer to turning any of this around, but if you find that you get little emotional support from your family and that you've had to parent your own mother or father, try to:

- Acknowledge your past—a bit of a self-absorbed family—for only then can you move on to healing your frustrations and learning from them.
- Acknowledge your feelings or visceral reactions (headaches, gastrointestinal symptoms, tight muscles, a lump in the throat, or anxiety). Be aware of the emotions that arise on autopilot (fear, loneliness, intimidation, jealousy, and sadness, among them).
- Decide to move on and change things for the better.
- Set appropriate boundaries and fortify existing ones. Otherwise, you risk "catching" the self-absorbed person's faulty feelings (including anger).

- Refuse to absorb their emotions. Don't unwittingly accept, incorporate, or identify with the angry person's projection because then you may act upon it with anger. This is called projective identification. Key clue: You suddenly feel angry when you weren't before, and the only thing that's different is that some other person has discharged anger onto you without your knowing it. Minimizing contact and shoring up the boundaries keeps this at bay.
- Hold family members accountable, if you must interact with them, for what they're responsible for doing or providing. Don't do their jobs for them (even emotional ones). Refuse to become codependent.
- Express yourself with "I" statements. Ask others to be as direct with you. Instead of "You were supposed to . . ." and "Why can't you ever remember to . . ." be much more direct with "I hope for . . . ," "I'd like . . . ," or "I want. . . ." It replaces mind-reading phrases such as "You did that because you can't stand to see me happy . . ." with more direct statements such as "I need to . . ." or "I need you to. . . ."

HIDDEN ANGER IN YOUR EXTENDED FAMILY

IF YOU FEEL like your family is no longer a haven, but a chasm of frustration, you're not alone. Years before I entered the Pennsylvania Senate and U.S. Congress, I was a regular guest on talk radio, where people would call in their questions to "Ask Dr. Tim," especially about news items. Loriann (no doubt taking notes for our future books even then) remembers an answer that often applied to many discussions—if you look deep enough into any family, you will find a certain level of dysfunction.

I honestly believe that. No family is a perfect match of temperaments, personalities, and circumstances. Our problems and our strengths combine to give our families their own personality (for better or worse). While some families openly express their anxieties or differences with one another, others hold thoughts and feelings inside. During family get-togethers or trips back home, they might pick up arguments where they last left off. Your parents may side with siblings, with whom you've never gotten along, and given these dynamics and stored resentments, it's unlikely you ever will. Sometimes, even a blood bond isn't binding enough. The reasons are both simple and complex.

In an extended family marked by indirect, covert hostility, those who continue to hide their anger feel inferior or inadequate, yet they gain power over others through their passive-aggressive control. They succeed, unfortunately, on four counts: first, they discharge their anger; second, they conceal it; third, they control the outcome, which reinforces to them the idea that this works; and fourth, they save face by being sly. If you know people who fit this troubling pattern, expect that in times of stress, the passive-aggressive behavior will only increase because it's a personality default, at the core of who they are and how they interact.

The Causes of Extended Family Problems

If your family style fits one of our four types—troubled, frantic, angry, indulging—then any frustrations may well stretch to extended family. An often callous world influences these families even further. I see it everyday with the constituent concerns brought to my offices. Generations ago, families were a much closer unit, with older members able to reach out to the less stable young ones trying to find their way. They bolstered them when life's storms blew through their lives. Youths and young adults found some comfort and stability in knowing the clear rules and expectations. Now people have little support.

Pure geography has eliminated the Sunday tradition of visiting one's relatives, and with frequent contact comes the ability to work out difficulty and learn to cope through tough times. Today, some families are caught in cyclical problems that cell phones and emails do not mend. In fact, email, with its immediacy and brevity, can make communication worse because it's not accompanied by nonverbal interaction that could clarify or even tone down meaning. If you state something emphatically in person, your smile and pleasant demeanor carry part of the message. All that is missing with technology-driven communication. Consequently, misunderstandings occur and hurt feelings well up. As our definition states, over time, this can lead to veiled hostility, and misinterpretations can erupt in anger. Simple instant messages can be like a Rorschach test where the reader projects his own meaning onto them. Resentments, past or perceived hurts become toxic, eating away at your happiness and affecting those around you if you're out of sorts or just plain negative.

Barbara LeBey writes in *Family Estrangements,* "Resentment escalates into grudges, then to rage and hatred, then to damaged and often completely ruined relationships." "Knotted relationships," she says, exist because of two factors—the need for control and the need for approval. "Passive hatred" develops such that family members can't even revel in another member's happiness. "This is a common occurrence when rivalry develops between siblings. Later in life, one sibling is unable to enjoy another sibling's success."[6] And it carries forth into subsequent generations—sisters and brothers comparing notes on whose children won which awards or got accepted at what college. Instead of cheering on your nieces or nephews who succeed, you feel jealous, withhold praise, and silently resent their good fortune. It's so juvenile, but we've all known cases where this has happened.

Covert Coalitions

Beyond geography and lack of traditional support, another factor afflicting families is *coalitions*, a family-therapy term for subgroups of family members. These are people who spend more time than not with one another, agree with and often back each other, and unfortunately resist confronting each other when there is a problem. Once established, coalitions endure. They can feed on faulty thinking and hidden anger. Not everyone lives in denial of what's honestly going on, however. One family member, maybe an adult sibling or an aunt or uncle, continues to be the scapegoat or the butt of old family jokes. Technology enables the gossip or joking to continue ("Oh, do you remember when Aunt Sally did . . . ?"), and when families do physically gather, you can imagine the reaction that any recipient of this taunting might have—something akin to "Not again . . . give it up already." Negative humor, as we know, is a form of passive-aggression, unless the person who is the main character in the joke is laughing with you as well. The "I was just kidding!" is the excuse people cop once they're caught scapegoating someone else.

Covert coalitions take hold when families gather, even in celebratory moments such as weddings or bar mitzvahs, that have the ability to polarize people. At these events, you're reminded of your differences whether it's your cousin's alternative lifestyle, a break from the family's religious tradition, or opposing political views. In already angry or troubled families, members tend not to embrace diversity and appreciate everyone's potential for growth and change, but see things one way or another, as if falling on the right side or the wrong side. Frantic families likely don't have time to embrace differences because they're too overwhelmed and overstressed already. Indulging families might confuse what role is appropriate, quickly surrender or spoil a person to cement connections distance has threatened.

Certainly, coalitions surface in crisis, too, as elderly members cope with failing health and resentment sets in within the clan over who is (and isn't) on the scene, and what decisions need to be made, or at funerals when memories of what was (or wasn't) stir strong emotional flashbacks to childhood. There's also considerable strife over money and inheritances proving this to be a time of entitlement and greed, obviously inciting anger. When this family's core behavior pattern fits the indulging family type, it's even worse.

Family members within a coalition derive a perceived present or future benefit. Some coalitions develop because of inherent similarities or closeness in age or interests. When there's little familiarity or comfort level with a person (sometimes the outsider or the newcomer), it's certainly harder to break in, and hidden anger can flourish. There are subtle and not-so-subtle techniques to put people through, a trial by fire before being accepted. We can attribute some of this to group dynamics. Anytime change is thrust upon a group, you might see some resistance. The minute a newcomer is thrust before a familiar bunch of people, there's a period of testing (resistance) or people become polarized. Remember movies like *My Big Fat Greek Wedding?* Any new daughter- or son-in-law surely understands the tension of trying to fit in, missing the context of situations or traditions, and worse, feeling distanced or pushed aside.

Occasionally with very angry families, acceptance never occurs. When these types of coalitions become unyielding and underhanded, charming yet cunning, they can destroy the overall family, and are often concealed at the expense of some family members' feelings (typically, those left out or the subject of gossip, innuendo, or scapegoating).

Recognizing Anger Triggers

What are the most common triggers of extended-family discord? Irrational beliefs; strong, negative emotions; the desire to control or jockey for position; forming triangles; sarcasm and cynicism; and self-absorption. Some family members feel wounded, without reason. When new members are born into the family, young children may act out, not understanding the attention shift. Being temporarily wounded is fine and is usually worked through, but research tells us that those wounds can lead to passive-aggressive behavior if the angst remains well into adulthood.[7]

Take your forty-five-year-old brother, who when invited to your daughter's fifth birthday, brings his photo album in order to show everyone his recent vacation voyages, and offers to take *your* guests out for a spin in his new convertible. Look closely enough to these behaviors, and you might see a grown sibling still competing against you for the attention or acceptance of relatives, certainly jockeying for position, self-absorbed, and with a desire to control the outcome (the child's party). Very likely there are strong, negative emotions at the core of this and perhaps more than a few irrational beliefs.

Anger That's Crossed the Line

When otherwise occasional behavior becomes a persistent pattern of subtle torment, the passive-aggression is really emotional or verbal abuse. There's no abuse meter, however, to demarcate that boundary. It's usually attributed to being overwhelmed, overstresssed, unhappy, frightened, continually perplexed or uncertain, and in many cases, ignorant of child development. Abusers still struggle with their own unresolved anger problems and resentment. When that struggle becomes so toxic, emotional abuse can last a lifetime in some families. So, how much should you endure? Too many people allow themselves to become the targets of someone's wrath until the pain becomes too intense. Don't let that be you!

In my practice, whenever I saw a family member "dump" on another, I couldn't help but feel that the person had little left to give. Their own emotional bank was depleted, so there was no patience, no unconditional love or acceptance, no empathy for anyone else. People like this will push someone close away to avoid the pain of rejection or to avoid what this person conjures for them out of their own memory bank. If they're the self-absorbed type, they may push other family members to meet their own needs with a "do this for me" attitude. The message behind such demands, on the receiving end, is very clear: "I must comply to be accepted, included, or loved." This, in itself, is very sad because at the core is the angry person's desire for love, but she fights against the very thing she cries out for.

No wonder relationships crack. Cruel words range from sarcastic remarks, unkind appraisals ("You're such a _____"), or vented regret ("I wish you'd never been born"). The same sentiment plays out in countless nonverbal ways: The absent or too-busy parent, the backstabbing sister or brother, the grandparent, aunt, or uncle with one more criticism but few compliments. Emotionally abusive people have a knack for pointing out what's wrong, never what's right. Being without such balance leaves family members with low self-esteem, trouble trusting or forming positive relationships, a negative worldview, poor social skills, body aches and pains, too few good memories, and of course, open or covert hostility.

Groups like Parents Anonymous teach that what you to do a child's feelings can hurt just as much as physical bruises. Kids depend upon their parents' reactions to realize their strengths, whether they're smart or dumb, good or bad, loved or unlovable. In the extended family, if a litany of bad appraisals continues, or if anything good about the person remains concealed, he or she will likely conclude the worst.

Your Reaction Matters

In a best-case scenario, prominent family members will leverage their influence over the difficult, depressed, or abusive family member so that the person concealing his troubles becomes aware and seeks solutions. In the worst case, you'll have to make some choices, occasionally difficult ones, about how you respond to the extremely difficult members in an extended family. A few suggestions:

- Understand what's at the root of the behavior. Knowledge is power. Power equates to some peace of mind.
- Rework strong feelings and unresolved anger. What's your anger about? What triggered it? What's in your control to change, and what is not? As the *Serenity Prayer* tells us: "God grant me the serenity to accept the things I cannot change, the courage to change the things I can, and the wisdom to know the difference."[8]
- Refuse to be sidetracked. Focus on the problem at hand and the best possible solution. Don't employ bad argument tactics such as throwing in extraneous arguments, blaming, assuming that you can read minds, denying your part, playing the martyr, whining, or putting up walls. Refuse to allow projective identification (defined in "Parenting the Vain Parent").
- Know when to back off, creating distance, especially so that your children don't see anger modeled before them or feel the anxiety from group tension. To overcome the little things, remember the big things—the commitment to family, faith, and values.
- Stay physically and emotionally healthy. Read this entire book so that you honestly understand passive-aggression. Read other books that we recommend or cite. Get help through individual therapy or join a supportive therapy group.
- Stay connected with cards, gifts on the holidays (see sidebar "Handling Holiday Hidden Anger"), occasional email. So long as it's positive, sensitive, and empathic, you're on the right course.
- Consider a permanent cut-off carefully. Permanent distancing may indeed be necessary for you don't want to check your self-esteem at the door every time you're near a family member or

coalition that discharges anger onto you. If it's a long-term pattern (spanning a decade), it's probably entrenched, unlikely to change on its own.

■

HANDLING HOLIDAY HIDDEN ANGER

"MY husband's brother was an angry child," wrote a woman after reading our first book. "Now, he's an angry adult exhibiting all the same behaviors. Many of us within the family have urged him to seek help, but he denies he's angry. It's gotten to where we must stay away because it casts a pall upon our holidays."

The holiday season frequently brings out the worst in families each year. Forget contending with the bustling crowds to find the right gift or the weekend you spent decorating, the real stressor during the holidays is family. And this coincides with a time when so many of us endure five weeks of excess—overtaxed schedules, unrealistic expectations, strained finances, way too much food and drink, and people whom they would ordinarily never have lunch with, let alone something as symbolic as a holiday meal. They find themselves stuck around the same table with their old unfinished arguments, their own lives, plus in-laws.

GIFT-WRAPPED ANTAGONISM

During the holidays, people conceal yet discharge their anger through "forgetting" to send a gift, giving totally inappropriate gifts such as a bottle of rum to the known teetotaler, or flexing their muscles with their purchase power. After a rather contentious divorce, one woman saw her daughter used as a pawn when the child's paternal uncle gave her a big-screen TV and video-game system for her bedroom. Not only was this indulging, but it also smacked of anger when you know the circumstances of the daughter's recently diagnosed learning and attention problems. The mom was having a hard enough time keeping the girl focused on school, and what's more, her ex-husband's extended family knew full well her stand—no game systems and no TV sets in the child's room.

Another man reported that his mother always gave his wife the stall tactic, never committing to holiday invitations until the very last minute. This failure to commit to any plan made holiday preparations burdensome because invitations to other family members were delayed, until the pattern became too irritating to ignore. Not knowing whether his mom was ambivalent about where to spend the holiday or whether she enjoyed the control that her silence granted her over the situation, the son asked his mother if she could please make a decision and inform them. She still stalled. Soon, the in-laws were the last to be invited to gatherings.

MANAGING YOUR EMOTIONS

For the holidays, assume that others will act the same but be ready to allow them to act differently. And you? Act differently indeed. Analyze from where any strong feelings emanate. Are you trying to create the Norman Rockwell holiday portrait that never existed in your own childhood? If your own holidays lacked warmth, maybe you're striving to create perfection. What about competition? In some families, siblings compete to see who can set the most elegant table, cook the best gourmet meal, or impress people with outlandish gifts. Why not embrace and celebrate individual differences?

Add in modern-day dynamics of stepfamilies, and you've got more holiday hot-buttons. Children who reside elsewhere may visit and feel like outsiders if there aren't enough beds, or simple conveniences like their bikes to enjoy recreation with the other parent. It's important to make everyone feel a part of things, talk about tensions before the holiday ever takes place, and ease transitions. Some families wisely opt to do something entirely different, such as renting a cottage where they can celebrate a holiday and also vacation together. Then, no one can claim home-turf advantage. Some ways to avoid a merry meltdown:

- Discuss as a couple how you'll handle the push and pull from extended family. What is it that you like most (and least) about these gatherings? Try to support your spouse's wishes for closeness or distance with his or her own family, especially if you don't have a strong opinion yourself.
- If you do feel a sense of obligation, alternate holidays with different relatives or in-laws, relegate holiday trips to brief visits, or have a separate celebration that enables you to choose a time that's a lot less hectic and stress-filled.
- Put your best behavior forward. Smile. Laugh when appropriate. Use empathy. Pay compliments. Offer to help with the meal or other tasks throughout the visit.
- Act differently. If your routine was to take a seat and watch TV, do something else. This will bring out different interactions and different dynamics will soon surface.

- Rein in your reactivity because your own anger escalates matters. Watch how you respond and what you convey through body language. If your sister pays you a backhanded compliment, don't get angry (old reaction). Don't begin defensive sentences with "You make me. . . ." Keep your defenses in check, and learn how to walk away and ignore (new reaction). If you must say something, use "I" statements. If an altercation ensues, remember the aftermath stage to clean up messes left behind.

- Determine to break out of any destructive coalitions. Listen when someone conveys heartfelt feelings that the age-old family joke really needs to be permanently sidelined. Likewise, don't participate in a triangle. If someone says, "Tell your brother . . ." calmly reply, "He's right over there for you to talk with."

- Be sensitive to those who are in transition from the death of a loved one, separation or divorce, or loss of a job, but also don't enable them to cast a pall upon the holidays either. Being kind does not mean that you must cater to anyone's melancholy. Rethink traditions and become more sensitive to others' feelings.

- Bolster yourself, realizing that if people choose to be cross, their actions or words do not change you intrinsically. Such antics merely invoke the past, since those who employ the technique can't accept the present. Resist the familial role if it's an uncomfortable one that pigeonholes you; it speaks of how narrow others are, with little reflection upon you.

- Do something helpful to take your mind off the day's longings if you are cut off from family. Volunteer at a soup kitchen. Help out at Children's Hospital or at a women's shelter. This keeps you busy, and you also extend yourself to others, boosting your self-confidence and helping you to feel gratitude for what you do have as opposed to longing for what you don't.

SEVEN

FACING HIDDEN ANGER
IN FRACTURED RELATIONSHIPS

Terry and Diana work side by side in their real estate office, only Diana thanks the heavens that she's out showing houses most of the time. While they started out as friends, Terry, knowing that Diana is a single mother supporting her children, frequently makes remarks that Diana's convinced are intended to remind her of that single, struggling status. Case in point: "Diana, wasn't it a beautiful weekend? The pumpkin farm was great. Kids and I spent hours." After Diana smiles back, Terry continues, "Oh . . . that's right, you were showing houses both days . . . must be lonely when the kids are off with your ex."

Terry can be socially proper when she wants to be. Diana often feels that the competitive world of who gets more closings each week extends to every conversation, with Terry, who starts out so innocently, then lobs a verbal jab when she gets a chance. Afraid she'll look petty, and knowing Terry would have a face-saving answer—"Oh, I can't keep your weekends straight" or "I was only talking about our visit to the farm, what's wrong with that?"—Diana remains silent but feels increasingly self-conscious. That's probably what Terry anticipated, and it makes Diana even more annoyed that such remarks succeed.

We often see passive-aggression and hidden anger in less solid relationships—some that appear to be on the brink of falling apart. Fractured friendships are the epitome of the incongruence we identified much earlier; that is, the other person says she wants to be your friend, but her actions don't. We see the same type of ambivalence and subtle meanness in children where they're trying to form friendships at school recess, during play dates, or during teams and after-school activities. And when connections end because of divorce or some other rupture of the relationship, two parties are left to look in another direction or reinvent their interactions, often when they are the most emotionally vulnerable. Their inability to openly express to one another the loneliness, despair, guilt, sadness, jealousy, or other profound emotion that the rift has triggered, leads to a level of simmering anger that doesn't take much of a spark to set off.

FRACTURED FRIENDSHIPS

BECAUSE SOME PEOPLE depend upon the companionship and support that friendly relationships typically provide, they can't come right out and unleash their frustrations openly when you've disappointed them, or when their expectations or needs aren't met. They are hurt or annoyed, nonetheless, that they can't get out of you or the friendship what they'd hoped to obtain. Concerned about fulfilling their need, afraid of loneliness or some other negative feeling, and avoiding direct conflict, they go underground, complaining to their friends, making caustic remarks or backhanded statements.

Who needs it, you might ask? Why doesn't anyone feeling the brunt of a friend's negative feelings, just dump the friendship? Answer: For the same reasons that anyone stays in an unhealthy relationship. Diana has some core needs, too, as a single mother. She probably doubts, at times, how well she's doing, and she might mistakenly believe she's just caught Terry on a bad day . . . or, as our example indicates, she's a little stuck since this is a workplace friendship. She needs the job. She must tolerate Terry's occasionally stinging remarks.

Friends who indirectly show their feelings also use the passive-aggressive strategy of silence, and the result inflicts frustration upon others. "In my feedback from hundreds of women, I learned that a key reason women felt hurt in a friendship was when a friend fell out of touch," says Marla Paul, who writes a syndicated column about friendship and who wrote *The Friendship Crisis: Finding, Making & Keeping Friends When You're Not a Kid Anymore.*[1] "They often wrongly assume it means the friend is angry at them or doesn't care. It can lead to their pulling away from the friend."

Also, because most women aren't comfortable with having angry or jealous feelings toward their friends, they shove those emotions aside, but they don't disappear, Paul says. "They erupt in sarcastic remarks or this pulling away from the friend that is much more hurtful than if they had had the courage to air their darker feelings."

Isn't it true that many broken relationships—and certainly fractured friendships—make us feel powerless? Yet, if we work things out after misunderstandings, disagreement, or years of silent (or not-so-silent) antagonism, we regain a personal sense of control, plus the bonds of a stronger friendship. You get out of any relationship what you put into it. Building a friendship is much like building any solid foundation—of a house, a business, or even your own physical strength training—there might be some growing pains at first, but the result is a friendship that survives.

When you feel tempted to drift away from a friend, challenge yourself to become more active in pursuing and keeping the relationship alive. Discuss any problems in a gentle, nonthreatening, supportive ("I'm on your side") way. "At the very least you can leave a phone message to say, 'I'm crazed right now, but just wanted to let you know I'm thinking of you. I'll call when things calm down,'" says Paul.

LETTING GO OF A FRIEND

SOME FRIENDSHIPS AREN'T destined to last. They may often meet their demise from purely circumstantial causes (see the sidebar "Helping Kids Create Strong Friendships"). Other reasons for friendship failure that we may not wish to face: passivity, negativity, ambivalence, or uncomfortable feelings about the friendship, including anger that has gone underground long enough that it surfaces. This can take a long time, too. According to research from the University of Virginia cited in *Psychology Today*, if you harbor concealed anger, your close friends might not pick up on it as easily as mere acquaintances will.[2] The reasons are fairly speculative, but people tend to view their friends and their actions more favorably because aggression and anger could threaten such close relationships.[3]

You might feel angry because you've put more work into the friendship than your friend has, and maybe quite frankly, your friend has been too self-focused lately to rally around your concerns or even ask how you're doing. Given our discussions of self-absorbed people remember that it's all about them leaving little room for the back and forth of normal friendship.

Of course, any of these scenarios could apply to you, meaning your friend could be as annoyed because you have let a friendship passively slide. Maybe you've been negative, indirectly angry, or a little self-focused?

Sociologist Jan Yager, PhD has written *When Friendship Hurts: How to Deal with Friends Who Betray, Abandon or Wound You* where she lists various types of friends that well . . . truly aren't. These include: the promise breaker, the taker (borrows something precious and "forgets" to return it), the double-crosser, the self-absorbed (sends you the invitation to her costume party so late that you have other plans, but this way you won't steal any attention either), the discloser (who can't keep a secret), the fault-finder, the downer, and the abuser, among others.[4] You could perceive many of these descriptions of so-called friends as passive-aggressive, particularly if their behavior was fairly well entrenched.

While some passive-aggressive friends may apologize when they feel contrition coming upon them (at the moment they realize that they want or need you and don't push you away), but self-focused, passive-aggressive friends will rarely apologize. Chronically depressed and passive friends will likely apologize a lot more than they need to.

How do you spot the pattern? Just as you would in other situations, you must tune your radar to recognize what your friend seems to need, fear, or avoid, and make note of the behaviors you see (our text boxes will help you with this task).

Does your friend put herself in a place of honor while you're left feeling stupid or inadequate? Does she derive pleasure from your misfortune or misery? That is, if you tell her that you missed a great opportunity, lost your job, or just sat in traffic during the commute from hell, might she reply, "I could have told you so," or correct you when she could have given you better directions in the first place? Once or twice, anyone can foul up or say something incredibly stupid, but if you spot patterns like this on a continual basis, beware. Hanging around negative people who don't wish to improve their demeanor can literally bring you down to their depths.

■

HELPING KIDS CREATE STRONG FRIENDSHIPS

AS many adults can attest, the bonds of childhood friendships can last a lifetime. Whether it's in your neighborhood or in school, you want your child to have close buddies, friends to rely upon, share confidences and interests, and just hang out with for a good time. You also want your child's confidantes to be positive, not negative influences. If we adults sometimes tolerate acquaintances or friends who get on our nerves, do we really think our children are that much better at solving the mysteries of friendship? Of course not, so they need a little guidance:

■ Teach your child about "friendshifts," that is how some friendships lose their zest because mutual interests aren't shared any longer. People join different teams, clubs, or churches. They move away, or sometimes they change what they're looking for in a friendship. It's not good; it's not bad. It just happens. This helps a child *not* to take it personally.

■ Build your child's social-language abilities. Learning expert Mel Levine, MD writes in *A Mind at a Time* that some children have trouble telling the difference between a joke and a serious statement, perhaps inferring that someone is angry when that's clearly not the case.[5] They might also find it difficult to match others' moods, reacting inappropriately. These misinterpretations can spawn a child's hidden anger.

■ Coach your child about how to deal with any anger and coercion unleashed upon them. Relational aggression, with adolescent girls in particular, has been on the radar screen for years, but now David Nelson and Clyde Robinson at Brigham Young University found that girls as young as three learn how to manipulate and use peer pressure to get what they want.[6] This type of subtle meanness manifests in directives ("don't play with her over there"), leaving someone off of the birthday party list, or an ultimatum ("if you don't do ___, I won't be your friend"). Boys can be equally cruel with their comments (homophobic or feminine insults, or intimating that they aren't "athletic" enough), but typically, boys are much more direct (likely to kick or punch, unfortunately). Other research from the university points to a familial link with discipline meted out by control and manipulation (what we'd call the angry family) or by passive-aggressive means such as withdrawing love and affection, evading eye contact, and instilling guilt in children.

■ Teach children how to respect diversity. Just as we wrote in *The Angry Child*, you can sometimes be angry, but you should never be mean. Here, we advocate telling your child that everyone can be different, but their differences don't give you the right to be mean and nasty. Show them that gossiping, forming cliques, or otherwise distancing themselves from other children when they have little reason to reject those people is simply quite shallow and not the way we treat one another.

■ Encourage give and take. While you want to discourage any selfish behavior, you also don't want your child to become any bully's doormat either. Reason with your child how it might feel to be ostracized or forgotten. Teach him or her kind words to use with other children.

■ Help your child to discover what strengths he or she has, as a friend, to offer others. A strong belief in self helps assuage any jealousy that erupts. Help him or her to feel successful at favorite leisure or recreational activities. This builds self-confidence, which later adds to your child's social strength.

THE ULTIMATE FRACTURES: SEPARATION AND DIVORCE

WE SEE MUCH hidden anger in marital separation because it's built up over time, causing enough damage that the parties often feel no way out beyond ending, or maybe taking a break from, their relationship. With new perspective and often with counseling, these men and women can grow beyond their frustration. Sometimes they can reconcile and learn what caused the wide chasm of bitterness and misunderstanding between them.

Even if they decide they can no longer salvage the relationship, they can also learn better ways of managing the intense emotions that ending a marriage stirs. Though plenty of people having separated or divorced may claim, "I'm not angry," neither of us has really encountered anyone unscathed by this process. Unless the union and all you'd done with your life in the company of this person meant absolutely nothing to you, the anger is there all right, only it may remain hidden.

In my practice, I met parents telling me that their son or daughter was fine with their getting a divorce. In 99.9 percent of the cases, I'm afraid that just wasn't so. The child may not show any visible signs, but rest assured there is some deep emotion there. It was either very visible or extremely well-hidden anger.

But as we've said so often, if you've contributed somehow to your anger or to your children's anger, then you have a greater capacity to be part of the solution as well. It's probably nowhere more important than in divorced families. When you don't do this important growth work—encouraging your children to do the same—learning to openly communicate and move beyond silenced anger, that's when we see children caught in the middle of a silent, or subtly antagonistic war between their parents.

WHY THE BREAKDOWN?

NEGATIVE, ANGER-CONCEALING people tend to recreate disappointing relationship experiences that parallel those previously disappointing ones in their past, according to Millon and Davis.[7] It may be traced back to a failed parent/child relationship or intimate relationship, and in turn, this helps to form their pessimistic worldview. If the patterns continue, you can see a host of fractured relationships on the horizon. Take the person who remarries an ex-spouse, trying to get a second chance or who remarries someone just the opposite of an ex to avoid recreating that relationship. If you've engaged in much introspection to analyze what went wrong in the marriage and what part each of you had contributed, it might be wise to marry the opposite personality. In cases where it's a knee-jerk response made out of frustration or blinded fantasy, however, it may recreate misery. Admittedly it's counter-intuitive to what you'd expect—that people would shy away from similar experiences on account of their disillusionment.

Despite being down on and ambivalent about life, passive-aggressive people feel that a new relationship will be different. Why? In our chapter on couples and marriage, we mentioned shallow reasons why people pair up—because they're turning blame for a problem outward, they're unhappy, and they're looking to be rescued. Or, maybe it's because they don't wish to change themselves (that's simply too hard, and they may think they're just fine the way they are) . . . so they figure they can change their partner.

These folks wear the rose-colored glasses quite well. The past doesn't impact their predictions so this time, they can capture what they've sought after in past relationships; they'll attain it in full measure. Not surprisingly, they wish to seize what they never attained as a child—unconditional love, affection, and attention; approval; and acceptance. With diametrically opposed needs, complete fulfillment remains illusory (e.g., they're dependent yet they crave independence, they desperately wish to be connected yet they see connection as dominance). While it seems that this dynamic fits intimate relationships best, it's by no means confined to those. This plays out in many other types of relationships, including those that people have with colleagues, friends, children, and extended family.

When the passive-aggressive person realizes he hasn't found the unconditional love, affection, attention, approval, or acceptance, he might become more entrenched (controlling, stubborn) in order to get his way, or he may move onto yet another target. Just as the inveterate job-hopper seeks greener pastures in which to ply his trade, the passive-aggressive person looks for another relationship to revive his (or her) hopes, a loving home, maybe even a new family situation to get things right. It's a march to the lawyer's office or courthouse as the first step toward attaining hoped-for happiness.

HIDDEN ANGER IN THE POSTDIVORCE FAMILY

NOWHERE ARE THE four types of families more evident than in those experiencing separation or divorce, in single-parent homes or in stepfamilies where anger is often the voice of all four emotions—pain, stress, desire, and power—that we outlined in the last chapter. These days, a single dad may be as overwhelmed as any single mom. After a long week at work, dad might enjoy watching the basketball game and grabbing a beer with some buddies on a Friday night, but he's afraid to leave his teenage son alone at the house where he might be tempted to throw an impromptu party or get into mischief. Mom might harbor real frustration because she's had to make lifestyle adjustments (maybe downsizing her housing, moving back with her parents, or sharing a place with another single mom) that pull at her emotions. In stepfamilies, where children never asked for any shift in the family makeup, hurt, confusion, and uncertainty trigger anger that goes underground. All of this strife occurs within the context of being a parent, the first and foremost responsibility.

When you think about family or any relationship, it requires nurturance. Even a one-parent, one-child family is still a family unit, though some might be tempted to view it as two individual people. When families merge, birth order shifts, step- and half-siblings complicate the family portrait. This can all be quite positive once sorted out and after everyone settles in. No matter what your family shape, setting aside time just to be together sends a potent nonverbal message akin to "You're worth my time" or in a new stepfamily "I want to know you better."

While you're often doing the best you can, you must also realize the strain you're under. Awareness is the biggest part of overcoming any obstacle. So, revisit our four family types.

We won't reinvent prior material here, but will highlight a few of the really crucial steps you must take to purge hidden anger, and keep it from reoccurring:

- **Do a new thing:** If you're separating or divorcing, this is new. Okay . . . keep up new, but "nice new." Shake up those faulty interactions by replacing old patterns of behavior that didn't work so well with something that does . . . or let's say behavior that "might" work. We realize the inherent conflict with our suggestion. We're asking grown adults and their children, who weren't functioning so well under the same roof, to do this apart, when they likely have even less willingness to get along, coupled with new hurts, wounds, and resentments. But hear this: if you want to be happy and move forward, you must—absolutely no exceptions here, you must—be willing to make changes in your behavior and in your reactions to whatever triggers your deepest hurts or stirs you to seethe inside.
- **Realize you are a troubled family:** You may be troubled in

numerous ways because if you're experiencing marital separation or divorce, that's one reason for the trouble. Any addictions, sustained anxiety, depression, or other mood disorder; physical illness or disabilities in yourself or your children; grief reactions; or job loss/change, and you now have added troubles. While no one is keeping score here, the more trouble, the harder you must work to overcome the pain and restore balance, cooperation, health, and happiness to your lives. Even in stepfamilies where the family additions are welcomed, a period of adjustment takes place.

- **Identify your anger:** You may also be an angry family, especially if one or both spouses' anger has contributed to the marital breakdown. We see this most often in cases of domestic violence or child abuse. Or, we see anger in stepfamilies, where unhappy members play "get back" for the changes brought about. Everyone's anger here is the voice of power, and everyone needs to learn healthier, more positive ways of expressing emotion. People frequently resort to passive-aggression because they feel they have lost control over some important aspect of their lives, and by covertly lashing out, they can cop a handy excuse. They never have to take responsibility. But the flip side: They never solve the real problem, either. They don't obtain true self-control but spin out of control with every passive-aggressive incident. When you find yourself using indirect methods such as triangulation (parent and child against former spouse or using children to carry messages), sarcasm or cutting remarks, silence or stonewalling, sighs, or hostile body language, realize you're angry, all right. You just need to see it.

- **Examine your lifestyle for frenzy:** It's not at all uncommon for the newly separated or divorced family to be managing dozens of more responsibilities. Change is everywhere. You may find yourselves looking for new housing, jobs, insurance, schools, legal support, financial resources, childcare, not to mention psychological support, and the list goes on. This list contains the relatively new items added to an already burgeoning to-do list filled with work, homework, after-school activities, parenting, and so on. Remember, there is no solution for the frantic family other than slowing down.

- **Watch for indulging patterns:** With separated or divorced circumstances, we often see parents indulge their children as a reflection of their not being around as much. Divorced and stepfamilies encounter an "I might as well do it myself" mentality whenever there is limited time for visitation, so a parent might rationalize "Just this once, I'll [do my child's chore complete his homework buy her what she really wants] because I hardly get to see the kids." Problem is "just this once" becomes two and three and ten times, equaling an indulging pattern. Be careful that you don't surrender for a connection with your children. Don't spoil them or confuse your role as parent because of your situation.

■ **Refuse to enable your former spouse:** Former spouses do this when they protect the other person from responsibility and the ordinary pitfalls of parenting. They might forgive child support in arrears, pay for the medicine or treatments that ought to be shared, or deal with a child's desires or battles in an attempt to go it alone. Sometimes this is based upon pride or because they don't care for any further hassles from dealing with their former spouse. But if you find yourself as a single parent at odds with your own limitations (financial resources and time, especially) or if you're at odds with your child who wants certain things, don't set yourself up to be Mr. or Ms. No to your child. The custodial parent always gets more flack for saying "We can't really afford that right now" or "Let's wait and see how that works out." But you're often shielding the non-custodial parent when you single-handedly assume the responsibility. Hurt feelings and anger set in between parent and child as well as parent and ex-spouse.

■ **Point out the positives:** Remember to offer praise before criticism. Ask for what you need. No calling names. Show children how to problem solve. Otherwise, they won't know how, or what working toward a solution looks like.

■ **Look for reasons to be optimistic:** Martin Seligman, PhD co-wrote *The Optimistic Child.*[8] Optimism is the antithesis of negativity, and when facing family upheaval, it's very easy to become pessimistic. Work at optimism. Jot down a gratitude list or verbally cite things that you're thankful for, even in ordinary conversation. Recognize your family and child's attributes and help all of you to be successful. Offer your support, too. Findings reported in the March 2004 issue of *Psychology and Aging* show that those with abundant parental support during childhood are likely to have relatively good health throughout adulthood.[9] Teach kids of all ages how to overcome their frustration by reframing negatives into positives or looking for the bright side. These are effective ways to prevent pessimism from setting in.

HOW THE ANGER PLAYS OUT

KIM'S MOM AND dad split up when she was six. They were separated for two years, and her dad got remarried a few months after their divorce . . . to mom's best friend. Well, they aren't best friends any more! Now that Kim is thirteen, she's pieced portions of the family puzzle together, but any way you put the pieces together, it adds up to a lot of hurt feelings and resentment. Kim never really understood why her parents split, why her mom's friend was suddenly on the outs, but now she senses that her stepmom had something to do with the split (hearing the word "homewrecker" applied to her stepmom probably helped that along).

She'd also hear things like "it's not your fault Kimmy," but that didn't assuage her belief that she'd been bad or that their family hadn't been "good enough." Kim was left to sort it out amidst the silent stares among the adults, and what little bit Kim's mom had to say was usually very negative (you can only imagine the trust broken in too many relationships).

Though Kim says mom "dragged" her to some counseling sessions when she was nine or ten, Kim told her mom she wasn't doing it again. The opposition to her mom, with whom she lives, is startling at times. "If you really cared about me you'd let me stay out longer with my friends," Kim yells at her mom most weekends. Other days, the "if you, then _____" phrase takes on monetary proportions when Kim surfaces her wish list to mom, only to hear "No," or "Ask at your dad's house," or "That's just not practical." But Kim, knowing that her two half-sibling twins consume a lot of her dad's and stepmom's time, feels that she can't count on them, either. She's ticked off, feeling sorry for herself a lot of days, and stuck in a mindset that everyone else's mom is more fair, their family is better, and no one is as poor as they are (a gross exaggeration, but Kim's take on the situation, nonetheless).

There's way too much hidden anger in these parents and in their newly created families. Kim feels disconnected with most of the adults, and it's no wonder why. Her mom stares down her dad and shields him from his responsibilities. Where she could share Kim's current list of teenage desires, she doesn't, taking more and more pressure upon herself, feeding her own hurts, sometimes playing the martyr. And, she ignores Kim's stepmom who used to be a close confidante. We can understand how she feels, but after seven years, mom ought to find ways of dealing with her nemesis. Dad has moved on to other interests and more importantly in Kim's mind, he's moved on with other people, who have gained what she dearly wanted and feels she's never had—a connected, intact family.

Families like Kim's struggle because of needs individual members have not surfaced or fears that stand as stumbling blocks. Some children may have concerns over affording a college education, or they may be afraid they'll be forgotten in a newly-formed family. It's all a recipe for hidden anger.

WHEN THE TORMENT GOES UNRECOGNIZED

UNFORTUNATELY, AS WE see in our example, hidden anger isn't readily recognizable, and family-court personnel typically aren't trained to spot how it manifests. Domestic-relations and hearing officers, special masters, and judges see so much anger before them, that everyone is impugned by poor behavior. From the get-go, you're considered angry until proven happy, and you're sometimes treated accordingly. Court personnel presiding over your problems on any given day may expect to see manipulation and nastiness. Why else would you be at the courthouse? If you could get along, you wouldn't be before them. But what if you are honestly conveying something negative about your spouse or ex-spouse? The person presiding may assume that you're just nasty—because all litigants are this way—so you must be manipulative, and therefore, the court can disregard your testimony, figure that your evidence is contrived, and come down on the most negative-sounding people that day. This is very much the adult version of "feelthink" (I feel it, so that's all the data I need for the decision).

In all of my years of private practice, the actions deemed most ugly occurred in family court. One family court judge moved to criminal division and liked it far better because this judge said that in family court they are not trying to solve anything. The people before you only create more problems. In criminal court, the one charged with a crime is at least trying to behave.

Loriann has written the second edition of her successful book *Surviving Separation and Divorce* [10] in which she cited research published in the journal *Family Relations* that while high-conflict cases in postdivorce are often assumed to be a shared interaction between two hostile former partners, it's not uncommon to find one enraged or defiant partner and the opposite party who no longer harbors anger and attempts to solve problems for everyone's sake, but to no avail. [11] Still too, many passive-aggressive parents know precisely which buttons to push on their ex-spouses or those they are divorcing. Too often, those buttons are the children.

If court personnel fail to recognize the attempts to gain power over others (namely the ex-spouse but even over the children) through manipulation and entitlement, they are likely to reinforce anger, spawning more of it. For instance, many custody actions are lodged because a parent has the "right" under state laws to file these types of petitions, but too few are thrown out for lack of merit. Or, when the case continues to a point at which it could be discharged by a master or judge, it's instead allowed to move forward, even lacking evidence or support. The net effect: warfare. This forces the more cooperative parent into a defensive posture and leads to hurt, in an emotional sense, with the time, attention, and worry put into a legal case, and also tremendous expense. Too often, cases lacking merit are merely "get backs"— passive-aggression at its worst—or what some dub *legal abuse.*

If you're the more rational, problem-solving parent and you don't fight back, your children may suffer, yet as soon as you fight back, the passive-aggressive parent gets you to play the game. Remember, with sometimes a lifetime of practice, he or she is better at it than you are. And even if you try not to play the game, the court system is set up to be adversarial so that everything lands you in that angry game (going back to our argument that you're angry until proven happy).

When game playing or less-than-genuine court actions slip through, the angry party gains tremendous payoffs. He or she essentially learns that discharging anger indirectly is perfectly feasible; no matter how irrational the "rationale" (more like irrational beliefs), the aggressor may feel that the anger is justifiable when indeed it's sorely out of place. In cases lacking merit, court personnel ought to do the exact opposite—empower the victim because when you remove the power from the aggressor, it makes life more peaceful, for everyone, including the judge. Certainly, it makes it a better world for the children who are fought over, and in whose best interest these matters are supposedly fought.

Kids in the Crossfire

The unnecessary custody battle example is the most prevalent passive-aggressive tactic in divorce, but so is withholding information the other parent needs for the children's benefit (homework, assignments, insurance information, possessions), refusal to cooperate or lend an answer, resistance toward following advice of authority figures (doctor's orders, treatment plans, teacher recommendations), obstruction (blocking a move, holding up a property or vehicle sale), and foot-dragging on any other need (delaying a child's bike or eyeglasses repair, forgetting to sign a necessary permission slip, or hanging up the telephone when the other parent needs an answer). Imagine, in a post 9/11 world, not being willing to share with your ex-spouse your children's whereabouts or flight information, or deliberately making contact between parent and child difficult. Some passive-aggressive parents have intercepted letters at the mailbox so that their child wouldn't hear from their mom or dad; they've refused to do something required for the child's health (for instance, putting off getting medicine because they resented paying for it when they already paid child support), or they undermine their children's futures by refusing to pay for any educational expenses, including a college education when very often theirs was fully financed by their own parents. Others deliberately alienate the other parent, often because they feel betrayed or abandoned (even if they were the party to leave or damage the union). Even more, passive-aggressive parents fail to act civilly when in the company of their child's other parent, or withhold ordinarily kind gestures or greetings out of their staunchly entrenched spite (failing to say "hello" or "thank you," ignoring major holidays or events such as Mother's or Father's Day when they could clearly afford a ninety-nine-cent greeting card or construction-paper creation so that the child wasn't empty-handed).

When a passive-aggressive parent also has self-absorbed personality traits, you'll see a lot of "saving face" maneuvers (postdating a check to make it look like the payment isn't late, promising certain indulgences to the kids), and when the hidden anger is mixed with immaturity, you'll see childish behavior (scribbling smart remarks in the check message line, making caustic comments out of jealousy, or being petulant). When one parent tried unsuccessfully to foul up his ex-wife's (and children's) holiday and couldn't accept that the judge denied his court motion, he demanded that the woman "bring the children to my doorstep as the judge said." Only problem: The judge never proclaimed any such action. Feelthink as we've discussed throughout this book, was fully operative in this man's angry mind.

All of these acts express underlying anger and unresolved problems. Chances are the problems were there long before the marriage ended, and as you can see, they often remain far past the divorce decree. The old cliché that you can run but not hide holds true, but sadly enough children pay the price because they pick up on such learned behavior. Kids become ambivalent, not knowing how to react to mom or dad (it depends upon the day, the mood). Such children constantly shift loyalties to survive emotionally between their antagonistic parents with their differing expectations. There's little certainty in these children's lives, and as we stated before, the child's anger becomes the voice of unremitting pain, stress, desire, and power. They have a lot to be righteously angry about with this warfare, and if there is no outlet for that anger, this sets the stage for hiding it.

Necessary Solutions

Some more forward-thinking court jurisdictions are instituting anger management and parenting-coordination programs to help bitter, passive-aggressive people gain insight, but all should pause when seeing these behaviors, delving a little deeper to see whose anger might really stand in the way of problem resolution. It may be deceiving, particularly if one party appears to have moved on (remarriage, more children), but this doesn't equate to an emotional divorce. Using the children or engaging in court battles keeps two parents engaged and also allows perhaps one of those parents to avoid real emotional work.

Loriann also wrote in the newer edition of *Surviving Separation and Divorce* that, "Unfortunately, there is still not enough awareness, particularly in our family courts, that this anger manifests itself physically, but also covertly, such as through legal maneuvering, mental abuse, property destruction, and economic impact."[12] Legal abuse, she writes, is hardly ever discussed. When the angry party succeeds in making life difficult for another, with what may appear to be the court's blessing, there is another payoff or secondary gain—inflated ego, which coupled with unremitting anger, is a recipe for a circular cycle that's hard to break. That's why newer approaches need to be explored to extricate families from getting stuck in the family court system, or for trained professionals (such as parenting coordinators in some states) to assess when the behaviors are primarily game-playing maneuvers and when they are merely reactive.

PROTECTING YOURSELF FROM A PASSIVE-AGGRESSIVE EX

BECAUSE IT'S EASY to get pulled back into situations and emotionally charged issues you worked so hard to extricate yourself from, protect yourself with these tips to keep hidden anger seeping back into your relationship with an ex-spouse:

- Watch out for "feelthink"—"I'm mad, and those are all the facts I need." If your emotions seem to justify your conclusions about your suspicions, jealousy, or other feelings, then your anger will likely seethe and spiral.
- Know that with self-absorbed, passive-aggressive spouses everything is supposed to work for them, to flow their way—not yours. They send off mixed messages like "I need your warm feelings and support" but at the same time "Move aside, you're disposable."

When your marriage ends, your ex may place no value on what the two of you or the bunch of you had as a family. This is another example of the self-centered attitude that it was all for their benefit, and when it ceases to be fun (or easy), they move on without much compassion.

- Realize that you may never have closure on what anger issue lurked in your marriage. The passive-aggressive person might not fully grasp the anger either. This can be terribly confusing especially if your ex remains angry toward you despite wanting out of the marriage. *"C'est la vie!"* Such is life, as the French say. Too often, the quest for understanding keeps you curious and intertwined. Cast curiosity aside for good.

- Resist playing the passive-aggressor's game. Become much less reactive. Sit on a response to a phone message, email, or nasty remark, for days if you must, until the powerful emotions that it stirred subside.

- Operate within your values. Never mind if she speaks poorly of you. Your behavior toward her is your choice. No one "makes" another do or say anything.

- Take action if dealing with a passive-aggressor becomes interminable. You may choose to represent yourself in some court matters so that you can speak directly to what's going on, providing that you feel confident enough and remain imperturbable. Or, you may need the services of mental health professionals, such as a parenting coordinator, who can size up the interactions and report to the court about the situation at hand. Look for a reasonable means to extricate yourself from "the game."

Solving the Hidden Anger Problem

EIGHT

UNDERSTANDING ANGER AS A DEEPER DISORDER

A T SIXTEEN, BLAKE shares a room with her fourteen-year-old stepsister after dad remarried a woman with a daughter also. Their closet serves as a constant reminder that Blake's size sixteen clothes hang opposite Megan's size six. To Blake, girls like Megan have it all—the body, the clothes, the turned heads the boys give her when she walks by, even the pearly whites. When their dentist pulled her stepmom aside to discuss the condition of Blake's enamel, the family began to question her habit of excusing herself after dinner, recent requests to buy clothes in increasingly smaller sizes, and their having to settle episodes of name-calling when Blake vents, quite frequently, upon Megan. Blake has signs of an eating disorder masking low self-esteem and hidden anger.

Joel, two years out of graduate school, has become angry over the corrective action-plan he was given at work. Simply put, Joel resembles disorganized chaos, with papers strewn all about his desk (never in file folders his boss has provided him), and with projects still on his computer's hard drive because he's never quite finished or turned them in. Through school, Joel struggled. He's not stupid, in fact, far from it, with an IQ in the gifted range, but his tendencies to put things off and to anger easily have finally gotten his attention. Joel has ADHD, diagnosed much later than most cases, but he's fortunate. His diagnosis and treatment will not only save his career but become a personal epiphany as he taps his strengths to overcome his weaknesses.

In each of these examples, hidden anger manifests quite differently, and in many cases it's not passive-aggression, though if you followed each of these individuals—and other indirect people—you might think they were being passive-aggressive, at least initially. This chapter discusses when anger crosses the line and is really something else, something that runs deeper and needs treatment. We encourage your continued reading about the disorders we touch upon, with resources we recommend in this book's chapter notes. Our overall message: Don't be afraid to acknowledge that anger can run pretty deep, and that it may be a much bigger problem than you alone can handle. Counseling and proper treatment spell hope. If someone you know or care about fits this picture, recognize the signs of the person's struggle. When you know that genuine improvement exists, you can turn that insight into action.

WHEN ANGER HAS CROSSED THE LINE

WHILE UNRAVELING THE signs and symptoms of passive-aggressive behavior and hidden anger, for the most part, what you might see or recognize has been problematic, but not pathological. In the appendix, you can read more about passive-aggression that reflects a deeper-rooted personality issue causing significant and enduring distress in a person's life.

But there are other problems where you'll see many behaviors we outline in this book. Quite often passive-aggression coexists with another, more deeply-entrenched problem. An important caveat: While this is a self-help book designed to offer comfort, if you're on the receiving end of difficult behavior or if you feel yourself struggling with anger, it can in no way help you to make a lay diagnosis of yourself or of anyone else. Only qualified mental health professionals can do that, and we urge you to recognize the limits of this book or any other resource. On the other hand, if reading helps you to put behavior into a better context, to be more empathic toward a person or problem, then that's quite positive. Don't confuse empathy with enabling because identifying a deeper-rooted problem is never a "get-off without-taking-responsibility" ticket. Indeed, some people see ADHD, depression, or other disorders as locks while others see them as a key. With that key, they can unlock a door opening the way to change and happiness.

■

ASSESSING ANGER

MANY people first consider informal feedback when they begin to acknowledge a problem. Has a significant other (or parent, child, friend, coworker) told you about your anger? Have you taken any informal quizzes such as the ones found in this or other books that indicate you have anger?

When feeling out-of-sorts is a lasting, pervasive problem, more formal assessments (tests) can be helpful, but these need to be administered by qualified mental health practitioners. Conducting an intake interview and mental status exam, commonly done upon a first visit to a clinic or practitioner, are examples of assessments, but so are pencil-and-paper or computerized tests. Some assessments are self-reported (the client answers test questions), and others involve a clinician asking questions and interpreting answers.

Consumers need to be knowledgeable and even a little wary when too much emphasis is placed upon testing or any label derived from it. Formal testing is only part of a diagnostic picture. Proper assessment creates added awareness for both the client and the therapist, and it often presents both with increased options for more effective treatment.

DEPRESSION

SO FAR, WE'VE detailed certain behaviors such as control, manipulation, self-absorption, childlike or immature conduct, and now we add depression. Our discussion here might remind you of our Eeyore category in Chapter 4, but clinical depression presents in different forms.

DEPRESSION

BELOW, WE'VE PROVIDED a list of traits that depressed people tend to exhibit, again based upon their core needs, which often have not been met, as well as what they fear or avoid. You may see some or all of these behaviors.

NEEDS	FEARS/AVOIDS	WHAT YOU SEE
■ Hope, support, security	■ Loneliness	■ "Glass-half-empty" mentality
■ Optimism, positives	■ Living or working without support	■ Low mood (especially chronic)
■ Self-worth	■ Unhappiness, difficulty	■ Addictions (self-medicating behavior)
	■ Failure, rejection	■ Low self-esteem
		■ Very passive nature

Depressive disorders strike an estimated 19 million people, roughly more than 9 percent of the population. Many others suffer silently so the number is likely much higher. Depression costs U.S. companies $44 billion each year in lost productivity, according to a study published in the *Journal of the American Medical Association* (JAMA).[1] In a marriage, the more anxious and/or depressed a spouse is, the more dissatisfied he or she may be with the marriage, according to research released in the *Journal of Consulting and Clinical Psychology* (October 2004).[2]

One in four women is likely to experience an episode of severe depression in her lifetime, but men are affected at such growing rates that the National Institute of Mental Health sponsors a "Real Men, Real Depression" Web site with personal stories of several men who have broken the social barriers that often keep depressed men from seeking treatment.[3]

Passive-aggressive or negative people frequently experience anxiety and depressive symptoms because, according to Millon, they feel their ambivalence through moodiness, being out of sorts, and worried.[4] Verbal venting or behaving in covert ways temporarily discharges pent-up anger, tension, and conflicting feelings. These personality types aren't beyond using anxiety (sometimes phobias) to escape the demands of others, Millon says. Phobias provide an innocent cover. Depression is common with persistently passive-aggressive people either in the form of major depressive episodes (intense but generally short-lived), bipolar disorder (formerly manic-depressive illness), or longer-term dysthymic disorder (chronic depression). There are other types of depression, which we'll touch upon briefly before these primary types. They include adjustment disorder, postpartum depression, and seasonal affective disorder. Any of these can have angry moods associated with them.

Adjustment Disorder

External stressors or difficult life transitions—death of a loved one, marital separation and divorce, miscarriage, chronic medical conditions, the loss of a job—can consume people enough that their mood suffers. *Adjustment disorders* tend to be a prevalent diagnosis when a person tries to make an adjustment to a real problem, but it can feel overwhelming when symptoms persist. Counseling provides the emotional support to get through the problem. Medication is sometimes prescribed to reduce the anxiety and depression that can prevent you from thinking, feeling, or even sleeping better. Sometimes, when people lack coping skills, when problems and/or low mood persists, or when genetic tendencies or biochemistry breaks down, this adjustment can evolve into a major depression.

Postpartum Depression

Following the birth of a child, *postpartum depression (PPD)* strikes one in eight mothers. This is not the same as "the baby blues," that are attributed to a temporary mood slide brought on by hormonal fluctuations. Though the symptoms of sadness, crying, irritability, and fatigue are similar, postpartum depression doesn't quickly lift, and subsequently, the mother feels more hopeless, guilty, exhausted, and intruded upon by repetitive, negative thoughts. Having a turbulent relationship with the child's father, stress, and little support contribute to the occurrence of PPD, as does a family history of anxiety or depression, but any woman can succumb to it. About one in one thousand women develop postpartum psychosis in which the mother suffers delusions and paranoia, often putting herself and her infant at risk. When this occurs, emergency treatment is called for right away. Nursing mothers are often reluctant to consider antidepressant medication, but certain medications can be administered safely, and help is available in other forms, such as talk therapy. The key is seeking help so that you don't suffer.

Seasonal Affective Disorder

Spring and summer may seem light years away, literally, for those afflicted by *seasonal affective disorder (SAD),* also known as "the winter blues," but research tells us it's a real phenomenon. Mood can falter and productivity plummet when the days get shorter. Some find it more difficult to concentrate as they also succumb to lethargy, carbohydrate cravings, and the real desire for isolation and sleep. Colloquially, people call this their hibernation mode, and while we all may have some of these symptoms during the winter months, SAD sufferers report interference with normal functioning each year. The lack of sunlight has major impact upon their body's circadian rhythms (their body clocks), but adding light therapy to their daily routine, in many cases, results in their symptoms remitting. You can most easily obtain this light through getting outdoors when the sunlight is plentiful. Start your day by allowing sunlight to filter in or by positioning yourself next to windows to do your work. Get out in the midday sun even for a brief walk (which has other health benefits, of course). Light boxes may offer another solution, and your doctor may recommend one. Be sure not to self-treat because you want to make sure that your symptoms are not something else entirely. If you are diagnosed with SAD, since studies continue, stay abreast of the latest research by contacting the National Organization for Seasonal Affective Disorder.[5]

Major Depression

As we said earlier, those experiencing temporary loss or life struggle may slip into a deeper mood disorder known as *major depression*. We characterize these sufferers as being down in the dumps, hopeless, discouraged, and indecisive, and as having lost pleasure in activities they once embraced. Many report increased irritability and persistent anger as evidenced by their low frustration tolerance, blaming, brooding, or feelings of guilt or worthlessness. Some depressed people seem to lose energy, while others appear restless; some lose weight, while others pack on extra pounds. Excessive sleeping or difficulty falling or staying asleep is also a frequent symptom. Frequently, there may be thoughts of death. These range from "I wish I'd just pass away and never wake up" to frequent, intense, lethal thoughts combined with a plan to commit suicide. Depression often takes a course where people "know" there are good things in their lives, and friends may repeatedly point out those blessings. But the depressed person still feels overwhelmingly sad, underscoring his sense of hopelessness.

Though suicidal ideation can be transient, it's serious when you see a person stockpiling medications, purchasing or gaining access to a weapon, isolating or harming themselves, giving away prized possessions, expressing sudden interest in wills, insurance policies, or burial plots, making more permanent plans for the care of children or pets, taking risks or abusing alcohol or drugs, or making statements such as "I wish I were dead" or talking of "ending it all." Especially if a close friend or family member committed suicide, or if the person has recently suffered a job loss, relationship breakup, serious torment, allegations or investigations regarding misconduct, it's important to monitor the depressed individual. In recent years, physicians and researchers have found that when chronic pain intrudes upon life, people also become so overwhelmed by grief, panic, and anger that they warrant careful monitoring for serious depression.

Depression rates can double when one has another chronic illness, for example, heart disease or cancer. Untreated depression contributes to the worsening of conditions and doubles the healthcare costs. Additionally, the number of people seeking treatment for depression is much lower than the incidence of it. Fewer than one-fourth receive treatment and even fewer receive *appropriate* treatment. The rest self-manage or deny their symptoms in the first place. Researchers have linked sustained stress to an increased risk for depressive and anxiety disorders because of its impact upon brain chemistry. Depression can also be a side effect of medications administered for other physical illnesses or conditions.

Early intervention is crucial (especially with children) to stop the development of more serious mood and mental health problems. With each subsequent major depressive episode, the risk of recurrence climbs; thus, patients need to be aware of the symptoms and treatment options. Individual, group, and medication therapy are all very effective treatments. Antidepressants such as selective serotonin reuptake inhibitors (SSRIs) work to increase levels of serotonin, a neurotransmitter in the brain. There are many other medications that impact brain chemistry. Often antidepressants lift a person's symptoms enough so that he or she can work with a therapist, but they are usually more effective long term when combined with talk therapy. Cognitive-behavioral therapy has an impact on your thinking, helping you to reorganize your thoughts and the ways in which you interact within your environment (your behaviors). This in turn helps you to feel better. A therapist will challenge any self-defeating beliefs, pick up on passive-aggressive patterns that lead to self-sabotage, help you to explore better ways of expressing your thoughts and feelings. Your negativity radar will become less activated, and with proper treatment, you'll be more open and expressive about what ails you, meaning that you'll conceal anger much less. Step by step, your mood ought to improve.

Bipolar Disorder

When depression coexists with extreme changes or elevations in mood, thoughts, feelings, and behaviors, it falls into the bipolar category. Formerly called *manic depression, bipolar disorder* typically includes periods of *mania* or *hypomania*, a lesser version of the symptoms, which can include anger (sometimes aggressive, sometimes hidden); extreme optimism, euphoria, energy, and self-confidence; risk taking, lack of inhibition, and impulsivity; racing thoughts and speech; marked changes in appetite and decreased sleep; distractibility and the inability to focus; peculiar thoughts and behavior; and alcohol and/or substance abuse and addictions.

Several good books exist on this topic in which you can read about individuals as they journeyed through this. Kay Redfield Jamison, a professor of psychiatry at the Johns Hopkins University School of Medicine, wrote *An Unquiet Mind,* recounting her years before, during, and after her diagnosis. She writes that, "There is a particular kind of pain, elation, loneliness, and terror involved in this kind of madness. When you're high it's tremendous. . . . But somewhere this changes. The fast ideas are far too fast, and there are far too many; overwhelming confusion replaces clarity. Memory goes. Humor and absorption on friends' faces are replaced by fear and concern.

Everything previously moving with the grain is now against you—you are irritable, angry, frightened, uncontrollable, and enmeshed totally in the blackest caves of your mind. You never knew those caves were there. It will never end, for madness carves its own reality."[6]

In *Bipolar Disorder Demystified,* Lana R. Castle puts her journey on the page to explain living a bipolar life. "Your jokes become insults. Your openness becomes rudeness. Your laughter becomes too loud. Your bottled emotions strain to blast forth," she writes. "Eventually, your mood either escalates into mania or you burn yourself out and fall into depression."[7] When a person with bipolar disorder says or does things that he ultimately regrets, his mood frequently plummets to self-blame—anger turned upon one-self. A negative mindset takes hold, filled with "Why me?" or "What did I do to deserve this?" or "Why can't this go away?" Resentments surface and without knowing it, the person's defenses kick in. He might act out against authority, and very often these acting-out behaviors take on a more aggressive look than a covert one, but since emotions get a bit scrambled, the person might not be fully aware of what's bothering him, what triggered it, and more importantly, what to do about it in the moment. Chronic irritability may be associated with bipolar disorder.

Bipolar disorder can begin with an early onset in childhood or adolescence with most initial diagnoses in early adulthood (late teens or early twenties). High-achieving and particularly creative people have a higher incidence of bipolar disorder. There are different types that may mean little to outsiders but perhaps a lot to the client and treating professional. Bipolar I is more the classic manic-depressive with the extreme highs and deep lows. Bipolar II, a milder form of the disorder, presents with hypomania in place of the mania. Cyclothymic disorder is a mild but chronic form of bipolar disorder.

Most adults function normally between episodes, even for years at a time. The average number of episodes over a ten-year period is four depressive and/or manic (hypomanic) episodes. Some people, however, experience only manic episodes with no depressive episodes at all. Since some symptoms mimic other conditions, proper evaluation is essential to achieve the right diagnosis. Mood-stabilizing medication and talk therapy help many to manage their condition and lead happier lives. The good news is that bipolar disorder is now one of the most treatable of psychological conditions.

Dysthymic Disorder

When depression lingers beyond a two-year point, and the person feels in a low mood more days than not, he may have *dysthymic disorder* (sometimes called *dysthymia*). Colloquially, we call it *chronic depression* because it does linger, and in many cases, it can present mildly enough that the person gets up, goes off to school or work, comes back home, and it's barely noticeable. The sufferer or his inner circle may feel "that's just the way he is." When you or a loved one is socially withdrawn, irritable, constantly tired, or when self-esteem is low, chronic depression could be the culprit. Dysthymic individuals often show distress within interpersonal relationships, work performance, and in an apparent lack of *joie de vivre*. They may have few friends or outside interests, and given their passive nature, they don't act to improve their circumstances. It sneaks in for the long term. When we described the "Eeyore" in our work chapter, it's possible that this glum, sluggish worker struggles with chronic depression. Terrence Real, a psychotherapist, writes about the covert nature of men's depression in *I Don't Want To Talk About It*. Depressed women may weep, but Real points out that men mask symptoms with work, exercise, spending, and drinking because this distracts them from their sadness.[8] Though possibly effective in the short term, it still conceals the problem.

Because negative outlook, passivity, and irritability play roles in this type of depression, it's not uncommon to see passive-aggressive thinking or behavior take hold as the person's default mode. In a scientific study published in the *American Journal of Psychiatry* in 1993, chronically depressed subjects scored significantly higher for using the individual defenses of devaluation, passive-aggression, and hypochondriasis (complaining of constant ailments) as well as acting out and projective identification.[9] The researchers found that dysthymia might lead to the development and use of these defense mechanisms, and that these maladaptive defenses might produce the depressed mood. This fits with other research where passive-aggressive people realized in childhood that they could usually count on parental attention when they were ill or injured, so complaining is a learned behavior that's been positively reinforced over the years.[10]

In a third model presented in this 1993 study, the authors suggested that dysthymia and this defense profile were related to poor self-esteem regulation, with the prediction that treatment to restore this regulation could alter both the chronic depression and one's penchant to use defenses such as passive-aggression.

Michael E. Thase, MD, a professor at the University of Pittsburgh School of Medicine, wrote *Beating the Blues: New Approaches to Overcoming Dysthymia and Chronic Mild Depression*. When there has been acute or chronic stress or trauma, an early major depression, or a genetic predisposition to anxiety and mood disorders, as well as the diagnosis of attention deficit hyperactivity disorder (ADHD), these factors may put a person at higher risk.[11] Additionally, medical illness, medications, pessimism, and poor thinking patterns can do likewise. We've discussed negativity and the self-perpetuating cycle that it can become, and the real red flag here is that if you don't take care of negative thinking and hidden anger, life may forever seem half-empty.

Antidepressant medication, along with supportive counseling, can significantly ease chronic depression's grip, and, according to Thase, often cure it, but if left untreated it may remain. Frequently, dysthymia coexists with other problems such as anxiety and phobias, personality disorders, and substance abuse. In up to 70 percent of dysthymic patients, there is also evidence of major depressive disorder, known as *double depression*.

■

SELF-CARE THROUGH DEPRESSION

SELF-CARE skills are no replacement for getting the proper medical or psychological treatment you need and sticking with that care. But anyone suffering from depression can assist in his or her treatment by eating a nutritious diet, exercising, staying connected (not isolated), and getting into optimistic pursuits and activities. Aerobic exercise has a tremendous impact on mild to moderate depression, according to material presented in the *American Journal of Preventive Medicine,* January 2005. Researchers found that thirty minutes of such activity three to five times weekly cut depressive symptoms in half.[12]

EATING DISORDERS

SOME OF THE characteristics of eating disorders involve hidden anger. Both anorexia nervosa and bulimia are physically harmful and potentially life-threatening conditions, and those who succumb are sensitive to rejection, need approval, and feel resentful. While these eating disorders are often associated with women, particularly adolescent girls, they also affect men. You'll find eating disorders in those who must maintain an ideal body weight for particular professions, such as modeling, ballet, gymnastics, and being a horse-racing jockey. You'll also find these disorders when men or women become obsessed about their bodies or when they harbor anger turned inward against the self.

There are two types of anorexia nervosa—the restricting type and the binging/purging type. A hallmark of this disorder is that one weighs below 85 percent of the normal body weight. Those who restrict their diets tend to be compulsive, introverted, fairly passive and dependent, and have low self-esteem. They also may resent parental control over their lives, craving independence. With bulimia, the diagnosis meets similar criteria except that one's weight doesn't necessarily fall below the 85 percent point. Many bulimic patients induce vomiting and abuse laxatives or diuretics (like those with the binging/purging type of anorexia) in a secretive manner. Here, we see the indirect personality style and hidden anger manifest. Bulimia sufferers tend to avoid conflict, live stressful and negative lives that are out of control. Harming themselves this way restores their self-control, at least in their minds.

Beyond obvious medical intervention, those suffering from eating disorders need to acknowledge the passive-aggressive role they play in refusing assistance from authority figures. Like many who conceal their anger, they desperately seek acceptance and approval yet they lack the skills of problem solving, assertive and expressive openness, and relaxation. They need to jettison perfectionism and become comfortable with a healthier body image, acknowledging their hunger as much as their anger. Often family counseling and having a positive environment, along with individual therapy and medical treatment, can restore good health to those who suffer from eating disorders.

SELF-INJURY

ANOTHER HARMFUL BEHAVIOR that has risen dramatically is cutting or other self-afflicted harm. While this afflicts mostly adolescent girls or adult women overwhelmed by emotional turmoil, stressed by life situations, and conflicted about their body image, *Time* reported that a growing population of boys has turned to self-mutilation. All cry out for help by cutting, bruising, or burning themselves because they cannot articulate their thoughts, feelings, and need for love and acceptance.[13]

The behavior develops until it's a person's primary outlet for dealing with life's frustrations. Many who use such self-injurious behavior want to feel more, or want to blunt their emotions, and they see their acts as an outlet for acute hidden anger and self-loathing. Very often clothing conceals the wounds, inflicted where others won't readily find them. Some cutters have bottled up their emotions so tightly that they actually relieve their emotional pain by the physical act, during which they feel numb or empty inside, and after which they feel much calmer and at peace (a sensation brought about by the body's natural opiates released upon bodily injury). Sadly enough, this relief is only temporary and doesn't solve the true problems that will surely surface again without therapy.

Of course, proper treatment of self-inflicted harm is multifaceted, often treating an underlying depression or anxiety disorder, while using behavioral interventions to control the self-mutilation. By learning to express one's anger, shame, guilt, or other intense emotions, the individual can regain lasting, healthier control over life. *Bodily Harm: The Breakthrough Healing Program for Self-Injurers* by Karen Conterio and Wendy Lader, PhD with Jennifer Kingson Bloom is a thorough resource about self-mutilating behavior that's fast becoming a most disturbing epidemic.[14]

■

SIGNS OF ATTENTION DEFICIT HYPERACTIVITY DISORDER (ADHD)

- Difficulty paying close attention to details; makes careless mistakes
- Difficulty sustaining attention and organizing tasks/activities; easily distracted by extraneous stimuli
- Doesn't appear to be listening when spoken to; doesn't follow through on instructions/duties
- Often forgets or loses things; disorganized
- May appear not to be present emotionally; silent
- Often avoids or dislikes tasks that require sustained mental effort
- Impulsive and/or hyperfocused at times; fidgety; "on the go" a lot
- Needs much stimulation; seeks conflict (such as arguments)
- Interrupts; impatient; trouble delaying gratification
- Talks a lot; processes verbally
- Gets stuck in thinking; holds strong opinions; appears uncooperative
- Below-average communication skills

ATTENTION DEFICIT HYPERACTIVITY DISORDER (ADHD)

ADHD REFERS TO a set of behavioral symptoms that usually begins in childhood, when it's often first diagnosed. About half of all ADHD children continue to show their symptoms into adulthood. Roughly 5 percent of the adult population has ADHD, but one-fourth of those (or fewer) are actually aware of it. Since more children have been diagnosed with ADHD in recent decades, parents have stepped forth affirming "that sounds like me," and since we know that ADHD characteristics may run in families, a child's diagnosis uncovers adult cases.

How can this remain hidden? Because the symptoms weren't intense or frequent enough to cause academic or social impairment, or if they did exist, the person found coping strategies that worked well enough to get by. Or, teachers treated it as a behavior problem and spouses got fed up without understanding why.

Accurate diagnosis of adult ADHD follows a paper trail of lackluster grades, poor driving records, or behavioral difficulties with friends, siblings, parental, or academic relationships. If not disclosed while a child is undergoing evaluation, it often presents when adults hit an impasse. Their résumé looks choppy with six jobs in four years or their impulsive or inattentive behavior lands them in trouble (a wrecked car, an unplanned pregnancy, racking up debt, being fired from a job). Their performance at work can appear erratic, such as the salesman who is great on the road, but terrible at sitting down and doing the follow-up paperwork. Not every ADHD child appears hyperactive and that contributes to its being overlooked. With adults, hyperactivity (if present) takes on the appearance of impulsivity, rash judgment, poor follow-through, and a short temper.

First the downside of ADHD: because these behaviors can cause problems without awareness and proper coping strategies, many with ADHD find themselves angry, a kind of a primal protective device to keep other emotions at bay. The behaviors are reactive because often the person may jump right to anger given their impulsive response to their frequent frustrations. In other words, you'll see a quick temper.

Russell Barkley, MD, author of *ADHD and the Nature of Self-Control,* believes that the biological component of ADHD makes anger difficult to process. His book is filled with the brain-based neuroscience of these mental processes explaining why the ability to contemplate the past to understand the present and future gets a little scrambled.[15] Those with ADHD must work harder to orient themselves to the future because their condition puts them squarely in the here and now. Barkley sees ADHD as a self-control problem largely because the person has difficulty modulating angry experiences and feels overwhelmed much of the time. Thus, we might see behaviors such as procrastination, avoidance, and brooding because it's harder to let matters drop. Most of us use coping strategies when we're annoyed. Something tells us to count to ten, take a deep breath, walk away from the conflict, or use imagery to soothe ourselves. That *something* doesn't alert the ADHD person as fast, or sometimes at all. The result can feel like a flood of unwanted stimuli turning frustrations into battles.

With a harder time focusing, even if a person learns anger management strategies, he may find them harder to implement. This is why some children with ADHD may *appear* passive-aggressive, as if they have the tools or knowledge, because teachers or parents know darn well that they have taught it, and they have even seen the kids use it. Spouses get angry because after asking their ADHD partner to clean up after a meal, for instance, they'll spot crumbs on the counter and feel angry inside. Here, too, the ADHD person must first notice the crumbs on the counter in order to wipe them away. Those without the condition then assume that "Joe is acting this way on purpose." When there's no follow-through it looks like defiance.

Similar dynamics play out in a marriage or adult relationship where one partner has ADHD and the other does not, creating an imbalance because the non-ADHD partner feels more responsible, and reminds and cajoles the other. When a person with ADHD is first in love, the excitement or novelty of it all provides constant stimulation. He thrives on the newness and tends to hyperfocus on his love object with much attention, flowers, wine, and romance. When love settles in and time passes, the person's interest or focus may appear to wane, not surprisingly leaving the one accustomed to being wooed a bit unsettled and confused when a birthday or Valentine's day goes forgotten or a promise to do something special such as a favor went unattended. Frustration, maybe even anger, sets in.

Also, if he doesn't pick up on social cues that other people recognize more readily, the ADHD adult may be drawn to the wrong kind of mate, fail to realize it's a poor match. He could find himself in shouting matches because he's drawn to such stimulation, which also could include taking risks (extreme sports, corporate deal making, or simply driving too fast on the freeway). What no one might realize is that ADHD is the culprit.

The positive side of ADHD: Having this can work well in some professions (but can be a real detriment in others). An emergency-room physician would thrive in a fast-paced, constantly changing environment. A brain surgeon, on the other hand, requires hours of careful concentration and the ability to shut out all distractions. Having flexible hours so that you can work when most alert, or having a job requiring a lot of movement and activity, instead of being confined to a desk, is great for the ADHD worker. As one's career progresses, the help of a good assistant or staff is invaluable. In many, but not all, cases medication can help by stimulating the parts of the brain controlling executive functions that channel attention, so that it's easier to learn skills to gain focus and organization. Life settles down, mood often improves, and study or work becomes more efficient and successful. But medication is rarely enough, and it's tough to learn these things on your own. The medication can help you to concentrate, but you still have to overcome years of learned bad habits. Many with ADHD use cognitive-behavioral therapy to help with anxiety, impulse control, managing their emotions, and organizing their lives. Counseling can also be useful to learn how to reframe things and work with your strengths. Learn how you can accomplish something, tap into your strengths, and compensate for any weaknesses. Many creative and successful people have had ADHD. Keep developing new strategies that move you toward your goals. For example, young people applying to college or adults seeking employment should phrase things in the positive. Rather than admit that their notes are scattered during a meeting, they should say, "I work best if I use a tape recorder to ensure I capture all the important details." Keep practicing the positive.

■

HELPING THOSE WITH ADHD

IF you are close to someone with ADHD, feel good about helping so long as you are not enabling or protecting the person from natural consequences. Here are tips to keep anger at bay:

FOR CHILDREN AND ADULTS:

- Help to identify stressors or obstacles; model problem solving.
- Maintain standards for personal responsibility, proper grooming and behavior, academic achievement, or household help. ADHD adults often thank their families for setting standards. While they may not have adhered to them on their parent's time frame, when *they* recognized the need for organization, cleanliness, and relationships, their parents had paved the way.
- Focus on the positive. Compliment rather than complain. A long litany of grievances wears anyone down. Tell the ADHD child or adult what *to do,* not what he shouldn't do.
- Don't take inattention personally. If you require the person's attention, maintain eye contact. Involve as many senses as possible because people process things differently, through auditory, visual, or kinesthetic processing. They'll find it easier to pay attention if you try to match their styles. You might ask "Do you *see* what I'm saying to the visual processor, "*tell* me more" to the auditory processor, and "I don't *feel* good about that" to the kinesthetic processor.
- Use cues since transitions are tough and especially important if you're requesting something when the ADHD person is embedded in an enjoyable task. Discuss signals that you can give, even out in public, that might show how you really have something important to relate. Cues also work to signal that one of you

needs a time-out to prevent the emotional overload or frustration that can occur.

■ Be as specific as possible to ward off forgetfulness. "Please grab your backpack" says precisely what you mean whereas "get ready for school" is way too vague.

■ Keep it concise. A laundry-list of questions or requests will get lost in the person's databank (brain). Write things down if necessary.

■ Remain consistent. Structure and consistency go much farther than waffling or ambivalence that may give children false hopes. The ADHD child may persist in trying to get his or her way, and if you're not careful, your indecision or lack of backbone may set up poor outcomes, over time.

■ Monitor balanced diet, getting enough sleep, promoting exercise, and limiting too much exposure to electronic stimuli, especially with children. Promote meditation and other means of calming the mind to improve mood and focus.

■ Invite the ADHD person to join you in a relaxing activity. It's often hard for them to settle down. Children, especially, have a hard time turning off their switch from active play to passive activity. If you take the lead and teach relaxation, you'll likely calm anxiety, anger, and impulsivity as well.

■ Encourage the person to stick with things because there is a penchant to quit and then there's no chance to excel at a particular sport, subject, or task.

FOR ADULTS:

■ Set realistic expectations. Many with ADHD are bright and intelligent, but they've had their disappointments and obstacles that may appear to be nothing to you. Ask things of them that tap into their strengths, and don't set them up for failure by insisting that they accomplish something in their weaker skill-set.

■ Calmly remind them when household requests or other tasks remain incomplete or unattended. Don't belittle the adult with ADHD or accuse her of bad intentions.

■ Break tasks into parts rather than one huge job. Write down steps to processes or keep track of lists in writing.

■ Don't distract the person if he or she is working. Keep outside stimulation down (e.g., keep the TV off while balancing the checkbook).

■ Remind the ADHD adult of his numerous strengths because he may easily ruminate solely on negative self-talk when things don't go so well. Find and practice strength-related habits, as this boosts self-esteem so that negativity doesn't set in for the long haul.

- Refuse to allow ADHD to be used as an excuse for laziness or lack of personal responsibility. ADHD adults must show up for work and/or academic programs, take part in home life and parenting. They cannot push their responsibilities onto others. Spouses can quickly lapse into the "mothering" role, but that can lead to an unequal distribution of responsibility.

- Don't discriminate. Plenty of famous, inventive, and successful people have had ADHD over time. Having the diagnosis does not suggest lack of intelligence. While the Americans with Disabilities Act (ADA) protects their rights, many are reluctant to disclose their condition for fear of stereotyping, stigma, or judgment.

- Educate yourself about the condition. *ADDitude* magazine features insightful articles. The A.D.D. Warehouse (www.addwarehouse.com) contains a myriad of resources. And CHADD (Children and Adults with Attention Deficit Hyperactivity Disorder) offers meaningful support. [16]

- Don't allow the condition to split you as a couple. Just as the ADHD person must find her way to success so can the two of you find solutions for a rewarding relationship. *Delivered from Distraction: Getting the Most out of Life with Attention Deficit Disorder* by Edward M. Hallowell, MD and John J. Ratey, MD contains this and other good tips.[17]

OPPOSITIONAL-DEFIANT DISORDER

ACCORDING TO CHADD, 40 percent of those with ADHD also have oppositional defiant disorder (ODD). A lesser number of children may also have conduct disorder, in which more extreme anger and aggression surfaces.

ODD involves a perpetual pattern of negativistic, hostile, and defiant behavior that includes arguing with adults and defying their requests; frequent loss of temper and frequent conflicts; deliberate annoyance of people and testing the limits; blaming others for one's mistakes or misbehavior; low self-esteem and low frustration tolerance; precocious use of alcohol, drugs, or tobacco; and acting stubborn, touchy, angry, resentful, or vindictive.

It sounds pretty similar to the passive-aggressive behavior we've described throughout this book. In a sense, it is, but it's exclusively a diagnosis for children and adolescents. This type of behavior is more prevalent at home, but it may impair home, social, academic, or occupational functioning. ODD isn't the proper diagnosis if there is a coexisting mood or psychotic disorder, and if conduct disorder is also present. School counselors and other clinicians are trained to look for ODD when ADHD is present, but it doesn't mean that it always coexists. Sometimes when childcare has been disrupted by a string of different caregivers, or when there has been harsh and inconsistent parenting, ODD surfaces.

Cognitive-behavioral therapy, and sometimes family counseling can help to remedy this oppositional pattern in kids. You've got to actively build the child's trust, and encourage the child to openly but responsibly express negative, hostile thoughts. Adults need to model respectful behavior and show how to reframe a complaint into a polite request. Keeping a journal in which the pages get filled with the angry thoughts helps. Having parents and teachers share values as they mete out discipline does also. For instance, it's much better to explain: "Here's why this rule is in place . . ." instead of resorting to an authoritarian "No, that's the way it is." Problem is, ODD kids often wear you down. Frequently, behavior-modification contracts effectively reward appropriate behavior with specific privileges or money. Learning to cooperate and resolve conflicts is crucial for a child with ODD, so be sure to review the problem-solving steps in this book.

PERSONALITY DISORDERS

IN THE APPENDIX, we briefly discuss personality disorders, what they are, the types, and how anger manifests in some of them. This book is not designed to go into detail about problematic personality traits that veer into this area. However, you should know that when you see persistent and pervasive anger that doesn't meet the criteria of another diagnosis (such as those we have discussed in this chapter), then it's *possible* that you're looking at anger within the realm of a personality disorder. Of course, you cannot make that determination. If you see entrenched traits that make life very troublesome, then at least you'll know that you can't possibly solve the dilemma on your own, and you might temper or adjust your approach.

With the various types of personality disorders, anger can provide energy—negative energy, of course—and the false sense of being in control, having power over a situation, or, anger can be a reaction with others. Since those with personality disorders lack coping skills and become easily frustrated, anger may compensate for their deficits. Because there is a lot of incongruence at times, you might see a smile but very much feel their suppressed anger. We've listed additional resources in the back of the book to assist you in learning more about these characterological issues (a more polite phrasing for *personality disorders*).

IN SUMMARY

IF YOU'VE READ this chapter and identified with some of the signs of deeper disorders, don't be too dismayed. If you're the one with the problem, take some time for soul-searching to reflect upon your struggles and the strategies you've tried that frankly have not worked so well, such as blunting your emotional pain in some unhealthy way or hiding your anger. If you're the cause of your own anger, that's okay. At least you can do something about it. Getting help through the right therapy spells hope. It's like driving and getting lost for a while. First, you must recognize that you're lost. Next, you try looking at a map. And if that doesn't get you where you need to be, then you ask someone who has been there before who can give you better directions. In essence, that's what therapy is like—finding new direction and better ways of getting to your destination!

NINE

ENDING
ALL ENABLING

"**Y**OUR HONOR, MY client contends that he couldn't make it to the pharmacy to get the child's medication and inhaler," said Attorney Aldridge. "There wasn't enough time."

"This was at eight o'clock that evening, correct?" asked the family court judge.

"That's correct."

"What time does the pharmacy close, and how far is it from Mr. Smith's home?"

"Nine o'clock, your honor, and I believe the pharmacy is forty minutes away."

The judge hastily scrawled notes at the bench. His looking up signaled to opposing counsel to summarize the plaintiff's testimony at this hearing.

"The child's mother would state that this pharmacy in question is twenty minutes at most from her husband's apartment, and that there is an even closer one, your honor. Here is the route printed from MapQuest. Returning Alyssa in the midst of an asthma attack instead of caring for her needs directly posed a potentially dangerous situation in that . . ."

"I object, your honor."

"Overruled."

"It posed a danger because it delayed treatment for a chronic medical condition, and caused Mrs. Smith to miss work the next day caring for the child, seriously jeopardizing her job. This was Mr. Smith's visitation time. They weren't discharged from the emergency room until five a.m. and the hospital bill could have been avoided with reasonable conduct. Furthermore, Mr. Smith has refused on numerous occasions to follow the court order paying for such expenses, and he's withheld insurance cards for their three children though we've asked repeatedly for them."

"How many times have you asked for this information, counselor?"

"Three times within the past six months. Once by telephone, once via email, and one time I surfaced the request to Attorney Aldridge."

"Excuse me, your honor, Mr. Smith never remembers receiving any correspondence nor speaking with Mrs. Smith, and I can't recall that conversation."

"Can't recall?" the judge asked, looking over his glasses.

"Well . . . I am not sure."

The judge sighed. "I'll take this testimony under advisement and have a decision for you shortly." With that he got up from his leather chair and headed for his chambers.

Twenty-five minutes later, he sent a member of his tipstaff out to hand the court order to the attorneys. Crossed out of the motion were the words "finds in contempt," "counsel fees," and "extraordinary medical expenses." In big bold letters, as if written with a Sharpie marker, was the word "DENIED," then "defendant should make reasonable efforts to have necessary medications on hand and provide Mrs. Smith with medical insurance cards within thirty days."

WHAT IS ENABLING?

How many times have you asked your child, spouse, or maybe even an employee or coworker to do something, and when it didn't get accomplished, you stepped in and did the task yourself, or you merely overlooked the oversight? In the example above, not only did Attorney Aldridge enable his client by possibly feigning ignorance to protect him from consequences, but the judge was the ultimate enabler, allowing this man to get away with excuses. Opposing counsel had begun to show a pattern of "being difficult." When the judge asks for compliance from a person with a history of withholding, obstructing, and/or causing inconvenience, what do you think the result will be?

If you thought along the lines of "it will only encourage him to be *more* difficult," then you're exactly right. When anyone makes life unnecessarily easier, it feeds the passive-aggressor's ego, thus making "next time" even more predictable.

Occasionally, if there's an extenuating circumstance, just doing it yourself often seems the easiest solution. But what if you lose track of the times you've stepped in, finished the work, mitigated the consequences of uncompleted tasks for the other person, and occasionally succumbed to stress because you have way too many responsibilities, no assistance, and often no appreciation? In other words, you consistently bail a person out of responsibility, work, and consequences, and solve the person's problems for him or her.

There's probably not a soul alive who hasn't enabled others at one time or another by solving their dilemmas, making life easier for them, or allowing one's own needs to take a backseat to their agenda. After all, it may seem faster to just step in, as we indicated. You might look bad because of a missed deadline, and you might have requirements or quotas to meet—thus, you're in a jam. But if you smooth over someone else's anger, covering up its tracks, time and again, you're in the same category of the well-meaning person who is codependent on an alcoholic, a tobacco user, drug addict, or otherwise addicted person. You're enabling them to perpetuate a destructive pattern even when you think you're being helpful, or in some instances, fair.

Over time, you can become as frustrated or annoyed as the angry person. So, the boss gets tired of yet another knock on the door and hearing that the report will be delayed, the judge rolls his eyes peering out at the same litigants, and the teacher sighs when the assignment is now three days late. The boss, the judge, and the teacher need to deal directly with the resistance; letting it slide makes matters worse.

By enabling, on a repeated basis, you're reinforcing the very behaviors that you would truly like to eradicate. When you ignore resistance and step up to the plate yourself, the person prone to passivity and ambivalence has little reason to become active, decisive, or cooperative. Rather, these types lapse into a dependent mode that might remain the norm well into the future, especially if these patterns begin in youth. This fosters codependency because most passive-aggressive people enjoy your taking care of them. They achieve this by wearing you down with their pattern of behavior, making you uncomfortable enough that indeed you act. Only if you do step in, and continue to act for them, then they'll never have to step in themselves. Remember, enablers empower others. Passive-aggressors who results this way with their dysfunctional behavior.

By enabling, on a repeated basis, you're

reinforcing the very behaviors that you

would like to eradicate. When you ignore resistance and step up to the plate yourself, the person prone to passivity and ambivalence has little reason to become active, decisive, or cooperative.

WHO ENABLES?

IN HER BOOK *Whose Life Is It Anyway?* Dr. Nina Brown explains very well how people "catch" someone else's projected anger, perhaps identifying with part or all of it, and actually taking it on as part of themselves.[1] If you do this a lot, that's a form of enabling and you might fit into one (or more) of the five types of enablers we have established and listed below:

The gullible: If you trust that others will do or say things with goodness all the time, you might fall into this category. Not that thinking positively is bad, but one also needs a healthy sense of skepticism to protect against harm. We need to see the darker side of human nature as well as the good. If you find yourself being naïve, easily fooled or fleeced because of your innocence, you might believe a passive-aggressor's alibis, excuses, or twists of the truth, thereby enabling him and his hidden anger. If you're the victim of your brother's nasty barbs, you might fume because while you see what's happening, your parents or other siblings do not. One could argue that they're enabling him by turning the other shoulder or tolerating such behavior. Or at work you might see an employee who says, "I'm trying my best" rather than focusing on getting the job done right. He wants *you* to change and for you to judge him based upon his motives, not on his results. If you buy into this, you're enabling him.

The caretakers: Who can find fault with a person who is always taking care of others? This is the person who overlooks things just to be nice to them. Say that your father always takes the family out on the town each New Year's Eve, but one time, you wish to ring in the New Year in your own home. Only, you're afraid of Dad's reaction and the sarcastic reminders that will come down upon you later when you fail to follow his wishes. This isn't an isolated incident. Here, he has taken care of you in one sense, and your reluctance to stand up to him, stifling your own emotions, takes care of him. Your silence may only enable more "gifts with strings." It could also lock you into a more dependent role when you're striving to be your own person.

The needy: Do you rely upon the approval of others so often that you end up feeling taken for granted or used? Do you find yourself stepping in, maybe doing more work for others, or shielding them from unpleasant consequences? Take the child of divorce. Dad raised you, and well, mom's just a little tough to take with her indirect anger. Still, she's your mom, and you haven't had the relationship you'd like to have. Her leaving the family hurt, thus you put up with a lot in order to spend time with her. Low self-esteem, trying to prove yourself worthy, loneliness, or being in a vulnerable spot sometimes leads to this type of enabling, whereby you overlook increasingly poor behavior because your payoff is your honest hope that this time you'll win the person's acceptance regardless of the cost.

The peacemakers: When people know that you'll go to just about any lengths to smooth over tension and avoid conflict, you become a safe dumping ground for another's hidden frustration because you swallow the anger for them, rather than bring it to anyone's attention. We know the health consequences of harboring your own anger over time, let alone how detrimental it can be if you take on more than your share. There's a lot of potential here for sarcasm or verbal abuse, that is, taking the punches to save someone else all the while reinforcing the link in the other's behavior that anger gets results.

The guilt-ridden: "Don't you want my birthday to be special by doing this one little favor for me?" "Look how you made me feel." "You always (never) _____." What you just read is a list of manipulative phrases that play upon people's guilt and push buttons that the manipulator may even have installed. This puts the recipient in an awkward spot, feeling uncomfortable, embarrassed, maybe mortified. You have to follow through on the person's expectation or request because if you didn't, you would be filled with remorse. One boss kept overlooking missed deadlines. His aide told him that it would look bad if she got fired. In all honesty, the boss knew she had a point. His only recourse was to eventually make finding a new job *her* idea so that he wouldn't have to fire her.

Which of these five types have you been? Have you bought excuses like the gullible? Stepped in with action to be nice and take care of the lazy person? Provided the shoulder for the whiner or clinger, the ear for the lonely heart because you need her as much as she needs you, while neither of you gets your lives together? Have you been the doormat for the abusive one, avoiding conflict, but seen the situation get dirtier, like a carpet after more muddy shoes? Or, have you overlooked behavior hoping to offset any forthcoming guilt that would make you squirm?

It's not altogether uncommon to find one or more types of enablers operating because we all adapt to meet the challenges of dealing with the angry person or situation. Recognizing this pattern is helpful whenever one person's behavior impacts others. Indeed, we teach people how to treat us by what we put up with and what we refuse to tolerate.

Our court example comes to mind because you can often find concealed anger cloaked beneath a senseless lawsuit, nuisance court motions, or any kind of troublemaking where one person is trying to "stick it" to another or cause great inconvenience for someone out of spite while copping a convenient excuse to make it seem innocent. Systems, much like people, should respond in ways that end the passive-aggressive cycle. Decision makers within systems can do this only by recognizing and gaining a full understanding of hidden anger.

YOUR PART IN ENDING ENABLING

IF YOU DEAL with passive-aggressive or anger-concealing people at home, at work, at school, or in life, maybe you're saying, "But it's that person, that silently vengeful person, who has the problem—not me!" Truth is, that silently vengeful person has likely annoyed you because you lacked better coping strategies. So . . . you're now a little angry, too, inside. Maybe you have enough angry people in your midst to qualify as a collection, but unfortunately this collection isn't easily jettisoned on eBay! Perhaps there are things that you're doing, even unwittingly, to set yourself up for mistreatment, and just maybe these passive-aggressors exploit your weaknesses, installing and later pressing your buttons, which are too easily pushed? Being persistently reactive or negative is simply dreadful, for it leaves you vigilantly on the defensive. You become wary of such people, unsure how to please them, and ultimately avoid all interactions with them.

Are You an Anger Target?

You've read our five types of enablers, but maybe there is still a missing link. Could it be that you think you're the victim of hidden anger when actually you're a bit angry yourself?

Martin Kantor writes about *pseudovictims* of passive-aggression as those who wrongly believe they've been abused by the behavior when in fact they are not. "Pseudovictims give few people the benefit of the doubt . . . every innocent question contains a hidden attack," he writes.[2] Using one of our examples, if the son who saw the New Year's treat as negative did this after one or two such incidences, he might qualify here because he approaches every favor, deed or remark, from an already negative or angry attitude. Anything looks bad at that point! So, it's important to keep your thoughts and feelings in check.

Kantor describes *nonparticipating victims* as being sometimes fairly oblivious to what's happening. Our needy and peacemaking enablers may fit with this. Nonparticipating types might not connect their headache, insomnia, or other ailments to the abuse they're receiving. They might not see that they have become the victims of someone else's projected issues, emotions, or core conflicts that arose years before any relationship with this person began.

Others, meanwhile, fully recognize the passive-aggression directed toward them but blame themselves for it, feeling overwhelmed, lost, and depressed. Kantor calls these *participating victims* or those who become or remain victims because they enable passive-aggressive behavior to continue. All of our five types of enablers participate in and can perpetuate hidden anger.

■

JOURNALING TO DISTINGUISH PASSIVE-AGGRESSION

AS you conclude this book, you'll have a good sense of whether someone's behavior fits with our descriptions. It's not always easy to assume motive or intent, however. In fact, it can be dangerous to cast it as anger. If in doubt, write the situation down from the other person's perspective. This helps to spot a person's righteous anger or maybe take his culture into account as the reason for his indirect demeanor. List what happened, when, how, where, and whoever else was affected. Include what led up to the incident, as well, and how it was taken care of. This last part helps you to determine any role you play in fanning another person's anger. Be as specific as possible and write your sentences or phrases using "I" statements.

To journal, "He made me mad" tells you very little later of what transpired when "I felt used and taken for granted as if my feelings didn't count for very much" details much more. Describe the person's nonverbal behavior as well as spoken comments or actions. Capture the dialogue if you can. The secondary gain for you is that if the situation with the angry person gets troublesome enough that you seek counseling, you can take this journal with you for insight into these interactions.

RESPONDING TO CRITICISM AND GOSSIP

ANGRY PEOPLE NEED to express themselves, if appropriate, and surface their frustrations without the venom. They need to give others feedback without attacking them. Feedback, when offered with positive intent, fosters growth, exploration, intimacy, and problem solving. Most importantly, people who conceal their anger must get to work. This isn't the case of the overinflated tire that will explode. These folks need to control their dysfunctional emotions and solve problems. Frequently, they don't work on the source of their frustration, and criticism springs forth. If you don't handle the criticism (or gossip) well, the angry person may succeed at turning you into an enabler in order to keep their anger going.

WHAT IS CRITICISM?

CRITICISM IS THE total opposite of feedback, too often stemming from an angry place in one's mind or heart. That anger never stands alone. Something triggers it—jealousy, loss, revenge, shame, regret, embarrassment or humiliation, low self-esteem or self-hatred, or even a deeper problem of depression or lack of self-control as we noted in the last chapter. Bottom line: whoever lobs the critical remark feels bad, squirms with those bad (sometimes mad) emotions, and now mistakenly feels better because you or someone else has become the dumping ground.

YOUR RESPONSE

ONCE YOU UNDERSTAND the criticism, then you have a better idea of how to respond. Knowledge is power, and the more you understand the dynamic of what causes the criticism, the better able you'll be to prevent it or escape from it.

Instead of getting equally annoyed, angry, self-doubtful, or confused, it's quite useful to develop coping strategies to ward off these negative side effects of criticism. For instance, stay focused on your goal. Doing just that was what allowed Martin Luther King to put up with violence and remain peaceful. Here are some other strategies or perspectives to consider:

1. **First, check out whether any criticism has validity:** Is there even a morsel of truth to what the angry person said? This morsel might be small, and if it was lobbed indirectly with hostility, it wasn't delivered well, but it may have emanated from righteous anger and deserves a useful place in your own thinking, feeling, and behavior. It could foster your own growth, in other words. Unfortunately, criticism and growth are not mutually exclusive just because of criticism's angry origins. For instance, instead of "I'm tired of doing the laundry for you" (criticism), try "we need to work out a plan of sharing the laundry." (solution)

2. **Second, the criticism might have nothing to do with you:** Let's face it: people can become ticked off just by the way you walk into a room. You can often see it in their body language, and you can certainly detect their hidden resentment or jealousy by the way they speak. They have their own thoughts and moods that they project onto the situation. Watch how secretly annoyed people take little responsibility. They rarely speak using "I" statements but begin sentences with the accusatory "You," as in "You make me feel _____" or "You did _____." They might begin questions asking "why," a word that immediately puts another on the defensive. When someone feels threatened, she often measures herself against others. In this person's own mind, she's coming up short. Rather than sit with that sense of insecurity, she casts it off. Sometimes, if you're a more conscientious person who achieves goals, knows your own direction, and has your act together, you become the most convenient target for the passive-aggressor. Again, the passive person who struggles with appropriate self-expression can't sit with the anxiety your presence or your achievements stir. Once again, it may *seem* as if it's about you—the angry person may *say* it's about you—the nonverbal behavior *indicates* it's about you—but it's not about you at all! It's about the other person. When you hear a criticism come your way, decide whether the person might actually be criticizing himself. The need to put others down reflects low self-esteem or their being stuck in a situation they'd rather not be in. Often the only way the critical person can think well of herself (or in the circumstance) is to make someone else feel worse.

3. **Third, don't fan criticism but learn to defuse it:** Ignoring often takes away the power of such a put-down. That's so pivotal when dealing with passive-aggression and hidden anger, but sometimes, you can't ignore it. Know, however, that your reaction either spawns more criticism (anger) or eases into something more positive, such as a solution, an understanding, a connection or bond, or progress toward a goal.

4. **Fourth, recognize that criticism builds and can become self-fulfilling:** Think about how self-fulfilling prophecies work. Most are setups. The dynamics for a critical person are quite simple: negative thoughts or emotional insecurity lead to saying or doing something that produces responses to confirm these beliefs and/or insecurities. For instance, twenty-year-old Gwen finds that her older brother Jason just got engaged to Emily. For two decades, Gwen has been the only girl in the family. This is going to take some getting used to! If Gwen harbors no anger and openly shares her feelings, she might acknowledge thoughts about her "turf" or status changing, or that she wonders what might happen if Jason's fiancée Emily impresses people or gets more of the attention? Sounds good, but openly expressing anxiety like this requires a hefty dose of self-awareness. Passive-aggressors lack self-awareness because they're very accustomed to sweeping away their true feelings and fears, even from themselves. They disconnect from feelings to avoid dealing with anything unpleasant.

5. **Deal with criticism directly:** Tell the critical person: "I can learn more from you if you teach me rather than criticize me." If someone tells you what you're doing right, you'll repeat those things because that guides you. Otherwise, you remain locked in fear, afraid to act. You wait it out, and then you get criticized. The pattern repeats and repeats if you don't take care of it. Here, Gwen needs to deal with her insecurities and jealousy. She needs to welcome Emily, not attack her. But if she's not aware of the jealousy, her actions will not welcome her, but undermine her appearance, personal decisions, and so on, implying that she's not good enough for her brother Jason.

DEALING WITH GOSSIP

THOUGH IT'S INDIRECT, criticizing requires a small amount of confrontation. If the fear of confrontation mounts high enough, the passive-aggressor may unload his frustrations on a third party through gossip. Of course, this triangulates matters. What's more, it's often coupled with more passive-aggression by distorting the truth, embellishing minor incidents, playing victim, or undermining the person being talked about so that she loses stature or gets annoyed (because the truly angry person can't bear to feel the angst directly).

In our example, if relatives ask Gwen where Emily is registered for wedding gifts, and Gwen lies and says that they're not registered, she can secretly smile inside as Jason and Emily open seven toasters or things they absolutely don't need. But since a façade usually lasts only so long, Emily might eventually catch Gwen and call her on some action. Now Gwen has all the convincing evidence she needs thinking, "I always knew Emily was a troublemaker!" Voilá: the self-fulfilling prophecy! Gwen set in motion a series of events that built upon themselves, and a dynamic stemming from insecurities eventually came full circle.

What we just described with the self-fulfilling prophecy happens all the time in stepfamilies, when stepchildren often resent the intrusion of a stepparent; in schools with new students facing existing classmates and cliques; at work with a new employee; or as we've seen, in most any situation when a new member joins the group.

Hanging onto anger creates an illusion of being in control. In the example above, Gwen felt as if things were happening to her family, beyond her grasp, which caused her discomfort. When trying to regain her balance, her anger gave her ego a boost (falsely so, of course). It restored the illusion of control. Temporarily, Gwen met her goal. If others bought into the gossip, they enabled Gwen. On the other hand, if they called her on it or stood up to Gwen right away with "I kind of like Emily," "I don't see it that way," or "It just doesn't matter to me," then they stemmed the anger behind her gossip.

In the long run, Gwen's anger created more problems than it solved, and her thinking and actions provided no lasting satisfaction. That's the way life plays out for many passive-aggressive people who discharge their negative energy through hidden means.

CHOOSING YOUR REACTIONS

How would you have reacted if you were Emily—or Jason—to Gwen's being mean-spirited? We advocated against fanning the flames of criticism but encouraged you to learn from it and/or defuse it, because anytime you react, especially in a less thought-out, knee-jerk fashion, your response will likely be to attack back in defensive mode. "Well, you made me mad" or "There you go again" almost guarantees that your conflict with the other person will escalate. Sometimes no matter which way you turn, it seems like a bad choice. Passive aggressors are skilled at placing people in double binds or no-win situations. If Emily or Jason very calmly stated their hurt and disappointment, that, too, would play right into Gwen's setup. With a calm, more collected reaction, the anger doesn't flare as much.

Of course, you are no one's doormat. There are times when you need to assert your position or confront another person about their remarks or behavior. If you do it all the time, it will look like you're reactive and that the passive-aggressive person can easily find and push your buttons. Hence, you are enabling them. So, rein in your reactivity and choose those reactions carefully. Let some remarks, innuendos, or harmlessly stupid actions slide. Save your energy for things that matter most. Here is another family scenario and several reaction choices:

> When the family gathers, your older cousin, who has no children, once again undermines your authority when you appropriately discipline your daughter. "Cuz" makes thinly disguised comments about "today's parents." Last time the clan gathered, she showed everyone embarrassing pictures of you from high school. Before that she criticized the casserole you brought, and another time she came late when you hosted the holiday. How do you respond?
> a. Ignore her and walk away.
> b. Overlook her behavior because you understand the pain of her being childless.
> c. Offer up something embarrassing she did as a child.
> d. Demand, in front of everyone, that she stop treating you this way.
> e. Take her aside and tell her that you won't tolerate disrespect, especially in front of your child. Tell her that if it continues, you'll leave the gathering early.
> f. Remember all the times you teased her as a child and remind yourself how it's fair payback.

If you chose *e*, taking your cousin aside, you're correct. Ignoring her might be appropriate if it's an isolated incident. Our scenario indicates otherwise. Meeting her hidden anger by taking a cheap shot only puts you on her level, puts her in a weak spot (which she'll loathe), and plays her game (thus enabling her). Understanding her pain is one thing, but plenty of people have regrets and don't discharge anger at others because of those regrets; thus, overlooking your cousin's behavior because of her pain enables her perhaps the most. The thought that it's fair payback compares childhood to adulthood, akin to comparing lemons to watermelons.

Though telling her what to do is exactly what she resists (and she might keep it up out of spite), clearly communicating what is and isn't acceptable to you tells her what she's done, what you expect, and what the consequences of any continued action will be. It also gives her a choice—the independence that these folks crave. Be specific and follow through if you offer ultimatums. Make sure that whatever you promise you can enforce. Otherwise, you walk away weak and malleable. And you once again enable.

OTHER BAD CHOICES

When choosing your reactions don't attack the person's character. Kids make the mistake of attacking all the time, and unfortunately, adults do it, too. "You're a liar!" one might yell. "Like you're so honest. You couldn't tell the truth if your life depended on it!" Now *that's* attacking character.

Becoming less reactive takes true practice because passive-aggressive people have graduate degrees in raising your blood pressure and anxiety. You can't impact their behavior. You may even feel emotionally drained, but if you invest your energy in changing your own behaviors and reactions, you have a shot at turning around a covert dynamic—not a guarantee, but at least a shot. This is important because essentially, this is the only real control you have: to control yourself, and it's key—pivotal in fact—to stopping your enabling. At the very least, by choosing better reactions you ease the momentary anger and avoid creating another buildup or spark. In fact, sometimes it's best to put some space or time between the problem and your response.

To learn from your mistakes, take note of how you've responded to a troublesome person in your past. Ask yourself what you stand to gain by any action you take and whether that action meets your goals. If you do nothing else, try this: make a conscious effort to respond in a totally positive way. Remember that we tend to rehearse (over and over) our negative patterns, reinforcing them. "So I said ____ and I showed him!" Instead, we need to mentally rehearse the positive (over and over) to break the habit. That's the only way. Insight isn't enough. "Deciding to change" isn't enough either. Move from poor reactions to positive ones.

If you've been reactive before, stay cool this time. Listen, rather than attack. Reflect what the other person has said, rather than offer your own interpretation. Use empathy, rather than anger. Model the assertiveness and respect you'd like to see instead of passive-aggression. Don't talk to the other person's anger. Talk to the resolution.

Get him to talk when you can't stand him? Yes. Use empathy? Yes. Even though deep down these people are way out of line, if you truly wish to turn the tables on this irritating behavior, you need to appreciate their emotion—best done by being as empathic as possible in as even a tone and temperament as you can muster. You'll ruin it if your body language sends an incongruent message from your words. Softly couch what you have to say. Be direct.

Take the information in this small section and craft a script for yourself. Rehearse what to say, how you'll say it (including body language). Practice alternative reactions that the other person may have so that you aren't surprised. Here's another chance to test your reaction:

Rick, Jodi, and Ed all report to the same project manager, out of the San Francisco headquarters, while they're stationed in Hartford. Though three on a team forms a triangle, this crew has worked supportively, preparing important presentations for a product rollout. Funds have gotten tighter, however, and their manager informed them that the budget allows only two of them to attend the big event. As the last hire, Rick will be left behind.

Time runs short. Rick left around noon to fetch everyone's sandwiches. 12:45: no Rick in sight. The team had a 1:00 phone conference. At 12:58, Rick sauntered in with two lunches. "Where's yours?" Jodi asked, knowing she'd only be able to nibble a few bites. Rick replied that he wasn't hungry, and while starved, she and Ed put their food aside for the important call. Later, Jodi noticed a red ketchup stain on Rick's shirt, not there all morning. Not hungry, huh? No wonder he was late!

The next morning Rick came in ninety minutes late, very unlike him. Then, Ed searched the office for a report they absolutely had to have. Later that afternoon, they found it, not in its usual place, and only after frantically recreating some of its contents, wasting precious time.

What do you think is happening here? How would you react? No multiple-choice list. That would be too easy! Instead, take a sheet of paper before you move to the next paragraph and write down possible phrases you could use to confront Rick, because with such an important work event approaching, the team isn't working efficiently.

What's going on? It's a pretty good guess that Rick is acting out his conflicting feelings without ever openly acknowledging them, or he's very aware of his feelings and thinks "if you're getting all the glory, do all the work yourself." Of course, his reaction only shows his immaturity, which will hold him back from any chance at traveling next time (if there ever is a next time).

For responses, if your list contains something like "Rick, why are you acting this way?" the buzzer just sounded. "Why" will only put Rick on the defensive. If you wrote, "Rick, we know you must be disappointed not going to the rollout, but we need you," you're getting closer. Assuming that you know Rick's feelings could put you in a one up/one down position. Rick may resent that and need to save face, thus hiding behind his cubicle and emotions. If Rick is young and naïve, he might deserve such a learning-curve approach, but he also needs to know his behavior has been unacceptable and that he cannot do it again.

If you started soft, something akin to, "Rick, we were working so well together, and your contribution has been tremendous. Lately, though, I sense we're not the same team. Is everything okay?" you're much closer. Now, it's Rick's chance to talk, and hopefully he will because you've used "I" statements, praised him and shown concern. Rick's in a much better position to apologize for the fact that he hasn't acted like himself, admitting his disappointment, so that you could follow up with "You've got a point about that Rick. You've worked so hard, and I wish everyone could attend. When we're not working together though, we all risk failing and facing the consequences if this product launch doesn't go well."

Placing yourself in a situation with "we" rather than "you" again softens things. Phrases such as "I agree with you," "you've got a point," or "tell me more about that?" are all good approaches because they align you with the other person. Asking an open-ended question also encourages the angry person to express whatever he has stored inside.

An important point, though, is that you're not a therapist so empathy only goes so far. If you're the coworker or the boss, it's helpful to see some things as misunderstandings, realizing that everyone is entitled to a bad day. But you also need to set clear limits.

Should Jodi or Ed have gone to each other with their concerns first? If they both voiced their concerns, Rick would feel two up/one down, it would triangulate things, thereby freezing the conflict in place. The closest path to a person is a straight line—a more direct, more personal approach at least as a first course of action. Letting off steam might feel good in the moment, but it's bad for long-term relations. Business has a bottom line though, and if their project was looming the likelihood that Jodi and Ed would communicate about this is great. When that happens, be extra cautious not to jump on a bandwagon where your own anger gains momentum, for it colors your reaction and complicates things.

Remember, anger-concealing people have been trained not to show their true emotions. They're scared or hurt, jealous or frustrated, selfish or mean. They need to talk, and for you to listen. Don't go around them; go to them. Even if they are disrespectful, you should set a respectful, not confrontational, example.

Gently easing information out of them sure beats going to battle. Each situation is different, but sometimes using humor to disarm an angry person softens things also. Just make sure that the humor is not mean-spirited because the purpose is to be respectful. Having said that, it's *usually* safer to poke fun at yourself. Indeed if you can find it within yourself to work with any angry person at the very first signs of passive-aggressive behavior, it might make future interactions much more positive.

If you do nothing else, try this: Make a conscious effort to respond in a totally positive way. If you've been reactive before, stay cool this time. Listen, rather than attack. Reflect what the other person has said, rather than offer your own interpretation. Use empathy, rather than anger. Model the assertiveness and respect you'd like to see instead of passive-aggression. Don't talk to the person's anger. Talk to the resolution.

SPECIFIC REACTIONS

THROUGHOUT THESE CHAPTERS, we have focused upon five groups of needs alerting you to what the passive-aggressive person frequently fears or avoids and what behavior you'll typically see as a result. Here, carrying through with our anti-enabling agenda, we help you to moderate your reactions specifically to the five categories.

Reacting to Control

Certainly, we all should listen well and extend some empathy to the controlling person. This, as we've indicated, is one of those skills to use with all passive-aggressive or secretly angry people. Equally important to the person who avoids being hurt and fears failure is getting "on their side." Next, being direct, clear, and very specific as you communicate what you need, want, or think helps to achieve calm confrontation. If you can help the controlling person to feel successful, or at the very least not diminish his or her sense of competency, you'll achieve more harmony as well. Where control manifests in eating disorders or in some other unhealthy pattern, encourage the person to seek treatment. Otherwise, refrain from enabling.

Reacting to Manipulation

Since the manipulator is quite skilled at pushing your buttons, sometimes plotting to do so as a "get back," it's really important to rein in your own reactivity and not seek revenge yourself. Doing this while you continue to be vigilant requires setting firm boundaries and defining the consequences. This type of passive aggressor avoids responsibility and doesn't easily admit to problems. Coping with someone else's needs or concerns? That's difficult, too. Thus, accept no excuses when the person shirks responsibility. Also, hold firm to your beliefs, make direct requests, but do be willing to cooperate and even show how to solve problems in order to create win-win situations (this helps to counter the "my way or the highway" attitude). Because the person fears being found out or confronted, tackle any lies, distortions, illogical thoughts, or harmful motivations with calm, again modeling problem solving. Reject the behavior, not the person. Remember to praise more, criticize less, and of course, use empathy. When necessary, act decisively because the manipulator may try to thwart your goals. When the going gets rough, avoid jumping on the bandwagon or forming coalitions. In fact, just avoid triangles all together by dealing directly, not indirectly.

Reacting to Childlike/Immature Behavior

At the core of the immature passive aggressor is a strong need to recreate parts of childhood and receive acceptance. These folks feel dependent, yet they do yearn for a little freedom. But with fears of losing favor, never being able to "get it right," and maybe being loved conditionally, they're certainly looking for others to take care of them most of the time. In one word: don't. Do not parent them. Focus on the here and now, and unless the person in question is indeed a minor, you should gently remind them of their adult independence, responsibilities, and choices they can make to improve their happiness. It will be challenging because you'll hear about their aches, pains, and ailments, many times in a whimpering fashion. It gets annoying after awhile, and it's oh-so-tempting to step in and make their decisions or lighten their load. But this will only enable them. Instead, try to show them the shift from problem-focused to solution-focused thinking.

If you remind them that they are accepted—faults and all—and that they have what it takes to express themselves appropriately, plus make their own decisions, you will lead them down a more mature path. In fact, encouraging all people who conceal their anger to appropriately assert themselves is not only wise, but very much needed. When you understand that being assertive was often prohibited in childhood, it may give you the extra incentive to work with this person to develop this necessary skill that could halt his or her passive-aggressive ways.

Reacting to Self-Absorption

In prior chapters, we've discussed how to deal with the workplace "star" and the self-absorbed family member, so we remind you to revisit those tips. But since this is a fairly prevalent passive-aggressive pattern, we offer a few general pointers. For starters, refuse to be too impressed because if you are, you're feeding their ego (enabling). When you have too-high hopes, perhaps believing in the favors promised or becoming star-struck, you'll be that much more disappointed when you realize that there are different rules— those that apply to the self-absorbed person, and then those that apply to everyone else. You'll be equally struck by their lack of empathy for your concerns and to the mixed messages they send when their words don't match either body language or actual behavior.

These folks yearn for attachment, security, and happiness that they somehow lost in their earlier years, and continually they create situations where others will notice them. Their stories and travels, life experiences and education far surpass yours, and if you don't dutifully fawn over them, they'll grab your attention until you do. That's why you'll see an exquisite discomfort with competition, because any attempt to steal their stage will most likely be met with hypersensitivity and indirect anger caused by their rather irrational fears.

Realize that it may take time to experience the full effects of the self-absorbed person who gradually ingratiates herself. But over time, you'll sense that she's always right, it's all about her, and the relationship seems off balance. While these folks form triangles (sometimes helping them to keep the stage lights), don't do likewise. Don't argue over who is right, who knows more. Ignore what you can, but calmly confront any attempts to show off at someone else's expense. Avoid becoming dependent when they believe they should lead and you should follow. Try as best you can to channel the vain person's strengths for everyone's benefit, but if problems occur where the self-absorbed adult becomes emotionally abusive or cannot delay gratification to look out for the needs of a child, for instance, counseling and intervention could help. Narcissism like this is a difficult personality pattern to deal with, and it's best to have some support along the way.

Reacting to Depression

Each case of responding to depression in someone you know will be different, depending upon the severity. It's best not to offer advice but to show through your own example how you can reframe negative occurrences into the positive. This also helps the person to brainstorm for ways to feel more competent, the hallmark of good self-esteem. Trust us, the depressed person can still spot phony praise or support, so just don't go there. Reinforce the steps that reflect responsibility and positive, healthy action. Listen, but if you do inquire, ask open-ended questions to facilitate the depressed person's sharing. Finally, encourage this type of passive aggressor to seek treatment for depression and/or any addictions.

■

GETTING HELP, GETTING OUT

IF it's truly difficult to cope with someone else's hidden anger, you may need to seek help or devise an escape plan. Passive-aggressive people take great delight in sending you into orbit by their behaviors. Psychiatrist Scott Haltzman, coauthor of *The Secrets of Happily Married Men*, says it never helps to say "You're the problem" or "There's something wrong with you."[3] Instead, point out the results of the problem, how upset other people get, how hard it is to enjoy time together, or how frustrating things appear. Remember the strategies of calm, assertive (not aggressive), respectful confrontation. Often, you don't know how deeply seated a person's anger might be, but there's usually a lot of hope for positive resolution. If relationships get too dicey, seeking therapy or workplace intervention is a good form of triangulation to spread the problem to another person trained to help with troublesome relationships and behaviors. If you approach people's anger from the problem/solution mode, Haltzman says, "Therapy becomes a forum to help them make life more manageable, and they won't feel like you're trying to manage them."

If the behavior is well entrenched, however, your approach to the passive-aggressive person, hoping he or she will work through the problem or "get it," may be dashed because anger-concealing people can hide things well, even from themselves. There's nothing to discuss, from their point of view. When this occurs and the passive-aggression is simply too painful to be around, it's time to implement an exit strategy.

When out with a friend or family member, devise a signal or saying such as "Honey, don't forget to check your voicemail tonight"—anything that only the two of you realize is a sign that says "let's get out of here." Coping with hidden anger is one thing, but becoming a martyr plays right into and replicates the pattern. That's not healthy for anyone involved.

DEALING WITH THE MANIPULATIVE CHILD

NOT EVERYONE ON the receiving end of anger is the same as we've just seen. Nicholas and Jody Long believe that teachers are in an ideal position to become counter-passive-aggressive since they have the power to question and evaluate their students' work and behavior. They detail what they define as counter-passive-aggression in *Managing Passive-Aggressive Behavior of Children and Youth at School and Home,* calling it the missing puzzle-piece. When a passive-aggressive student relates to teachers (or parents), over time, the adults end up behaving similarly. They might step back, realizing this isn't their typical mode. "Many times the adult is shocked and appalled to behave counter-passive-aggressively and is dismayed to have acted in such a childish and nonprofessional way," the authors write.[4] This is another example of how anger can sneak into your own demeanor if you're not careful.

You can see, then, the connection between learned or witnessed passive-aggressive behavior and how one comes to hide anger as an adult. Expressing feelings directly is often very threatening for the child of passive-aggressive parents. She fears reprisal so she meets her parent's emotional level so as not to upset them by appearing happier when mom or dad is down, or by feeling sad herself because that may not sit well, either. Every child yearns to receive positive parental feedback, only when your parent hides anger, you never know quite where you stand. It's confusing and hurtful. Child or teen culture today doesn't promote a lot of interpersonal education either.

Computers, video games, hand-held entertainment, and cell phones have spawned a generation brought up without the skill of calming and entertaining themselves without electronic stimuli. Instant messaging and text messaging on cell phones don't foster social skills. There's no nonverbal communication going on when you're typing in messages to a friend, no one to sit with you in silence and listen unconditionally with eyes riveted and body turned in. The best prescription: turn off the electronic stimuli.

Despite everything, children latch onto hope that things will get better because they want so badly to have positive feelings. Adults, noticing that their relationships aren't as healthy as they could be, often latch onto this hope as well. Hope is good, but staying stuck for too long is not.

■

CLASSROOM MANIPULATION

HOW do you maintain your composure in the classroom when one student defies your authority? "You can't send me to the office 'cause I'll tell the principal you threw a book at me!" In the university lecture hall, an interrupting student picks apart your research or an online student tries to run the class. Teachers mask anger, too. In adult education, picture your instructor, joking with a group of students. Everyone tosses around a few tame remarks, and suddenly the instructor replies, "You don't have to be mean." Anger-concealing people take offense when clearly none is intended. It comes across as sly and confusing to others.

Well-hidden anger elicits reactions from subtle to strong. Students carry their reactions with them after the bell rings. If you think you're dealing with disguised anger at school, try the following tactics:

- If you're dealing with childlike angry behavior, ask if they'd like to be treated like a child or an adult. Then add, " . . . because if you want me to treat you like a child, then I will _____," and when they say, "No! Treat me like an adult," give them a more direct answer.
- Be sure it's anger, because anger is always attached to another negative emotion. Children with learning disabilities, ADHD, or sensory-processing concerns might appear defiant when they are merely shutting down due to classroom challenges or the teacher's requests. A disorganized or slow child might have legitimate difficulties with attention and brain-based executive functioning but appear to be passive-aggressive, lazy, or oppositional. Investigate what else might be going on before labeling the behavior.

- Check on self-esteem. Hidden anger may really be a child's low self-concept, having slipped into a negative expectancy set; if you expect a certain behavior from the child, over time, the child internalizes that and gives you just what you expect. Pessimistic students often perform beneath their potential.
- Stay in control of the class by controlling your reactions. Any anger or attention you give to certain passive-aggressive behavior reinforces it. If the offending student looks for a stage upon which to perform, take away that stage by dealing with the child privately, not in front of the group. Once you become annoyed, the situation resembles a power struggle, the student becomes defensive, you may respond more quickly with anger, and this becomes a cycle.
- Use your own feelings as a guide. After a stressful incident, how do you feel? Was it a struggle? Did you feel powerless? Confused? If your current methods aren't working, identify ones that will. Target the behaviors you wish to change without tackling too much. Choose no more than one or two, at first.
- Invite the sarcastic or cynical student to stay after class. When students show their egos, resentment and irritability, they often haven't been heard. Listen to them. Do this privately so that other students aren't swayed by their cynicism. Tell students that you care about them and their performance, acknowledge their difficulty, and vow to get through it together. Don't use this as a time to lecture or threaten. Build a relationship first. Use a suggestion box by which you invite students to freely share so that they feel heard.
- If the angry student creates a distraction, acknowledge their struggle before the group to solicit peer support. "It looks like Johnny is having a hard time focusing on our work," you might say. "He's acting silly but I know he wants to get a good grade because we've seen his good work. I wonder what we can do to help him."
- Build empathy in students by assigning them to write out the perspective of the other person. If children tattle or repeat an embarrassing incident from the playground, make this a teaching moment that effectively stops such a hidden undercurrent.
- Rearrange seating to facilitate open expression and positive communication. Students who face one another are more willing to share, remain open, and drop their defenses. Forming a circle reveals body language so that anger is acknowledged, not hidden.

■ Hold everyone accountable to certain standards. Make those standards and expectations clear as to what is acceptable behavior and what is inappropriate. This counters the common refrain "I didn't know."

■ Ask for assistance. If it's hard to manage large student groups with overtones of hostility, consult the administration. Ask for an assistant or parent volunteers. Break the class into small groups. Ask that other teachers pull children aside for "specials" or individualized instruction during these times.

■ Don't abandon the child to homebound instruction. If he's bad enough to not make it in the class, he won't make it alone with a tutor.

TEN

REWRITING YOUR OWN ANGER SCRIPT

How does it feel to have learned more about hidden anger? Did you ever feel like going "on strike" from completing this book? If so, what prompted that? Knowing these answers helps you to determine your next steps.

It's great that you've kept reading, especially if some of the material might have been uncomfortable. It shows that you're open-minded, willing to learn and grow. Here, we'll build on that. If you're still identifying how you feel, see if the sidebar "Building an Emotional Vocabulary" contains words that apply, maybe multiple or conflicting words that describe your feelings.

■

BUILDING AN EMOTIONAL VOCABULARY

SOMETIMES just labeling any negative feelings removes the fear of expressing them. Do any of these words or phrases apply right now, or when you're angry?

agitated • alarmed • ambivalent • at a loss • apprehensive • ashamed • belittled • bossed around • burdened • cautious • conflicted • confused • controlled • culpable • cut off • degraded • demoralized • desperate • despondent • devastated • disappointed • discounted • disgusted • distant • down • drained • edgy • enraged • exasperated • exploited • exposed • foolish • frustrated • guarded • guilty • helpless • hesitant •

horrified • imposed upon • incompetent • indignant • inept • insecure • insignificant • intimidated • intruded upon • jealous • jittery • left out • let down • lonely • miffed • mischievous • mistreated • misunderstood • nauseated • neglected • needy • obsessed • overlooked • over-whelmed • pessimistic • picked on • pressured • provoked • put down • reluctant • repelled • resigned • resistant • restless • run down • seething • shamed • shocked • smug • sorrowful • stuck • suspicious • tearful • threatened • timid • tired • turned off • uncertain • unwanted • unwelcome • used • vulnerable • wary • worried • wounded

COMING TO TERMS WITH DIFFICULT FEELINGS

MANY OF THE feelings in the "Building an Emotional Vocabulary" side-bar aren't easy to admit. Awareness is a huge first step in solving hidden anger. Lingering anger does great personal harm to your overall health and longevity, and especially to your relationships, reputation, and career. Everyone has experienced anger to some extent, but you must be able to put your arms around these feelings in a figurative sense; otherwise, you risk mis-managing anger in the future.

Sometimes knowing what you don't want can also help you become more contented. Having felt isolated and lonely, for instance, might help you to become more accepting and tolerant because you know that your buried anger has previously pushed people away. Knowing what it's like to be silent may help you to finally assert yourself, and having taken offense to minor slights may help you realize that a negative mindset breeds anger—if you let it. No matter how anxious or angry you've been in the past, it doesn't have to outline your future. If you've caused problems because of concealed resentments or struggles, you have as much, if not more, ability to shift things in a more positive direction, using that energy for your own betterment. If you have failed to take any action, vow to comply or cooperate. Two critical tools—productive, open expression and problem-solving skills—will make the way much easier.

ENCOURAGING OPEN EXPRESSION

IF YOU WEREN'T allowed to express strong emotions or your parents eas-ily washed away your anger with lines like "you're not really mad" or "now, now . . . that's not how you feel . . . you're not really angry . . . " then using descriptive words and sharing feelings doesn't come easily. It's a pattern that you risk perpetuating unless you explore more open communication. Convinced you can't do it? Do you want your children to mask their true feelings as you did, gaining a sense of power by being clever or oppositional? If so, they'll feel empowered one minute, demoralized the next for having pulled the wool over *your* eyes or having been less than honest with *you*. Let them achieve comfort with ordinary, garden-variety anger—you, too—by practicing these expressive techniques:

Know what you can change: Do this by defining your trigger emotions with specific words. For younger children, buy a feelings poster, seen in pediatric, therapy, or school offices so that kids with limited vocabulary can point to a vast range of smiling or frowning faces.[1] Start with short phrases such as "this makes me feel hurt," and nothing more.

Take action that can change things: Be responsible for your feelings using "I" statements. No exceptions. "I feel afraid," "I'm feeling hurtful," or "I feel silly (worthless, sad, guilty, sorry)" discharges your angst, and conveys much more to the person involved to work with you toward a solution. This avoids name-calling, swearing, sarcasm, and other indirect discharges of anger. "You make me so angry" puts the other person on the defensive and solves nothing.

Make sure that thoughts, feelings, and actions convey the same meaning: When they don't, others sit in a tenuous spot wondering if they should call you on the contrast between what you say and what you do. In their minds, you become more difficult.

Review your style: If it's authoritarian, with the need to rule, it discourages honest expression. Indulging or permissive, indifferent or disengaged styles aren't optimal either, for they never teach. An authoritative style allows you to exercise control but in a warm, responsive, encouraging way. This invites discussion and builds bonds as opposed to closing down communication and pushing others away.

Extinguish *shoulds*, *musts*, and *oughts*. Whenever you find yourself thinking, "I *ought* to be silent," "Good people *should* smooth it over," "I *must* keep the peace at all costs," realize your inner critic calling out. Stop the thought. Express yourself, or respectfully wait for the right time to speak up.

Let occasional mistakes slide: We all have bad days. Especially with children, berating only adds to their sense of helplessness. Shame keeps the anger churning. Belittling shuts down communication, and when that's lost, so is any influence the adult might have upon a child. With no means for honest expression, people hide their feelings, becoming dishonest.

Practicing open, positive, and helpful expression is an important first step to turning around your indirect style, but success isn't acquired in one afternoon. It probably took a long time to go underground with your anger; it will take additional time to unearth the patterns, stop counterproductive thoughts, and apply new, problem-solving behaviors. Keep at it!

TEN STEPS TO SOLVING PROBLEMS

INDIRECT ANGER STEMS from ignoring problems. When you realize how powerful and productive you become as part of the solution instead of contributing to a dilemma, you become goal-focused, finding out details before responding in a knee-jerk, negative fashion. Possessing knowledge helps you to make wiser choices so that ultimately you can claim the influence you'd like to have over your own life, rather than see others act because you have not.

Sometimes, no matter how hard people try, they get stuck, often because no one ever taught them problem-solving steps. Other times, the heat of an incident blinds them to productive approaches. Practice these problem-solving skills and teach them to children as well:

1. **Focus on resolution, not attack:** Choose one issue to resolve. Use "I" statements; not "you" statements. If you're so angry that you could react using negative words or actions, take a deep breath. Resolve to solve the problem at hand.
2. **Gather the details:** Identify exactly what you're arguing about—not a side issue, but the issue at stake.
3. **Name your goals:** Long term, what would you like this situation to look like when the problem is resolved?
4. **Brainstorm potential solutions:** Sometimes anger flourishes because people feel there is one ultimate answer. There are many paths to the same point.
5. **Evaluate your options:** Write down the pros and cons of each idea. How feasible and realistic are they? Discard ideas that set yourself up for failure because they're too difficult or because the drawbacks outweigh the benefits.

6. **Think through the obstacles:** Will your favored option get you to your ultimate goal? What stands in the way? What worked well in one situation might not work now.

7. **Choose the best plan:** If you've followed these steps, make your decisions accordingly. Commit your solution to paper.

8. **Implement your solution:** You'll never know if it's really right until you test it. Allow plenty of time to see it in action.

9. **Review it periodically:** Understand this is an ongoing process. This allows you to adjust it with new knowledge you've gained after you put the plan into action.

10. **Fine-tune your solution as needed:** If it works well, great. If not, modify it so that it works more to your liking and helps you reach your goal. If it's an abysmal failure, forget it. Refuse to get discouraged and stop thoughts like "it will never work" from clouding your optimism. Testing and retesting instills confidence and moves you toward resolution, whereas negative self-talk perpetuates problems.

If you follow our ten-step approach, we hope you are bolstered by new knowledge and confidence that this process creates opportunities, instead of closing doors when problems continue. Need more practice? Get a copy of *Successful Problem Solving: A Workbook to Overcome the Four Core Beliefs That Keep You Stuck* by Matthew McKay, PhD and Patrick Fanning, who highlight competence and self-worth, discuss their views about problem solving, and allow you to journal some of your own.[2]

■

POSITIVE VS. NEGATIVE MENTAL ENERGY

MARTIN Seligman, author of *Authentic Happiness,* teamed with Chris Peterson, a psychologist at the University of Michigan, to create the Values in Action Strength Test to identify a person's signature strengths. Knowing these, they say, makes it easier to achieve happiness throughout life.[3] Many psychologists and life coaches help clients play to their strengths, pointing out not-so-obvious mismatches between career or lifestyle demands that don't fit those core strengths. Adjust or remove these obstacles and you often remove misery, empowering people to action. If you feel competent in at least a few areas, this often compensates for those where you need improvement.

Additionally, we advocate taking stock in what enhances your mental energy or drains it. Negative, demanding people, assumptions and second-guessing, a frantic pace or cluttered environment, financial stress, too much mindless exposure to electronic stimuli, obsessive worry or negative self-talk, and unresolved conflict take its cumulative toll. Replacing these "brain drains" with positive people, neat, organized surroundings, facts and praise, activities such as reading or listening to educational/inspirational books on tape, financial savings, flexibility in one's daily schedule, and the resolution of unresolved conflict empowers your mental energy. Remake your mood with kindness to stay as positive as possible. Keep a gratitude list, pay people compliments or leave kind messages, smile, extend courtesy to other drivers, praise before criticizing, and generally do good deeds each day to carry out kindness, the antithesis of hostility. In fact, it's easier to make a change in a positive direction than to eliminate something negative, at least at first.

ASSERTIVE SELF-HELP STRATEGIES

WHEN YOU SOLVE problems and empower yourself, your anger slowly dissipates because you've replaced it with something far better. You're unlearning some of the patterns that have rendered you stuck. But in the heat of an irritating situation, you need short, specific, and easy-to-remember tips—a new menu of options.

Below, using our already familiar charts, we break down some of those "stuck points" to help you select better alternatives and complete the work regarding hidden anger. No matter what your needs, fears, or what you avoid, it's wise to do five things when you're tempted to conceal your frustrations and hostility:

1. **Accept your anger:** Don't jettison it through unkind remarks, gossip, disgruntled body language, or some other concealed means. Also, tell those around you (friends, loved ones) directly that they're *not* the cause of your irritations or anxiety. Most people will make allowances, but if you aren't honest, they may feel responsible, particularly children who often internalize what they see and hear of their parent's anger.
2. **Identify what triggers your anger:** Anger doesn't make a solo appearance, but usually stems from a lonely, jealous, sad, embarrassed, or otherwise uncomfortable place. Learn to identify your trigger emotions and deal directly with those feelings.
3. **Stop habitual negative thoughts:** These pop into your mind and end up thwarting you. Think self-fulfilling prophecy; resist self-fulfilling prophecy.

4. **Resolve to act assertively**—not passively, aggressively, or passive-aggressively.
5. **Practice running the proactive tape not the reactive one:** Otherwise you dwell on the negative and rehearse those thoughts.

CONTROL

NOW THAT YOU can look back upon things you needed as a child, or perhaps still do need, hopefully it's easier to understand why you're afraid of certain situations and veer toward avoiding them. Next time you feel yourself wanting to take charge, stop and think about what you've learned about control. Try a new strategy that's less likely to keep your hidden anger brewing.

YOUR NEEDS	WHAT YOU FEAR/AVOID	NEW APPROACH TO TRY
■ To have upper hand	■ Taking chances, risks	■ Identify your payoffs or what you get out of being stuck, express these.
■ To be in control	■ Being hurt or blamed	■ Cooperate; solve problems.
■ Success	■ Fear of failure and competition	■ Work on your thinking; see shades of gray or in between all good or all bad.
	■ Dependence	■ Commit to action, follow-through, and personal growth.
	■ Losing control	■ Try new approaches; develop a plan with more risk and fear involved.
		■ Seek treatment if you're truly stuck in an unhealthy cycle.

Colin always had a fear of being blamed. His fear of failure stemmed from having no assertive skill set. Without the proper tools, Colin has coasted, first through school, now working for the same small accounting firm he temped at during summers. His choice was the safest, but Colin grew jealous of friends on the fast track with stock options and corporate perks. When his wife Jenny got a promotion, Colin said he was thrilled, but his actions betrayed his words. Inside, everyone else's successes tore at him. The struggles and bitter words tore at their marriage, too. Finally, in couples counseling, Colin admitted that he felt Jenny had eclipsed him. Jenny hadn't understood why her opinions counted for nothing and why a simple request for Colin to pick up the dry cleaning seemed as if she'd asked him to scale a skyscraper. Now, she saw glimpses that Colin's needs weren't being met, and Colin realized his responsibility to become more open, less controlling when he shut down or saw a simple favor as a demand. He discovered that in order to turn these problems around, he needed to feel more competent, gain some successes. To do that, he'd have to take some risks, find a job that met his needs, and really work on stopping automatic, knee-jerk thoughts that tripped him up. He also needed to focus on the higher goal of being part of a couple, supporting, *not* undermining that.

When you feel yourself going to great lengths to remain passive to control a situation, it may well be the moment you most need to act. Many disgruntled workers shut down their performance, hoping their bosses will fire them. Unhappy spouses stomp off during an argument or put-upon teens "forget" to do a chore. These misuses of control reduce action and the risk of solving problems. In a relationship, they reduce the threat of intimacy. Can you see how counterintuitive and counterproductive this is? Nothing is resolved; instead, it adds to the next buildup, hastening a quicker spark next time. In most cases, there *is* always a next time.

Parents and teachers come across as controlling (sparking more of the same) if they adopt a "because I said so" attitude. Use phrases like these only when absolutely necessary, as in "run . . . the building is on fire!" Remember that the authoritative style, as opposed to an authoritarian one, allows you more room to operate fairly. You're still in charge, but not at the expense of good relations with your children or students.

MANIPULATION

IF YOU'VE TRIED to exert pressure to force a particular outcome before, these new tactics may work far better, because they take into account what you need, what you're afraid of, and what you have tended to avoid when angry.

YOUR NEEDS	WHAT YOU FEAR/AVOID	NEW APPROACH TO TRY
	■ Uncertainty	■ Focus on solutions, not obstacles
■ To manipulate or control the outcome or the process	■ Having to cooperate, give and take; having to deal with others' expectations, needs, or concerns	■ Assert, rather than demand
■ To win, have fun through fighting/hurting	■ Authority, perceived or real	■ Cooperate; be willing to meet halfway.

YOUR NEEDS	WHAT YOU FEAR/AVOID	NEW APPROACH TO TRY
■ To push people's buttons, extract revenge	■ Confrontation	■ Listen; let others speak for themselves.
■ To set agenda	■ Being found out	■ Count to ten; take deep breaths; relax.
■ To hide true emotions	■ Intimacy, dependency	■ Halt knee-jerk, immediate actions.
■ To blame, find fault	■ Guilt, self-blame	■ Increase your frustration threshold.
■ To be intentionally ineffective, independent	■ Admission of the problem or any anger	■ Keep your eyes on the problem so that you're not swayed by "getting back" at the person.
■ To keep responsibility at bay	■ Responsibility	■ Take responsibility for problems you created or put off.
		■ Match thoughts, feelings, and actions.
		■ Be a team player acknowledging others' opinions as equally valid as your own.

The need to manipulate the outcome is very similar to the need to control because of an internal pressure to win at all costs, born out of fear and what you often avoid. Pat seemed to engage in battle for the sport of it. A divorced dad with a twin boy and girl, he took great pleasure in evoking reactions from his ex-wife Olivia, discovering the easiest way was to refuse to cooperate as a co-parent and refusing to comply with ordinary expectations most any dad encounters—dropping his son off at little league or his daughter to a softball game and making an issue out of purchasing a few toiletries for his children. By complicating things, Pat essentially crafted Olivia's response most Monday mornings when he'd find an email reading him the riot act for being so damn difficult. "I'm not angry . . . you're the one upset," Pat would typically reply, yet nearly every weekend with his children, Pat dug deeper into this type of resistance, manufacturing the outcome.

Sometimes, "conflict avoidant" is an apt description because those who need to control the outcome shy away from the uncertainty that open expression brings. Crafting Olivia's response almost guaranteed her reaction (the certainty that Pat needed), and made it easier than the work of being a co-parent. Little will turn this around until one of them changes the dynamic—Olivia becoming less reactive and Pat voicing his concerns directly to her, not through manufacturing the outcome and making a statement through resistance.

I once worked with parents battling over which church service their children would attend. Mom tried to "guilt" Dad into doing things her way. I got them to refocus first by asking, "Do you want them to believe in God?" Next, "What are the core religious beliefs you want your children to have?" Then, I asked, "Do you want them to practice their faith?" About five questions later, I asked, "What service should they attend?" and by this time, after being able to agree on a few preliminary items, it wasn't hard to find a workable solution.

CHILDLIKE/IMMATURE BEHAVIOR

WE CERTAINLY ARE creatures of our past; thus, unmet needs in childhood often drive our adult behavior. When that happens, stop to recognize the source, acknowledging what you fear or avoid. Try out a new strategy to move you forward, not several steps back.

YOUR NEEDS	WHAT YOU FEAR/AVOID	NEW APPROACH TO TRY
▪ To recreate earlier experience in childhood	▪ Being loved conditionally	▪ Take responsibility for your own issues.
▪ To be seen as the "good boy" or "good girl"	▪ Losing rank in family	▪ Believe in yourself.
▪ Independence yet feels dependent	▪ Powerlessness	▪ Overcome learned helplessness.
	▪ Never getting it right	▪ Practice decision making skills; be decisive.
	▪ Responsibility	▪ Practice relaxation techniques when you feel anxious.

At fifty-eight, Brenda is a member of the sandwich generation, with a daughter in college, and an elderly father in assisted living. She constantly butts heads with her brother Daniel, twelve years younger, since nothing he does suits her. Her criticism leaks out because Brenda remains silent, as the martyr. She comes across as an adult daughter desperately seeking to be daddy's little girl, right to the end. To hear Daniel tell it, she's always been two-faced. When they were kids, Brenda would act as a second mother, swatting at him when their parents left the room, but acting protective when they returned. Since Dad was tough, too, Brenda may have gotten the message that she needed to act a certain way to win praise. As a result, she's hung onto that, still carries a grudge toward Daniel and is overwhelmed. Underneath it all,

Brenda longs for closer family ties, but sets up a self-fulfilling prophecy because good daughters "should do everything well." Rather than trust her inner experience, Brenda denies her feelings. Defenses rooted in childhood to protect her from unavailable, unreliable, punitive parents have limited, if no, usefulness in adulthood. Brenda might feel quite liberated if she moved from where her emotions weren't appreciated and used the best parts of her anger as a motivating force not as a destructive one.

SELF-ABSORPTION/VANITY

NEXT TIME YOU feel selfish desires come over you, recognizing what you really seek in any given situation is far better than acting out of anger. Acting differently might very well allay your fears, put an end to what you have previously avoided, and help you to find the attachment, attention, or security you quite possibly have wanted all along.

YOUR NEEDS	WHAT YOU FEAR/AVOID	NEW APPROACH TO TRY
■ Attention, often to be the center of that attention	■ Loneliness	■ Cooperate consistently.
■ Security	■ Living or working without support	■ Recognize other people's right to shine.
■ Attachment	■ Unhappiness	■ Take an active interest in others and their achievements; offer praise, empathy.
■ Happiness	■ Failure	■ Live by the rules; deal honestly.
■ Self-advancement	■ Losing	■ Respect other people's boundaries; realize everyone gets a turn.
■ To be loved	■ Responsibility	■ Stop faulty, negative thoughts.
		■ Work on being less sensitive; laugh.
		■ Seek treatment for addictions.

Remember Pat and the twins? He was selfish to make his need to get back at his ex-wife take precedence over his children. Pat unnecessarily drove his son and daughter to avoid him because their weekends became negatively charged, only ameliorated with a few cold beers during a football game. When they said, "We want to be with mom," he blamed Olivia. Pat would do well to cooperate with Olivia, but also to meet his kids' needs. First, he should seek help for any drinking because that stands in the way of change. Had Pat dared to get close to his kids, he could have found the attachment, attention, love, and security he craved. Lessening his sensitivity and lightening the mood with laughter might have established closer connections as well.

We all know a vain person who feels he knows what's best for others because . . . well, everyone ought to be thankful for that wisdom! Being so smart, though, often lands this person in a lonely place. If you're the parent of a self-absorbed teen, some inflated self-worth is normal (though you work to modify it). Teenagers, with less understanding of the world and their place in it, focus on themselves often to the exclusion of others. You've heard about the book titles like *Get Out of My Life, but First Could You Drive Me and Cheryl to the Mall?* Getting kids to help others through volunteer work or other forms of outreach helps to round out their world until maturity takes its course.

DEPRESSION

EVERYONE GETS DOWN about life or circumstances some of the time. Very often, with positive thinking and other action steps, we can alter our mood, tackling our fears and meeting needs that have led us to a blue mood. Try these strategies, and if you still feel stuck, seek help from a qualified professional.

YOUR NEEDS	WHAT YOU FEAR/AVOID	NEW APPROACH TO TRY
	■ Loneliness	■ Focus on the positive; reframe negatives.
■ Hope, support, security	■ Living or working without support	■ Use exercise and positive mood-boosting strategies.
■ Optimism, positives	■ Unhappiness, difficulty	■ Seek treatment for addictions.
■ Self-worth	■ Failure, rejection	■ Use positive self-talk, relaxation techniques.
		■ Take proactive role in life.

When self-esteem and self-confidence wane, and especially if you've experienced loss in your life, it may seem harder to turn negative feelings into positives. Anger often lurks behind passive, negative, and depressive symptoms but can be remedied with positive thinking and a helpful technique called reframing—mentally turning negatives into positives.

Sometimes other people's negative perceptions stay with us. Karina's brother taunted her with nicknames like "beanpole" because of her thin frame. She found herself shying away from men because she bought into the notion that she was unattractive. Getting herself to go to college parties raised her anxiety. Karina needed relaxation techniques (i.e., deep breathing) in conjunction with reframing and positive self-talk. After practicing several times, she found that she stayed at parties longer, enjoying herself instead of bolting for the exit.

Take baby steps to become more self-confident, acting as if you're already self-assured. This moves you beyond your comfort zone. You've limited yourself playing it safe, remaining stuck with certain misperceptions. Simple changes build upon themselves so that you develop coping skills that will really pay off if anxiety or adversity strikes again in life, which is almost a given. You'll feel much more capable and much less depressed.

■

ASSERTIVE THINKING AND PHRASING

BEING assertive means that you act in your best interests without violating others' rights. It's the belief that everyone is equally worthy with the same opportunity to agree or disagree, voice a "yes" or "no." Assertiveness equates to being firm but tactful, and it conveys openness, problem solving, compromise, and negotiation. You know it when you see it with matching body language, comfortable posture, firm handshake, appropriate eye contact and voice intonation. When you hold firm to your values, that's being assertive, and so is taking responsibility for yourself and your actions. Start with a small assertive act like calling customer relations or questioning a clerk in a store. Accept responsibility for low grades or mistakes at work.

If you struggle to become more assertive, practice these lines to short-circuit that critical inner voice. Use these when you're tempted to blame or drop hints instead of speaking up. There is no one right way of being assertive. Try these in place of less assertive standbys:

ASSERTIVE THOUGHT OR PHRASE:	INSTEAD OF:
I would like to _____.	You should _____.
I'd appreciate your understanding that I'd like _____.	If you don't _____, I'll _____.
Everyone has a unique contribution.	It must be done this way.
I will improve my performance.	It's the teacher's fault.

ASSERTIVE THOUGHT OR PHRASE:	INSTEAD OF:
It's _____ that bothers me, frankly.	Oh, everything is just fine.
Let's review this now and see what we can do.	"It's done . . . too bad . . .you lose."
I want to weigh all the information before I decide.	I don't have time now. Or [silence]
I know I made a mistake, and here's how I'll correct it.	People are out to hurt me.
Deciding has been a problem for me. It might help if we could sort it out. Could you help me with that?	Give me a break. I just can't do this.
When I don't know where you are, I get worried.	You were supposed to call from your friend's house. You're just so darn irresponsible.
I can see that. I should think about it. I'd like until tomorrow to get back to you.	I don't know. Whatever. [shutting down on because of pressure]
I know I haven't been myself, that I've been cranky and critical lately. I just want you to know that it's not you. I'm doing the best that I can right now.	Look what you've done to me. You make me so angry!
I'm sorry I didn't come to you sooner. I should have.	Well, you would have gotten upset. I know it.
The human resources office can help us resolve this.	You should go for counseling.
I'd really appreciate your spending Saturday with me because it's my birthday, and I'd love to get together.	Doing anything this weekend?

WHEN ANGER LINGERS

EVEN THOUGH YOU may have used your anger for self-shielding, protective purposes, there comes a time when staying bottled up is simply too painful to perpetuate. You've held feelings inside to your maximum limit. Still, how can you sustain the wish to become more open and contented without nagging patterns interfering with progress?

Defeating your inner struggles with independence versus dependence, support versus resistance, cooperation versus refusal, passivity versus active management of your life, well . . . it can seem daunting. You're to be congratulated for giving it a try!

Anytime you embark upon change, it helps to have the support of family and friends. Being open with them—perhaps using phrases we've offered or your own variations—may help elicit this. Hopefully, you arrive at this juncture of your own accord, not at the behest of a spouse, an employer, or someone else. Those who resist change won't usually be too committed to trying new thoughts, using assertive phrases, or acting any differently than they have before. What we're saying essentially is that you've got to be squirming, somewhat uncomfortable with the status quo, to give change a try. Predictably, when you make that commitment yourself, you get much, much more out of the process.

DECIDING UPON THERAPY

SOME PEOPLE MANAGE to solve their struggles without the help of therapy, but many decide to give counseling a try. A good therapist can help you determine what keeps you from moving beyond faulty thinking, limits your actions, and nudges your reactions out of defense mode. By working with a caring, knowledgeable professional, you learn more about how to halt your anger without causing emotional unrest and to visualize what a happier, less angry life would look like.

Some who opt for counseling see the process as a useful opportunity to reparent themselves, particularly if they can connect some of their lingering anger to childhood. Viewing therapy this way helps many to become less self-critical and self-sabotaging, to actually commit to counseling as a journey of self-exploration. A counselor, for instance, can show you that expressing yourself yields far better results than walking out on a coworker or girlfriend, that your old default reasoning of "it's no use" sets in motion a self-defeating cycle, and that your not wanting to feel difficult emotions stems from messages your parents may have instilled within you. Role-playing conflict takes the fear out of it. With practice, even the most conflict-avoidant person can become comfortable with challenge.

Does stigma stand in your way? We've made great strides to acknowledge that people need occasional counseling just like they need to visit the medical doctor complaining of a cough. Yet, some embrace the notion that needing therapy suggests something pejorative, like being "nuts" or "crazy," or in need of "a shrink." Toss stigmas out the window where they belong. Countless people go to counseling throughout their lifetimes. Most say it was refreshing, that they, surprisingly, discovered more strengths than they first thought they had, and that the experience overall was positive. Just as you may not click with a primary care doctor or your child's pediatrician, the same goes with mental health practitioners. So, if you've had a prior experience that didn't live up to your expectations, don't let this deter you. Another professional relationship may click quite well.

If you're using your health insurance to cover counseling visits, check with your plan for in-network providers, but if you wish to pay out of pocket you've just broadened your choices. There are community mental health agencies that offer therapy on a sliding scale if cost stands in your way. Ask others, consult a hospital referral line, or contact mental health organizations for recommendations. You want a counselor who can help you feel comfortable yet also effectively challenge you, to move you beyond angry and stuck. For children, school counselors can be helpful as an initial go-to person, and many groups exist within schools to sort through problems with the help of the counselor or school psychologist.

What type of professional you see is an individual choice. If you require medication, a psychiatrist is a medical doctor trained to diagnose mental health conditions and prescribe proper medication, but you will often work with another type of professional for talk therapy or group counseling. If you would like to learn as much as possible about yourself through psychological testing, ask if the provider is qualified to administer such assessments. Many more psychologists (those with PhD or PsyD credentials) provide testing. Pastoral counselors add a religious perspective to their counseling work. Otherwise, marriage and family therapists (MFT), social workers, or clinical social workers (MSW or LCSW) and licensed clinical or professional counselors (LCPC or LPC) have at least two years of postgraduate coursework and experiential knowledge to help most people with lingering anger issues.

What to Expect

After establishing rapport, work with your therapist to establish goals as you unravel why you're seeking help. Therapy doesn't always tell you what to do. Some types, however, are much more directive and provide specific advice and plans for change. Therapy affords you the space to come to realizations yourself. A good counselor will help you to move from talking about how things were or are to how you feel. Talking is great, and it can definitely fill the time, but moving beyond "fact talk" fills the therapy hour with your feelings where the real work of exploring your frustrations takes place. Your therapist will pick up on any uneasiness and not move you faster than you can safely handle.

Therapists will respond differently toward you than others have in your past—that's the truly cool part! What feelings weren't allowed when you were younger will most assuredly be welcome here. If you're accustomed to being criticized or rejected, you will be validated. What space you had to fight for among self-absorbed parents, siblings, or bosses, will be all yours. There's no need to overadapt. If you're afraid of feeling powerless, unsupported, or foolish, you needn't worry. You truly hold a lot of influence in this process. Just feeling some different dynamic often shakes up the faulty pattern that has prevented you from expressing yourself.

Expect that your therapist may occasionally challenge you to spark recognition and help you to see how you might inadvertently paste someone else's face onto an innocent party, how you can adjust troublesome or self-defeating beliefs, and how you can role-play and practice new behaviors, responding to situations with less pent-up anger. New reactions may create changes in others who, in turn, change their behavior. Your counselor may help you to role-play anticipated (or unanticipated) reactions as well because if you are dealing with a significant other who also hides anger, that angry person might not have the same impetus for change.

Though not there to be your buddy, nor there to assist you in covering up or avoiding tough issues, your therapist's purpose is to help you change where you need to change. He or she may also realize that if part of what's brought you into the office is your ambivalence, then ambivalence may tempt you to quit when difficult feelings surface and you're afraid of rewriting your anger script. It's hard to clarify your own standards if you never had any firm foundation. Maybe your parents kept you guessing, and some of this stems from having nothing upon which to truly take a stand. Think about your therapy goals if ambivalence strikes, and know that it's a normal temptation to want to stay as is or to quit, but one that you can work through. Your therapist may point out observations; for instance, you may learn that indecision or keeping things to yourself is part of your process, where you routinely write out the way things seem in your head, yet fail to check these things out with other people. Not surprisingly, your beliefs aren't accurate, and this process causes problems. Quitting often happens as a pattern of "when the going gets tough, the weak run." Before you quit, ask yourself if it is indeed the wrong therapist, the wrong methods, or if it's you that needs to change.

Other Forms of Therapy

Some people choose to attend a therapy group as they wrap up the individual work they do. Group therapy can be particularly effective in treating substance abuse; other addictions; eating disorders; when overcoming certain losses such as a separation, divorce, or the death of a loved one; or when trying to improve certain abilities, such as social or interpersonal skills.

Group therapy works well, for it fosters cohesion among members carefully selected to participate by trained facilitators or coleaders. Sometimes, this leader may be your own therapist. The group approach runs effectively when you want to check out how you're coming across to others. Will, for instance, never felt too self-assured throughout high school and beyond college. He'd gone to the college counseling center a few times, but when he was out working, meeting new people, and still afraid to ask women out on dates or make new friends, his therapist suggested he try group counseling, where he discovered strengths and learned to improve his actions just by accepting the feedback from group members. In one session, the coleaders encouraged him to role-play with another member, and Will's confidence grew as he tested out how to phrase things and respond within such an emotionally safe setting. Will grew more confident and much less frustrated.

Group is also a good place to work through some of the issues that originated in your family, because amazingly enough, those roles seem to be recreated within the dynamics of groups. Members offer each other objective feedback, mutual support, different perspectives, and confidentiality because what happens in group stays within group. Counseling and education also become the focus of some groups as people gather around specific topics such as divorce, parenting, chronic pain, anger management, certain illnesses, or other issues. Fees for group therapy vary in different areas and can sometimes be less expensive than individual counseling.

Online therapy has come of age in our technological world. It can cost just as much as face-to-face counseling, and it's more suited for those who express themselves best through written expression and who need fairly straightforward, short-term, solution-based therapy or help with a life transition such as a job loss, a move, or another adjustment. It's *not* recommended when your anger has truly taken hold, when you're in crisis, or feeling depressed or suicidal, because these situations require face-to-face work. It's sometimes less favored among established professionals for various reasons, including the risks to confidentiality.

The length of treatment varies. When what brought you into counseling (presumably your anger or hidden frustration) is resolved or when you've met the goals you and your therapist set at the outset, then you may realize that you're feeling better. Counselors help you to acknowledge your progress and choose a time when you'll work to end regular sessions. When you reach a point at which you stand to gain more from independent work than from meeting each week with your therapist, it's time to phase out of counseling. This, too, can be stressful because it's a parting, but the door pretty much remains open for booster visits if you need these later.

Realize that very few people who attempt change get it right the first time. It takes practice, but change is not only possible, it's probable if you learn from each setback, recommit yourself, set specific, short-term goals, and surround yourself with the right supports. In other words, if you keep at it, you're there!

■

ELEMENTS OF CHANGE

JAMES O. Prochaska and his colleagues identified six stages that self-changers experience.[4] In *Changing for Good,* they explain that everyone who successfully effects change goes through: *Precontemplation,* where you aren't even aware of what habit/behavior to change until those around you draw your attention to the problem. *Contemplation* follows; here, you've figured that out and start thinking about ways to alter the behavior.

In the *preparation* stage, you plan to take action in the days or weeks ahead. During the *action* phase, you muster the most commitment to changing your behavior, expending much time and energy. *Maintenance* comes next because successful changers sometimes take one step back to every two steps forward. But they persevere, monitoring their progress, sometimes for a lifetime. Think of those who constantly monitor their weight or keep from taking a drink.

The sixth stage involves *termination,* a phase almost everyone loves to achieve, where you've extinguished an addiction or faulty habit. It's gone for good. The chain-smoker never yearns for a puff, or the anger concealer doesn't lapse into sarcastic gossip, shut down with "whatever," or put off a task that she really could accomplish.

Realize that very few people who attempt change get it right the first time. It takes practice, but change is not only possible, but probable if you learn from each setback, recommit yourself, set specific, short-term goals, and surround yourself with the right supports. In other words, if you keep at it, you're there!

No matter what the therapeutic approach, remember how important you are in the change process, and remember that as life experiences change you, you may be more ready than at other times to receive help. You are ultimately the very best expert on yourself—this is the message that Fred J. Hanna, PhD gives in *Therapy with Difficult Clients* in which he's identified seven precursors for client change. "A sense of necessity for change will not emerge if there is a greater necessity to remain the same," Hanna writes. That necessity is followed by a readiness to experience anxiety or difficulty, awareness, confronting the problem, effort or will toward change, hope, and having social support for change.[5]

■

FIXING YOUR FAULTY THINKING

WE all fall into faulty thinking, at least occasionally. Check to see if any of these faulty thought patterns play out in your life:

- **Feelthink:** Confusing emotions with thoughts and using feelings as the sole basis needed for understanding. "I feel it, therefore it is." The feeling is all the justification needed to keep anger brewing. It's the "I'm mad so you must have done something to make me mad." Separate feelings from facts in order to make changes in your faulty thinking.
- **Dirty-Lens Thinking:** Viewing everything through a very negative filter, as if there is an inch-thick coating of dust on the window and that's how you see the world.
- **Black-and-White Thinking:** Everything is one way or another with no shades in between. Job performance must be stellar or else it's terrible. Watch for "must," "should," and "ought" in your thinking. Life has shades of gray. So do many circumstances and situations.
- **Magnifying and Minimizing:** This is very similar to black-and-white thinking because a mistake, for instance, gets blown out of proportion with an overgeneralization. "I'll never succeed" or "It'll always be depressing here." *Always* and *never* are red-flag words that alert you to this faulty thinking.
- **Bag-the-Benefit Thinking:** Rejecting the good, embracing only the bad. We're not talking about a mere bad day but a constant pushing aside of the positive. All you're left with is discouragement, and it takes hold, spawning negativity.
- **Taking It Personally:** When you personalize something negative, internalizing it so that you feel responsible, it's a sign that your mood is at low ebb. Many chronically depressed or angry people resort to this thinking pattern.
- **Label Thinking:** Making a global assessment, typically a pejorative attack such as "He's a jerk" or "All stepmothers are witches," is quick, easy, but also unfair. If you're perpetually sarcastic and lob such low remarks, you're labeling.

FREEDOM AT LAST

WE'VE COME TO the end of our journey exploring hidden anger. We hope that through reading about anger's self-reinforcing nature, you realize the false illusion it often creates of being powerful and in control of a situation. No one is condemned to remain angry. We've not met any person who changed his destiny by staying the way he was.

Research out of the University of California at Berkeley revealed that core traits defining a person do change throughout life.[6] And, you've heard the colloquial definition of insanity: doing the same thing over and over, yet expecting different results. Don't let that be your modus operandi. Do a new thing!

Next time you feel tempted to sweep away a powerful emotion, silence your anger, or let it escape so that it won't easily be discovered, think about how you're using that frustration. Very often, it's to create this illusion.

Illusions aren't real. They're fleeting. Figure out what purpose your anger serves—because trust us, anger can serve very useful purposes. The problem isn't just your anger; it's your mismanagement of it. Be an engineer of your future instead. The result of figuring out what purpose your anger serves is such a valuable, freeing, and lasting part of this puzzle that the process of getting there is surely worth it. If you recognize what you get out of your anger, you've done a great thing for yourself.

What will contentment look like? Will it include happier relations, including more friendships, camaraderie at the office, a fulfilling marriage and intimate life with your significant loved one? Will your home be a safe harbor instead of a storm? How about academic success, a more promising career, financial and emotional security, or at least fewer hassles with those things? Will you be healthier, less shackled by the past, more inspired by the present and future? It's time to get off the emotional roller coaster. Ride's over!

Keep your eyes on the prize. Do it for yourself, your loved ones, and your career. Do it for your children, raising "can-do" kids who take on challenges and never think less of themselves if they can't. Want to really master problem solving? Teach the ten problem-solving steps to your children because anytime you teach someone else a skill, you reinforce it within yourself.

You can change. There is hope if you work toward the long-term goal of happiness. The work will continue because life is tough. But life is also very good. Reach for the higher-order goals in life as well. For many who are caught in an angry snare, their spiritual beliefs will help them along the journey of change.

After all, if your goal is to make people miserable, well . . . thanks for buying this book. You can put it down now, or give it to someone else.

If your goal is to be happy and healthy, however, you can find ways to achieve these things. Refer to this book—our tips and strategies, phrases to help you assert yourself, and explanations to understand confusing behavior—when you need an added boost or simply a reminder that there is a better way.

Yes, if you've identified anger's purpose or payoff in your life and visualized a better "next stop" along your journey, now you're in a much better position to attain what you really need in a more thoughtful, problem-solving way. You become a powerful part in realizing the life you may have always wanted. You can take care of yourself and can feel a tremendous sense of accomplishment. You can seize the life you always dreamed of, enjoying success, warm relationships, and happiness.

RESEARCH
REGARDING
PASSIVE-AGGRESSION

T HOUGH FREQUENTLY A subject for therapy, anger management wasn't always a topic for the bookstore, nor too well represented in textbooks. Since debate exists regarding the classification of passive-aggression, or even use of the term, we thought it best to explain why we used it in our title and why we encourage further study.

THE HISTORY OF PASSIVE-AGGRESSION

THE TERM PASSIVE-AGGRESSIVE has become synonymous with "difficult," and that was pretty much how the behavior appeared when first introduced in a *U.S. War Department Technical Bulletin* in 1945.[1] World War II Army psychiatrist Colonel William Menninger, who witnessed harsh reactions among troops as they adjusted to military life, advocated that the government provide psychotherapy and rehabilitation to those in the military. Col. Menninger is said to have coined the phrase because soldiers essentially followed orders but did so with ever-present hostility. Yet, those in uniform tried to project the image of the innocent, dutiful soldier. This smoldering resentment manifested in the classic pattern identified by both purposeful resistance and antagonistic compliance by putting off or forgetting to complete a task, doing so grudgingly, or doing a job inefficiently. In the army, there is little personal freedom yet much regimentation, and the need to "grow up fast." Those soldiers who couldn't cut it or merely wanted to flee, often showed their resistance by ignoring or resisting orders from a higher command, or merely wanting to escape altogether.

PASSIVE-AGGRESSION AND PERSONALITY DISORDERS

WHEN PASSIVE-AGGRESSION becomes a way of life, look to see how deeply it's entrenched. One of the best resources to learn about personality traits and disorders is through the work of Theodore Millon, PhD, DSc. Millon has written many books, and we have noted these for your continued reading as we list resources in our chapter notes.

What's a personality disorder? Simply put, it is long-standing, pervasive, and inflexible behavior or inner experience that differs vastly from one's cultural norms; frequent and intense at times; causing distress or impairment; and found in adults at least eighteen years of age. In other words, it's an adult pattern that doesn't budge much. Dealing with a personality-disordered person is difficult at best. By their very nature of being long-standing in duration, these characterological disorders are not generally diagnosed in children or adolescents (e.g., conduct disorder often becomes antisocial personality disorder at age eighteen).

Therapists look for patterns in a person's worldview, thoughts, and behaviors to judge whether these are enduring (not merely situational), frequent as well as intense. A person might meet this description, but if there is no impairment or distress, then it doesn't fit the criteria. In addition, if the patterns look odd to someone from a Western perspective, but it's perfectly understandable in that person's culture, once again, it's *not* a personality disorder. Right now there are eleven personality disorders reflected in the *Diagnostic and Statistical Manual of Mental Disorders, Fourth Edition, Text Revision* (*DSM-IV-TR*): antisocial, avoidant, borderline, dependent, histrionic, narcissistic, obsessive-compulsive, paranoid, schizoid, schizotypal, and personality disorder not otherwise specified (PDNOS).[2] Passive-aggression's place in this "bible" of mental health diagnosis is still evolving.

After the Veterans Administration identified and labeled passive-aggression, researchers began including it elsewhere. The American Psychiatric Association developed the first diagnostic manual (*DSM*) in 1952 with three subtypes of a passive-aggressive personality:

- "Pure" passive-aggressive style (pouting, stubborn, procrastinating, obstructing)
- Passive-dependent style (helpless, indecisive, clinging)
- Aggressive style (irritable, resentful, low frustration level, destructive, tantrums)[3]

Each of these styles could exist within the same person interchangeably. In the *DSM-II* (1968), the passive-aggressive type took only one form reflecting hidden hostility. Passive-dependent and aggressive styles were dropped.[4] Dr. Robert Spitzer, feeling that passive-aggression was a defense mechanism, was all for dropping it in the first draft of *DSM-III* (1980).[5] Others argued it was a pervasive, not merely situational behavior that could manifest in many settings. So, they included the diagnosis of Passive-aggressive Personality Disorder (PAPD), relabeling the passive-dependent type as *dependent personality*, and subsuming the former aggressive type under the *antisocial personality* description. After 1980, PAPD reflected an emotional tone, involving interpersonal conflict as well as resistance, which had always been a key feature.

When the *DSM-III-R* (revised edition) came out with fewer limits placed upon the diagnosis, what happened? Clinicians diagnosed more of their clients with PAPD because therapists truly saw these problematic behaviors on a routine basis.[6] Passive-aggressive individuals went through life vacillating, waffling between the polarities of dependence and independence, passivity and activity, and they tended to adopt a "down-in-the-dumps," negative outlook. In other words, they were the walking wounded.

In 1994, researchers added the word *negativistic* to the description, but with so many changes in definition and criteria, task force members feared that this new diagnostic category had not been sufficiently tested thereby questioned its reliability. In the absence of empirical data, the *DSM-IV* work group felt compelled to place it in the manual's appendix, relegating it to a host of disorders that needed further study. It became a provisional diagnosis with seven criteria to meet instead of nine in the *DSM-III-R*.[7]

■

PASSIVE-AGGRESSIVE PERSONALITY DISORDER (NEGATIVISTIC PERSONALITY DISORDER)

RESEARCH criteria for passive-aggressive personality disorder:

A. A pervasive pattern of negativistic attitudes and passive resistance to demands for adequate performance, beginning in early adulthood and present in a variety of contexts, as indicated by four (or more) of the following:

1. Passively resists fulfilling routing social and occupational tasks

2. Complains of being misunderstood and unappreciated by others
3. Is sullen and argumentative
4. Unreasonably criticizes and scorns authority
5. Expresses envy and resentment toward those apparently more fortunate
6. Voices exaggerated and persistent complaints of personal misfortune
7. Alternates between hostile defiance and contrition
8. Does not occur exclusively during Major Depressive Episodes and is not better accounted for by Dysthymic Disorder.

Source: *DSM-IV-TR* published by the American Psychiatric Association (2000)

VIEWING PASSIVE-AGGRESSION TODAY

CURRENTLY, CLINICIANS WHO see four or more of the seven traits (see the sidebar "Passive-Aggressive Personality Disorder") deeming them to be frequent, intense, and long-standing patterns that meet the criteria of a personality disorder can diagnose clients as Personality Disorder Not Otherwise Specified (PDNOS). Key passive-aggressive traits as of this writing include unpredictable moods, pessimistic outlook, irritability and hostile temperament (even nonverbally), surly demeanor (low frustration tolerance, high-strung, highly reactive), and a stubborn, fault-finding, and cynical nature.

Interpersonally, anger-concealing people display passive resistance when it comes to fulfilling routine requests—tasks we associate as "givens" in an occupational or social setting. Second, these individuals are unreasonably fault-finding and reject authority figures, shunning their directives, advice, and influence.

Negativistic people feel cheated. This is how the passive-aggressive person's mind works: "No one understands me. No one appreciates me, and by golly if someone else dares to do well in this world, I'm going to resent them and be jealous if they're more fortunate." Factor in feelthink as the passive-aggressive person reacts to "more fortunate." "More fortunate" is so subjective that the passive-aggressive person rejects, resents, and extracts revenge at times when others would not typically think or act this way at all.

What's more, the passive-aggressive/negativistic person may well undermine the enjoyment and goals of others, as Millon and Davis write.[8] There's also the pattern of contrition. After an angry outburst, it's not at all unusual for this person to feel guilty, try to placate others, or ask forgiveness—mollifying those she just put down, blocked, or tried to undermine. If these negativistic individuals attempt to do what others desire, they're quickly annoyed with themselves and shift swiftly to their own agenda.

In 1999, Scott Wetzler, a professor at Albert Einstein College of Medicine and a clinical psychologist at Montefiore Medical Center in the Bronx, and Leslie C. Morey, a psychology professor at Vanderbilt University, reviewed the evidence for dropping PAPD as a diagnostic label, noting that the removal of the diagnosis didn't reflect any true decline in those suffering from PAPD. What's more, they objected to the negativist terminology, stating:

"Not only do we believe that there is little gained by the term negativistic, but much has been lost by dropping the term passive-aggressive. Negativistic misses the fundamental internal conflict between aggression and self-assertion on the one hand, and fear and dependency on the other, whereas passive-aggressive beautifully captures this unique, apparently contradictory behavior and personality style."[9]

Lorna Smith Benjamin, PhD at the University of Utah has also written about personality disorders, and clinicians who wish to view her approach can order a video of *Interpersonal Reconstructive Therapy for Passive-Aggressive Personality Disorder* through the American Psychological Association.[10]

In *Interpersonal Diagnosis and Treatment of Personality Disorders (2nd Edition)*, Benjamin states that the "*DSM-IV*'s demolition of this disorder to the Appendix was a mistake" because she says that passive-aggression often complicates other disorders, including intractable depresssion.[11] Benjamin writes that passive-aggressive patterns demand targeted therapy because otherwise a therapist's interventions will prove useless. In practical terms, identifying passive-aggression is important because these clients are prone to cancel appointments, show up late, ignore payment, forget important forms, and even sue their providers, given the chance. The passive-aggressive patient agrees to comply with demands or suggestions, but later, fails to perform, even with the therapist.

Two other works to peruse are *Cognitive Therapy of Personality Disorders (2nd Edition)* by Aaron T. Beck, Arthur Freeman, and Denise D. Davis,[12] and *Passive-Aggressiveness: Theory and Practice* by Richard D. Parsons and Robert J. Wicks.[13] This last book is a collection of writings, including many theoretical approaches to passive-aggression.

TYPES OF PASSIVE-AGGRESSIVE/
ANGER-CONCEALING PEOPLE

SOME RESEARCHERS HAVE categorized types of passive-aggressive personalities. Millon and Davis describe four types of negativistic people.[14] Resistance typifies the *circuitous* subtype even unconsciously as people create problems and conflict but repress any awareness. Thus, they remain impervious to change. For the *abrasive* negativist, life is the constant discharge of one's own bitter struggles. This person is contentious, fault finding, and simply corrosive to be around. Telling people off is their right because they've been "victims."

The *discontented* soul isn't as "out there" in his or her verbal assaults, just more sly, masters of sugarcoated words or the not-so-subtle barb. When their camouflage is blown, you'll hear "you can't take a joke." This is true hidden anger. At work (or elsewhere), this manifests in critical observation because the discontented negativist feels she has worthwhile commentary, yet when it's received, you know there was no good intent at its core. This person might also rile you about others' faults when he or she has precisely the same personality attributes.

Lastly, Millon and Davis describe the *vacillating* subtype as experiencing sharp reversals of mood and behavior. They can be oppositional and disagreeable one minute followed almost immediately by self-confidence and decided cooperation. You'll commonly see adult temper tantrums as well as polarized behavior, shifting between the polarities of self (individuation) and other (nurturance), passive (accommodation) and active (modification), and pleasure (enhancement) and preservation (pain).

Martin Kantor, a psychiatrist, wrote *Passive-Aggression: A Guide for the Therapist, the Patient and the Victim* in 2002, offering six subtypes of his own.[15] *Paranoid* types blame to project their indirect host since they perceive themselves as victims. As Kantor writes, "I am angry with you" becomes "You are angry with me" and "I blame and dislike you for that."

With *narcissistic* types, entitlement drives their hostility toward others so that they matter above everything. Acting superior is less about boosting their lagging self-esteem, and much more to put and keep you in a place of their choosing. You'll see selfish behavior, lack of concern or empathy, and a lot of faulty thinking.

Kantor describes *depressive* and *hypomanic* passive-aggressive people under his *affective* umbrella. Depressed individuals disguise their anger with humor, sarcasm, barbs meant to demean or humiliate, whereas hypomanic passive-aggressives express their anger by "living well as the best revenge," in Kantor's words.

The *obsessive-compulsive* type sets out to deliberately annoy, always watching for your reaction to his passive-aggressive action or words. It wears you down, over time, through retaliation, foot-dragging, withholding, always having to be right, button pushing, tight purse strings, intentional accidents, and indecision (the knack of always keeping you guessing). The more they exhibit these behaviors, not surprisingly, you become more anxious.

Histrionics tease, demean, invalidate, envy, create competition where none exists, and when these tactics fail to work, they might turn on their theatrical bent with nonverbal behavior. Eyes roll in disbelief. An audible sigh says what words don't have to. A hostile headache Kantor points out halts sexual intimacy between a couple. All of these examples send negative, indirect messages.

Lastly, Kantor discusses the *sadomasochistic* type in his book, those who delight in the sadistic misery of others while spite drives the masochistic type. "Who cares if I suffer _____ fate, I'll show them" is the attitude you might see.

GENDER DIFFERENCES

SCOTT WETZLER ALSO wrote *Living With the Passive-Aggressive Man* in the early 1990s, claiming that passive-aggressive behavior was the number one source of men's problems in relationships and at work. [16]

Why did he focus upon men exclusively? "I don't think it strikes men more than women, but it's that men are clumsier about their passive-aggression," Wetzler told us. "They call attention to it, and it can be more irksome to those around him." Wetzler suggests that given gender-role expectations, some men may feel less comfortable when they doubt their own ability to lead, be assertive, and exercise power.

The American Psychological Association discussed gender differences and anger expression in the March 2003 of its publication *The Monitor.* Ongoing research shows that men and women are socialized differently and do indeed handle anger in vastly different ways. This report cited the work of Raymond DiGiuseppe, PhD at St. John's University in New York, where he was developing a new anger-disorder scale. Men and women both showed anger. The key difference was in expression. Whereas openly acting upon one's anger is more acceptable or expected for men, it's often seen as unpleasant behavior for women.[17]

IN CONCLUSION

SCOTT WETZLER ADHERES to the original "passive-aggressive" phrase. "I think passive-aggressive is the most descriptive term, much preferable to negativistic (linked to depressive temperament and irritability) or the more general concept of ambivalence," Wetzler told us. "It captures the inherent conflict and complexity, and most importantly, it identifies the behavior as a form of hostility, which is not obvious since it is disowned." In a nutshell, the term is "wonderfully descriptive," Wetzler says. "Not many terms make such a crossover, but when they do, it's because they resonate with the public."

Both Wetzler and Morey, in their research paper, stated their hope that the next *DSM-V* work group would carefully consider restoring passive-aggression as a personality disorder in its own right.[18] For many of these reasons, and because the term passive-aggression has been tossed around but rarely understood, we chose to use it while adhering to our own beliefs that there are other types of problematic hidden anger as well.

Notes

[1] U.S. War Department. (1945, October) *Nomenclature and Method of Recording Diagnoses.* War Department Technical Bulletin.

[2] American Psychiatric Association. (2000) *Diagnostic and Statistical Manual of Mental Disorders (text revision).* Washington, D.C.

[3] American Psychiatric Association. (1952) *Diagnostic and Statistical Manual of Mental Disorders (first edition).* Washington, D.C.

[4] American Psychiatric Association. (1968) *Diagnostic and Statistical Manual of Mental Disorders (second edition).* Washington, D.C.

[5] Wetzler, S. & Morey, L. C. (1999) "Passive-aggressive personality disorder: The demise of a syndrome." *Psychiatry,* 68, 49–59.

[6] American Psychiatric Association. (1987) *Diagnostic and Statistical Manual of Mental Disorders (third edition, revised).* Washington, D.C.

[7] Wetzler, S. & Morey, L. C. (1999) "Passive-aggressive personality disorder: The demise of a syndrome." *Psychiatry,* 68, 49–59.

[8] Millon, M. & Davis, R. D. (1996) *Disorders of Personality DSM-IV and Beyond (second edition).* New York: John Wiley & Sons.

[9] Wetzler, S. & Morey, L. C. (1999) "Passive-aggressive personality disorder: The demise of a syndrome." *Psychiatry,* 68, 49–59.

[10] American Psychological Association. (1999) *Interpersonal Reconstructive Therapy for Passive-Aggressive Personality Disorder with Lorna Smith Benjamin, Ph.D.* [Video] Washington, D.C.: American Psychological Association. Video Tape Series II.

[11] Benjamin, L. S. (1996). *Interpersonal Diagnosis and Treatment of Personality Disorders (second edition).* New York: The Guilford Press.

[12] Beck, A. T., et al. (2004) *Cognitive Therapy of Personality Disorders (second edition).* New York: The Guilford Press.

[13] Wicks, R. J. & Parsons, R. D. (1983) *Passive-Aggressiveness: Theory and practice.* New York: Brunner/Mazel.

[14] Millon, M. & Davis, R. D. (1996) *Disorders of Personality DSM-IV and Beyond (second edition).* New York: John Wiley & Sons.

[15] Kantor, M. (2002) *Passive-Aggression: A guide for the Therapist, the Patient, and the Victim.* Westport, Conn.: Praeger.

[16] Wetzler, S. (1992) *Living with the Passive Aggressive Man.* New York: Simon & Schuster.

[17] Holloway, J. D. (2003) "Researchers and practitioners are examining what works best for managing problem anger." *Monitor on Psychology,* 34: 3, 54.

[18] Wetzler, S. & Morey, L. C. (1999) "Passive-aggressive personality disorder: The demise of a syndrome." *Psychiatry,* 68, 49–59.

CHAPTER NOTES
AND ADDITIONAL RESOURCES

CHAPTER 1

[1] Harburg, E., et al. (2003) "Expressive/suppressive anger-coping responses, gender, and types of mortality: A 17-year follow-up." *Psychosomatic Medicine,* 65(4), 588–597.

[2] Murphy, T. F. & Oberlin, L. H. (2001) *The Angry Child: Regaining Control When Your Child Is Out of Control.* New York: Three Rivers Press.

CHAPTER 2

[1] Freeman, L. L. (2004, January/February) "Vital stats." *Health,* p. 192.

[2] Oberlin, L. H. (2005) *Surviving Separation and Divorce: A Woman's Guide to Regaining Control, Building Strength and Confidence, and Securing a Financial future.* Boston, Mass.: Adams Media.

[3] Tyre, P., Scelfo, J., and Kantrowitz, B. (2004, September 13) "The power of no." *Newsweek,* pp. 42–51.

[4] Gutfeld, G. (1998, October) Stop the madness! *"Men's Health,"* p. 118.

[5] Suarez, E. C. (2004, September) "C-reactive protein is associated with psychological risk factors of cardiovascular disease in apparently healthy adults." *Psychosomatic Medicine,* 684–691.

[6] Williams, J. E., et al. (2000) "Anger proneness predicts coronary heart disease risk." *Circulation,* 101, 2034–2039.

[7] Todaro, J. F., et al. (2003) "Effect of negative emotions on frequency of coronary heart disease." *The American Journal of Cardiology,* 92, 901–906.

[8] Browder, S. E. (2000) *The Power: 11 Ways Women Gain Unhealthy Weight and How You Can Take Charge of Them.* New York: John Wiley & Sons.

[9] Raikkonen, K., Matthews, K. A., & Kuller, L. H. (2001) "Trajectory of psychological risk and incident hypertension in middle-aged women." *Hypertension,* 38, 798–802.

[10] Williams, R. B., et al. (2001) "Central nervous system serotonin function and cardiovascular responses to stress." *Psychosomatic Medicine,* 63, 300–305.

[11] Lykken, D. & Tellegen, A. (1996) "Happiness is a stochastic phenomenon." *Psychological Science,* 7(3), 186–189.

[12] Bushman, B. J., et al. (1999) "Catharsis, aggression, and persuasive influence: Self-fulfilling or self-defeating prophecies?" *Journal of Personality and Social Psychology,* 76(3), 367–376.

[13] Merchant, A. T., et al. (2003) "A prospective study of social support, anger expression and risk of periodontitis in men." *Journal of the America Dental Association,* 134, 1591–1596.

[14] Wallis, C. (2005, January 17) "The new science of happiness." *Time,* A3–A9.

[15] Seligman, M.E. (2004) *Authentic Happiness: Using the New Positive Psychology to Realize Your Potential for Lasting Fulfillment.* New York: Free Press.

[16] Epel, E.S., et al. (2004) "Accelerated telomere shortening in response to life stress." *Proceedings of the National Academy of Sciences of the United States of America,* 101(50), 17323–17324.

[17] Schaubroech, J., et al. (2001) Individual differences in utilizing control to cope with job demands: Effects on susceptibility to infectious diseases. *Journal of Applied Psychology,* 86(2), 265–278.

[18] Cohen, S., Miller, G. E., & Rabin, B. S. (2001) "Psychological stress and antibody response to immunization: A critical review of the human literature." *Psychosomatic Medicine,* 63, 7–18.

[18] Song, S. (2004, July 19). "The price of pressure." *Time,* pp. 68–69.

Recommended Reading

Williams, R. & Williams, V. (1993). *Anger Kills: 17 Strategies for Controlling the Hostility That Can Harm Your Health.* New York: Harper Collins.

Williams, R. & Williams, V. (1997). *Lifeskills: 8 Simple Ways to Build Strong Relationships, Communicate More Clearly, and Improve Your Health.* New York: Three Rivers Press.

CHAPTER 3

[1] Murphy, T. F. & Oberlin, L. H. (2001) *The Angry Child: Regaining Control When Your Child Is Out of Control.* New York: Three Rivers Press.

[2] Vaillant, G. E. (1994) "Ego mechanisms of defense and personality psychopathology." *Journal of Abnormal Psychology,* 103, 44–50.

[3] Wetzler, S. (1992) *Living with the Passive Aggressive Man.* New York: Simon & Schuster.

[4] Rogers, F. M. (1967) Lyrics to the song "Everybody's Fancy," found in *Mister Rogers Talks With Parents.* Pittsburgh, Penn.: Family Communications, Inc.

[5] Long, N. J. & Long, J. E. (2001) *Managing Passive-Aggressive Behavior of Children and Youth at School and Home: The Angry Smile.* Austin, Tex.: Pro-Ed, Inc.

[6] Kubler-Ross, E. (1997) *On Death and Dying.* New York: Scribner Classics.

[7] Silver, L. B. (1984) *The Misunderstood Child: Understanding and Coping with Your Child's Learning Disabilities.* New York: Three Rivers Press.

[8] Main, M. & Cassidy, J. (1988) "Categories of response to reunion with the parent at age 6: Predictable from infant attachment classifications and stable over a one-month period." *Developmental Psychology,* 24(3),415–426.

[9] Millon, M. & Davis, R. D. (1996) *Disorders of Personality DSM-IV and Beyond (second edition).* New York: John Wiley & Sons.

[10] Millon, M. & Davis, R. D. (1996) *Disorders of Personality DSM-IV and Beyond (second edition).* New York: John Wiley & Sons.

[11] Rogers, F. M. (2000) "A point of view: Family communication, television, and Mister Rogers' Neighborhood." *The Journal of Family Communication,* 1(1), 71–73.

[12] Family Communications, Inc. offers a variety of anger-management resources for children (preschool through elementary age), including video materials in the Child Care Video Library series, books for children regarding domestic violence, as well as the Mad Feelings Workshop and Challenging Behaviors Training Kit for childcare providers and teachers,

www.fci.org.
13 Millon, M. & Davis, R. D. (1996) *Disorders of Personality DSM-IV and Beyond (second edition).* New York: John Wiley & Sons.

CHAPTER 4

1 Benton, S. A., et al. (2003) "Changes in counseling center client problems across 13 years." *Professional Psychology: Research and Practice,* 34(1), 66–72.
2 Ruderman, M.N., et al. (2002). "Benefits of Multiple Roles for Managerial Women." *Academy of Management Journal,* 45(2), 369-386.
3 American Counseling Association (2004, July). "In brief." *Counseling Today,* 35.
4 Mannix, M. & Smart, T. (Eds.). (2004, December 6) Stress relief. *U.S. News & World Report,* EE1–EE6.
5 Mannix, M. & Smart, T. (Eds.). (2004, December 6) Stress relief. *U.S. News & World Report,* EE1–EE6.
6 Rost, K. (2004) "Medical Care." *The Health Behavior News Service,* 42, 1202–1210.
7 National Institute for Occupational Safety and Health. *Stress . . . At Work.* [Brochure]. Department of Health & Human Services (NIOSH) Publication No. 99-101.
8 Leibovich, M. (2002, August 17) "Capital offenses: Snubbery in the first degree." *The Washington Post,* C1, C4.
9 Fox, S. & Spector, P. E. (Eds.). (2004) *Counterproductive Work Behavior: Investigations of Actors and Targets.* Washington, D.C.: American Psychological Association.
10 Wetzler, S. & Morey, L. C. (1999) "Passive-aggressive personality disorder: The demise of a syndrome." *Psychiatry,* 68, 49–59.
11 Brown, N. W. (2002) *Working with the Self-Absorbed: How to Handle Narcissistic Personalities on the Job.* Oakland, Calif.: New Harbinger.
12 McIlduff, E. & Coghlan, D. (2000) "Understanding and contending with passive-aggressive behaviour in teams and organizations." *Journal of Managerial Psychology,* 15(7), 716–736.
13 Cavaiola, A. A. & Lavender, N. J. (2000) *Toxic Coworkers: How to Deal with Dysfunctional People on the Job.* Oakland, Calif.: New Harbinger.
14 Cavaiola, A. A. & Lavender, N. J. (2000) *Toxic Coworkers: How to Deal with Dysfunctional People on the Job.* Oakland, Calif.: New Harbinger.

CHAPTER 5

1 Waite, L. J. & Gallagher, M. (2000) *The Case for Marriage: Why Married People Are Happier, Healthier, and Better Off Financially.* New York: Doubleday.
2 Combs, R. (1991). Marital status and personal well-being: A literature review. *Family Relations* 40, 97–102.
2 Kiecolt-Glaser, J. K. & Newton, T. L. (2001). "Marriage and health: His and hers." *Psychological Bulletin,* 127(4), 472–503.
3 Bookwala, J. (2005) "The role of marital quality in physical health during the mature years." *Journal of Aging and Health,* 17(1), 85–104.
4 www.smartmarriages.com
5 Vaillant, G. E. (1994) "Ego mechanisms of defense and personality psychopathology." *Journal of Abnormal Psychology,* 103(1), 44–50.
6 Hendrix, H. (1988) *Getting the Love You Want: A Guide for Couples.* New York: Henry Holt & Co.

[7] Gottman, J. M. & Silver, N. (2000) "The seven principles for making marriage work: A practical guide from the country's foremost relationship expert." New York: Three Rivers Press.

[8] Gottman, J. M. & Krokoff, L. J. (1989) "Marital interaction and satisfaction: A longitudinal view." *Journal of Consulting and Clinical Psychology,* 57(1), 47–52.

[9] Epstein, N., et al. (1996) "Assessing relationship standards: The inventory of specific relationship standards." *Journal of Family Psychology,* 10 (1), 72–88.

[10] Wetzler, S. & Morey, L.C. (1999) "Passive-aggressive personality disorder: The demise of a syndrome." *Psychiatry,* 68, 49–59.

[11] Millon, T. (1981) *Disorders of Personality DSM-III: Axis II.* New York: John Wiley & Sons.

[12] Diamond, J. (2004) *The irritable male syndrome: Managing the 4 key causes of depression and aggression.* Emmaus, Penn.: Rodale.

[13] Reichman, N., Corman, H., & Noonan, K. (2004) "Effects of child health on parents' relationship status." *Demography,* 41(3), 569–584.

[14] Whisman, M. A., et al. (2004) "Psychopathology and marital satisfaction: The importance of evaluating both partners." *Journal of Consulting & Clinical Psychology,* 72(5), 830–838.

[15] Glass, S. P. (2003) *Not "Just Friends": Rebuilding Trust and Recovering Your Sanity After Infidelity.* New York, Free Press.

[16] Wetzler, S. (1992). *Living with the Passive Aggressive Man.* New York: Simon & Schuster.

Recommended Reading

Doherty, W. J. (2003) *Take back your marriage: sticking together in a world that pulls us apart.* New York: Guildford Press.

National Fatherhood Initiative. *The 7 Benefits of Marriage for Men.* [Brochure]. National Fatherhood Initiative, www.fatherhood.org.

CHAPTER 6

[1] Doherty, W. J. & Carlson, B. Z. (2002) *Putting Family First: Successful Strategies for Reclaiming Family Life in a Hurry-Up World.* New York: Owl Books.

[2] Maddox, W. R, (2004, January 4) "A diet on activities." *USA Today.*

[3] Gillman, M. W. (2000) "Family dinner and diet quality among older children and adolescents." *Archives of Family Medicine,* 9, 235–240.

[4] Rogers, F. M. (1967) Lyrics to the song "I Like to Be Told," found in *Mister Rogers Talks With Parents.* Pittsburgh, Penn.: Family Communications, Inc.

[5] Pressman, S. D. & Pressman, R.M. (1994) *The Narcissistic Family:Diagnosis and Treatment.* New York: Jossey-Bass.

[6] LeBey, B. (2001) *Family Estrangements: How They Begin, How to Mend Them, and How to Cope with Them.* Atlanta, Ga.: Longstreet Press.

[7] Millon, M. & Davis, R. D. (1996) *Disorders of Personality DSM-IV and Beyond (second edition).* New York: John Wiley & Sons.

[8] Pietsch, W. J. (1992) *The Serenity Prayer Book.* San Francisco, Calif.: Harper.

Recommended Reading

Murphy, T. F. & Oberlin, L. H. (2001) *The Angry Child: Regaining Control When Your Child Is Out of Control.* New York: Three Rivers Press.

McGraw, P. C. (2004) *Family First: Your Step-by-Step Plan for Creating a Phenomenal Family.* New York: Free Press.

Brown, N. W. (2001) *Children of the Self-Absorbed: A Grown-Up's Guide to Getting Over Narcissistic Parents.* Oakland, Calif.: New Harbinger.

Roth, K. & Friedman, F. B. (2003) *Surviving the Borderline Parent: How to Heal Your Childhood Wounds & Build Trust, Boundaries, and Self-Esteem.* Oakland, Calif.: New Harbinger.

CHAPTER 7

[1] Paul, M. (2004) *The Friendship Crisis: Finding, Making, and Keeping Friends When You're Not a Kid Anymore.* Emmaus, Penn.: Rodale.

[2] Aaronson, L. (June, 2005) 'Guess who misses signs of anger?' *Psychology Today,* 33.

[3] Sternglanz, R. W. & Depaulo, B. M. (Winter, 2004) "Reading nonverbal cues to emotions: The advantages and liabilities of relationship closeness." *Journal of Nonverbal Behavior,* 28(4), 245–267.

[4] Yager, J. (2002) *When Friendship Hurts: How to Deal with Friends Who Betray, Abandon or Wound you.* New York: Simon & Schuster.

[5] Levine, M. (2002) *A Mind at a Time.* New York: Simon & Schuster.

[6]Nelson, D., Robinson, C. C., & Hart, C. H. (2005) "Relational and physical aggression of preschool-age children: Peer status linkages across multiple informants." *Early Education and Development,* 16(2), 115–139.

[7] Millon, M. & Davis, R. D. (1996) *Disorders of Personality DSM-IV and Beyond (second edition).* New York: John Wiley & Sons.

[8] Seligman, M. E. (1996) *The Optimistic Child: Proven Program to Safeguard Children from Depression and Build Lifelong Resilience.* New York: Harper Perennial.

[9] Shaw, B. A., et al. (2004) "Emotional support from parents early in life, aging, and health." *Psychology & Aging,* 19(1), 4–12.

[10] Oberlin, L. H. (2005) *Surviving Separation and Divorce: A Woman's Guide to Regaining Control, Building Strength and Confidence, and Securing a Financial Future.* Boston, Mass.: Adams Media.

[11] Kelly, J. B. & Emery, R. E. (2003) 'Children's adjustment following divorce: risk and resilience perspectives." *Family Relations,* 52(4), 352–362.

[12] Oberlin, L. H. (2005) *Surviving Separation and Divorce: A Woman's Guide to Regaining Control, Building Strength and Confidence, and Securing a Financial Future.* Boston, Mass.: Adams Media.

Recommended Reading

Elman, N. M. & Kennedy-Moore, E. (2003) *The Unwritten Rules of Friendship: Simple Strategies to Help Your Child Make Friends.* New York: Little Brown.

Baris, M. A., et al. (2001) *Working with High-Conflict Families of Divorce: A Guide for Professionals.* Northvale, N.J.: Jason Aronson, Inc.

CHAPTER 8

[1] Stewart, W. F., et al. (2003) "Cost of lost productive work time among U.S. workers with depression." *Journal of the American Medical Association,* 289(23), 3135–3144.

[2] Whisman, M. A., et al. (2004). "Psychopathology and marital satisfaction: The importance of evaluating both partners." *Journal of Consulting & Clinical Psychology,* 72(5), 830–838.

[3] Real Men, Real Depression website, the National Institute of Mental Health, http://menanddepression.nimh.nih.gov.

[4] Millon, T., et al. (2004) *Personality Disorders in Modern Life (second edition)*. New York: John Wiley & Sons.

[5] National Organization for Seasonal Affective Disorder, www.nosad.org.

[6] Jamison, K. R. (1995) *An Unquiet Mind*. New York: Alfred A. Knopf.

[7] Castle, L. R. . (2003) *Bipolar Disorder Demystified: Mastering the Tightrope of Manic Depression*. New York: Marlowe & Co.

[8] Real, T. (1998) *I Don't Want to Talk About It: Overcoming the Secret Legacy of Male Depression*. New York: Scribner.

[9] Bloch, A. L., et al. (1993) "An empirical study of defense mechanisms in dysthymia." *American Journal of Psychiatry*, 150, 1194–1198.

[10] Millon, M. & Davis, R. D. (1996) *Disorders of Personality DSM-IV and Beyond (second edition)*. New York: John Wiley & Sons.

[11] Thase, M. E. & Lang, S. S. (2004) *Beating the Blues: New Approaches to Overcoming Dysthymia and Chronic Mild Depression*. New York: Oxford University Press.

[12] Dunn, A. L., et al. (2005) "Exercise treatment for depression: Efficacy and dose response." *American Journal of Preventive Medicine*, 28(1), 1–8.

[13] Kluger, J. (2005, May 16) "The cruelest cut." *Time*, 48–50.

[14] Conterio, K., Lader, W., & Bloom, J. K. (1998) *Bodily Harm: The Breakthrough Healing Program for Self-Injurers*. New York: Hyperion.

[15] Barkley, R. A. (1997). *ADHD and the Nature of Self-Control*. New York: The Guilford Press.

[16] Children and Adults with Attention Deficit Hyperactivity Disorder (CHADD), www.chadd.org, 8181 Professional Place, Suite 150, Landover, MD 20785; (National Resource Center on ADHD, 1-800-233-4050).

[17] Hallowell, E. M. & Ratey, J. J. (2005) *Delivered from Distraction: Getting the Most Out of Life with Attention Deficit Disorder*. New York: Ballantine Books.

Recommended Reading

Kadison, R. & DiGeronimo, T. F. (2004) *College of the Overwhelmed: The Campus Mental Health Crisis and What to Do About It*. New York: Jossey-Bass.

Kreisman, J. J. & Straus, H. (2004) *Sometimes I Act Crazy: Living with Borderline Personality Disorder*. New York: John Wiley & Sons.

Kreisman, J. J. & Straus, H. (1989) *I Hate You, Don't Leave Me: Understanding the Borderline Personality*. New York: Avon Books.

Friedel, R. O. (2004) *An Essential Guide for Understanding and Living with Borderline Personality Disorder*. New York: Marlowe & Co.

Mason, P. T. & Kreger, R. (1998) *Stop Walking on Eggshells: Taking Your Life Back When Someone You Care About Has Borderline Personality Disorder*. Oakland, Calif: New Harbinger.

CHAPTER 9

[1] Brown, N. W. (2002) *Whose Life Is It Anyway: When to Stop Taking Care of Their Feelings & Start Taking Care of Your Own*. Oakland, Calif.: New Harbinger.

[2] Kantor, M. (2002) *Passive-Aggression: A Guide for the Therapist, the Patient, and the Victim*. Westport, Conn.: Praeger.

[3] Haltzman, S. & DiGeronimo, T. F. (2005) *The Secrets of Happily Married Men: 8 Ways to Win Your Wife's Heart Forever*. New York: Jossey-Bass.

[4] Long, N. J. & Long, J. E. (2001) *Managing Passive-Aggressive Behavior of Children and Youth at School and Home: The Angry Smile*. Austin, Tex.: Pro-Ed, Inc.

Recommended Reading

Brown, N. W. (2003) *Loving the Self-Absorbed: How to Create a More Satisfying Relationship with a Narcissistic partner.* Oakland, Calif.: New Harbinger.

Levine, M. (2003). *The Myth of Laziness.* New York: Simon & Schuster.

CHAPTER 10

[1] Feelings Posters are available from Creative Therapy Associates, www.ctherapy.com. 1-800-448-9145.

[2] McKay, M. & Fannin,G.P. (2002) *Successful Problem Solving: A Workbook to Overcome the Four Core Beliefs That Keep You Stuck.* Oakland, Calif.: New Harbinger.

[3] Peterson, C. & Seligman, M. E. (2004) *Character strengths and virtues: A handbook and classification.* New York: Oxford University Press.

[4] Prochaska, J. O., et al. (1995) *Changing for Good.* New York: Harper Collins/Quill.

[5] Hanna, F. J. (2002) *Therapy with Difficult Clients: Using the Precursors Model to Awaken Change.* Washington, D.C.: American Psychological Associations.

[6] Srivastava, S. & John, O. P., et al. (2003) "Development of personality in early and middle adulthood: Set like plaster or persistent change?" *Journal of Personality and Social Psychology,* 84(5), 1041–1053.

Recommended Reading

Ellis, A. & Tafrate, R. C. (1997) *How to Control Your Anger Before It Controls You.* Seacaucus, N.J.: Carol Publishing Group.

ACKNOWLEDGMENTS

S O MUCH EXPERIENCE and so many people have helped to develop this topic into what you're now reading. First, I'm grateful for the career experiences I've had, first as a psychologist and now as a legislator. In both roles, I meet people who are unhappy, but each job has been inherently different.

In graduate school, I trained to help people stop conflicts that led to problems, and later, people came to my practice so that I could help them stop their own bitterness. In politics, conflict innately exists, and to some, if you don't fight, it's seen as a sign of weakness. I thought I knew a lot about anger as a practicing psychologist, but I've learned more in these past few years in Congress, and working on this project has coincided with many of those lessons. Anger is everywhere in life, but in Washington, we sometimes delude ourselves into thinking that if we're angry, we must be right. We confuse passion with productivity, arguments with action, and rancor with results.

When I see anger used for the sake of wielding more power, it gets to me. I've gained a real distaste for nastiness, planned meanness, selected mistruths, and plotted misrepresentations so often set forth to derail a person or wear him or her down. That type of anger only spawns more anger, in other public servants, and within the American people. Ultimately, it will always backfire as it leads directly to universal mistrust. We don't need it. The good news is there are more good and honorable people than there are those who try to undermine with anger. I'm also glad we've written a book about stopping such anger.

Several people have worked diligently to develop the book you're reading. Our agent Kristen Auclair and our editor Sue McCloskey believed, also, that there was too much hidden anger and entrusted us to raise awareness.

My coauthor Loriann Hoff Oberlin has put many hours into this manuscript. Without her drafts and rewrites, this would never have become the book it is. While most authors research their topics, Loriann has gone a step beyond, investing even more energy and resources into the study of mental health in graduate school. I admire her enthusiasm for her work and appreciate her deliberate attempts to keep after me when I fell off task with my other duties.

Those duties do consume much of my time, and the fact is we all face stress that can be overwhelming at times. The key is to surround yourself with good people. In particular, my congressional chief of staff, Susan Mosychuk, and my colleagues in the House of Representatives have been there to help me over the bumps. There are too many to thank, but I'd like to mention Jo Bonner, J. Gresham Barret, Eric Cantor, and Mario Diaz-Balart. My heartfelt thanks to them.

My family deserves more appreciation than I can express on this page. To my wife Nan and daughter Bevin, who both have endured my absences, hectic schedule when in town, and the distractions of my work, they have my thanks for putting up with me. I couldn't do all of this without them, and by their presence, they remind me to recommit to core values, goals, and direction, almost daily. Finally, I am very grateful to my parents, who on a meager income managed to raise eleven of us, who all turned out to be successful. They taught the most valuable lessons of all!

—DR. TIM MURPHY

THIS IS THE book I've always wanted to write. Having started out as a completely different project for adults, I think we settled on an area that affects just about everyone, in almost every facet of life. There are many people responsible for shaping this project into what it's become, especially my coauthor Tim Murphy, who, given the demands of his schedule and congressional work, agreed that it would be an appropriate follow-up book to our first collaboration. Tim's concepts about anger and cognitive and behavioral processes, and feedback on the manuscript have once again taught me a great deal. Our careers may be in different places, but I'm grateful for the chance to learn from his years of experience.

Developing this has not been an easy process, and there have been amusing twists in how our individual writing styles have changed since we first met. Thanks, Tim, for pointing out that my immersion in too many textbooks had to go! I remember writing those margin notes to him (though I couldn't doodle nearly as well!) so many years ago. Turnabout is fair play, and we've managed to keep a sense of humor as we reviewed and revised this text.

Special thanks to Kristen Auclair, our agent, who believed in us and in the topic, and whose work at helping us to shape our proposal went beyond what we'd both expected. Sue McCloskey, our editor at Marlowe, acquired this book, added helpful insights, and moved it along so that it could reach the reading public in a timely fashion. Jeri Freedman offered much help in the shaping of this text, and the publicity staff deserves credit as well.

Many others were kind enough to lend their thoughts and assistance. Robert J. Wicks, PsyD at Loyola College in Maryland graciously loaned me his own copy of the book he co-wrote on this topic so that I could get a proper historical perspective of it. Scott Wetzler, PhD, who has also written about passive-aggression, provided additional insights to us. Our thanks to these people and to the many other authors extending their expertise and opinion.

My good friend Jodi Wood provided feedback and encouragement along the way, and certainly my professors at Johns Hopkins University have added immeasurably to my knowledge as I pursued my master's degree while writing this manuscript. I don't think I could have undertaken such a project without continuing my education in this field. To the librarians on campus, my thanks for pointing me in the right direction for databases and resources, and also to my classmates who offered thoughts pre-testing some quizzes. Finally, my husband Bob and sons Andy and Alex, who experience the ups and downs of the writing life along with me have my love and appreciation, always.

— LORIANN HOFF OBERLIN

INDEX

abrasive negativism, 214–216

academic achievement, 35–36

academic environment, 62

Academy of Management Journal, 63

accountability, 6, 116, 169, 184

action stage of change, 206

addiction, 105

ADHD and the Nature of Self-Control (Barkley), 155

ADHD (attention deficit hyperactivity disorder), 93–94, 96, 151–152, 154–159

adjustment disorder, 146

adolescents. *See also* children: in academic setting, 62; anger as natural in, 15, 51–52; household chores and, 107–108; overbearing parents of, 36, 50; substitute for absent spouse, 105–106; unmotivated student, 9; watching for red flags, 111–112

affective people, 216

aftermath stage of anger, 45

Ainsworth, Mary, 52

American Journal of Cardiology, 31

American Journal of Psychiatry, 151

American Psychiatric Association, 212–213

American Psychological Association, 63–64, 84, 217

anger: aggressive versus hidden, 4–5, 4–7; anticipated and appropriate, 14–15; detrimental health effects of, 25–26, 28–29; as habitual response, 37–38; inappropriate, 120–122, 144–152; learning and growing from, 39–40; overcoming, 201–205; overview, 3–4, 201; pervasiveness of, 3–4;

productive, 15–16; therapy for, 201–205; unmasking the, 18–20

anger script, rewriting your: acknowledging feelings, 188; assertiveness and, 187–188, 192–193, 199–200; childlike behavior and, 196–197; depression, 198–199; open expression and, 188–190; positive versus negative mental energy, 191–192, 193; problem-solving steps, 190–191; self absorption and, 197–198

anger types, 67–72, 75–81

The Angry Child (Murphy and Oberlin), xvi, 44, 104, 129

angry mind, thought process of, 29–31, 46

angry people: characteristics of, 45–48; happy people compared to, 38–39; inability to change, 37–38, 48–50; nature of, 37, 47–48; as noncompliant patients, 34–35, 75; transforming an angry childhood, 54–56; as undifferentiated, 87; watching for red flags, 112

angst and anxiety, 26–28

anorexia nervosa, 152–153

antidepressant medication, 149, 152

An Unquiet Mind (Jamison), 149–150

anxiety and angst, 26–28

assertive self-help strategies, 192–193

assertive thinking and phrasing, 100, 199–200

assessment, professional, 145

assessment, self-, 16–18, 60–62, 65, 191–192

attachment, hidden anger as search for, 52

attention deficit hyperactivity disorder (ADHD), 93–94, 96, 151–152, 154–159

authoritarianism, 189
avenger personality type, 68–69

backstabber personality type, 67–68
bag the benefit thinking, 207
Barkley, Russell, 155
Baucom, Donald H., 91
Beating the Blues (Thase), 151–152
Benjamin, Lorna Smith, 215
bipolar disorder, 149–150
Bipolar Disorder Demystified (Castle), 150
black-and-white thinking, 207
blamer personality type, 10, 46, 75–76
boa constrictor metaphor, xvi
Bodily Harm (Conterio and Lader), 154
book recommendation lists, 215, 222, 224,
    225, 226–227
Bookwala, Jamie, 84
boundaries: healthy adult narcissism and, 78;
    lack of, 27; as response to manipulation,
    179; and self-absorbed people, 80,
    115–116, 197; setting and honoring, 90
Bowen, Murray, 87
Browder, Sue Ellen, 31
Brown, Nina, 78–79, 166
buildup stage of anger, 44
bulimia, 153
Bushman, Brad J., 33
buttons. *See also* triggers: button-pushees, 37,
    174, 179; button-pushers, 79, 89; children
    as, 136–137; children as button pushers,
    45–46; holiday hot buttons, 123; manipu-
    lators and, 22–23, 167, 168; obsessive-
    compulsive type, 217; from original family,
    87; over reactive button pushing, 107–108;
    reprogramming, 121, 132

caretaker enablers, 166–167
The Case for Marriage (Waite and Gallagher), 84
Cassidy, Jude, 52
Castle, Lana R., 150
Cavaiola, Alan A., 80
CHADD (Children and Adults with Attention
    Deficit Hyperactivity Disorder), 159
change. *See also* anger script, rewriting your:
    anger versus, 37–38, 48–50, 52–53; ele-
    ments of, 206; fixing faulty thinking, 207;
    motivating, 108–109; realistic hope for,
    19–20, 205

Changing for Good (Prochaska), 206
childhood, 41–42, 43–45, 48–56
childlike behavior, 55, 72, 179–180, 183,
    196–197
children. *See also* adolescents: characteristics of
    angry, 45–48; chronic depression in, 52;
    and divorce, 135–139, 195, 197–198;
    encouraging open expression of feelings,
    188–190; friendship development tips,
    128–131; making time for, 106–107;
    manipulative, 36, 48, 182–185;
    overindulging, 27–28, 109–111; parenting
    parents, 113–116; watching for red flags,
    111
choosing your reactions, 173–181
chronic depression, 150–152
circuitous people, 216
Circulation (AHA journal), 31
classroom manipulation, 183–185
cognitive-behavioral therapy, 159–160
communication: congruence in, 18; listening,
    27, 66–67, 171; ratio of positive to nega-
    tive, 89, 170, 182; social skills and, 54;
    with teenagers, 111–112
compassion, 76, 184
conflict, dealing with, 91–99, 100–101,
    172–173
conflict, irrational beliefs about, 91
conflict avoidance behavior, 195
congruence, 18, 19, 189
contemplation stage of change, 206
Conterio, Karen, 154
control, 20–21, 173, 178, 189, 193–194
controller personality type, 69
coping strategies, 48, 52–53. *See also* anger
    script, rewriting your
Counterproductive Work Behavior (Fox and
    Spector), 68
couples: childhood anger and, 41–42, 55–56;
    childlike behavior in, 55, 72; debut of hid-
    den anger, 86; emotional distance, 91–93,
    99; family crises, 95–97; financial stress,
    93–94; finding love and support, 87–88;
    healing the relationship, 89–91, 100–101;
    infidelity, 97–98; irritability in, 94–95;
    miscellaneous escapes, 98–99; overview,
    83–86; test for problems, 88–89
covert coalitions, 118–119
C-reactive protein, 30

criticism, dealing with, 170–172
cultural conditioning, 32–33, 53–54
cyclothmic disorder, 150
cynic personality type, 70–71

Davis, Roger D., 52–53, 93, 216
depression: blaming and, 75; in children, 52; overcoming, 198–199; overview, 144–152, 215, 216–217; physical health and, 64; reacting to, 181; self-inflicted nature of, 33; workplace costs of, 63
destructive self-talk, 47
developmental stages, anger as part of, 51–52
Diagnostic and Statistical Manual of Mental Disorders, 212
Diamond, Jed, 94–95
DiGiuseppe, Raymond, 217
dirty lens thinking, 207
disappointment, coping with, 72–74
discontented people, 216
displaced resentment, 53
divorce, 130–136, 137–139
Doherty, William, 106
Donaldson-Pressman, Stephanie, 114
Driscoll, Richard, 69
dysthymic disorder, 150–152

eating disorders, 31–32, 99, 152–153
Eeyore personality type, 46, 71–74
elderly, watching for red flags in, 112
emotional distance, 91–93, 99
emotional vocabulary, 187–188
emotions, 25–28, 87, 97, 121–122. *See also* feelings
enabling, 163–170
Epel, Elissa, 34
Epstein, Norman, 91
excuses for bad behavior, 32–33
exercise and anger, 33
expectations, 73, 74, 85–86
explosion stage of anger, 44–45
extended families, 116–124

families. *See also* adolescents; children; couples: choosing your reactions, 173–181; crises in, 95–97; extended families, 116–124; influence of, 87, 121–122; overview, 102–103; preventing indirect anger, 111–112; triangulation in, 79, 118–119; troubled families,

104–105; types of, 104–111; vanity issues, 113–116
Family Communications, Inc., 223n12(Chpt. 3)
Family Estrangements (LeBey), 117–118
Fanning, Patrick, 191
faulty thinking, 207
feedback, 76–77, 81, 144–145, 170, 182, 204
feelings, 14–15, 46, 171, 188–190. *See also* emotions
feelthink, 46, 207
financial button pushing, 23, 93–94, 107, 109
forgiveness, 101
Fox, Suzy, 68
fractured relationships: children in divorce actions, 137–139; family court and, 136–137; helping children avoid, 128–130; overview, 125–128; protecting yourself, 139–140; separation and divorce, 130–136
Franklin, Benjamin, 33
frantic families, 105–107
freedom, xvi–xvii, 208–209
The Friendship Crisis (Paul), 126
friendship development tips, 128–131
friendships, fractured, 125–127

Gallagher, Maggie, 84
gender differences, 217
genetic anger research, 32
Getting the Love You Want (Hendrix), 88
Glass, Shirley, 97
gossip, dealing with, 170, 172–173
Gottman, John, 89, 91
grief counseling, 105
group therapy, 204
guilt-ridden enablers, 167–168
gullible enablers, 166

Haltzman, Scott, 181–182
Hanna, Fred J., 206
happy people, angry people compared to, 38–39
health-care providers, 35
health effects of anger, 25–26, 28–29, 33–35
Health Enhancement Research Organization, 63
Hendrix, Harville, 88
hidden anger: defining, 5–7, 212–218; protecting yourself from, 10–14, 49–50, 139–140
histrionic people, 217

holiday anger in extended families, 122–124
humor, healing with, 101
hypomanic people, 216–217
I Don't Want To Talk About It (Real), 151
immature behavior, 55, 72, 179–180, 183, 196–197
inciting anger in others, 12–13
indulgent families, 109–111
insecure attachments, 52
intent (motive): allowing positive meanings for, 87–88; of appropriate anger, 14–15; of backstabber versus avenger, 68; concealing with self-centeredness, 27–28; cynicism as payback, 70; in family anger situations, 43–44, 115; of infidelity, 98; journaling to determine, 169–170; manipulation, 5–7, 22–23, 38, 47–48, 76–77; of obsessive-compulsive type, 217; paying attention to, 26, 111–112, 166; repeated behavior as key to, 11; revenge as, 68–69, 93–94
Interpersonal Reconstructive Therapy (Benjamin), 215
irrational beliefs about conflict, 91
irritability, 94–95

Jamison, Kay Redfield, 149–150
journaling, 169–170
Journal of Applied Psychology, 34
Journal of Consulting and Clinical Psychology, 96, 146
Journal of the American Medical Association, 145–146

Kantor, Martin, 169, 216
Krokoff, Lowell, 91
Kübler-Ross, Elisabeth, 51

label thinking, 207
Lader, Wendy, 154
Lavender, Neil J., 80
learned behavior, anger as, 53–54
LeBey, Barbara, 117–118
Levine, Mel, 129
listening, value of, 27, 66–67, 171
Living With the Passive-Aggressive Man (Wetzler), 217
Long, Jody E., 51, 182
Long, Nicholas J., 51, 182
Lykken, David, 32

magnifying and minimizing, 207
Main, Mary, 52
maintenance stage of change, 206
major depression, 148–149
Managing Passive-Aggressive Behavior of Children and Youth (Long and Long), 51, 182
manipulation: controller-type, 69; destructive self-talk as, 47–48; as intent, 5–7, 22–23, 38, 47–48, 76–77; manipulative children, 36, 48, 182–185; need for, 21–23, 194–196; reacting to, 179; revenge as, 68–69; sarcasm as, 166–167; self-destructive nature of, 3, 5–10; silence as, 76–77
marriage. *See* couples
McKay, Matthew, 191
Menninger, William, 211
mental illness as family crisis, 96–97
Merchant, Anwar T., 33
Millon, Theodore, 52–53, 93, 212, 216
A Mind at a Time (Levine), 129
minimizing and magnifying, 207
The Misunderstood Child (Silver), 51
Morey, Leslie, 72, 215
motivating change, 108–109
motive. *See* intent
Murphy, Tim, xvii, 44
mute personality type, 76–77
My Big Fat Greek Wedding (movie), 119

The Narcissistic Family (Donaldson-Pressman and Pressman), 114
narcissistic people, 216
National Academy of Sciences, 34
National Institute for Occupational Safety and Health (NIOSH), 66
National Institute of Mental Health, 63, 146
nature or nurture, 32
needy enablers, 167
Nelson, David, 129
Newsweek, 27
noncompliant patients, 34–35, 75
Not "Just Friends" (Glass and Shaeheli), 97
nurture or nature, 32

obsessive-compulsive type, 18–19, 217
ODD (oppositional defiant disorder), 159–160
On Death and Dying (Kübler-Ross), 51
online therapy, 205

oppositional defiant disorder (ODD), 159–160
The Optimistic Child (Seligman), 134

parents and parenting, 111–116
Parents Anonymous, 120–121
Passive-Aggression (Kantor), 216
Passive-aggressive Personality Disorder (PAPD), 212–218
passive hatred, 117–118
Paul, Marla, 126
peacemaker enablers, 167
performance style quiz, 60–62
personal effects of anger, 35–37
personality disorders, 160–161. *See also specific disorders*
Peterson, Chris, 191–192
postpartum depression, 147
The Power (Browder), 31
precontemplation stage of change, 206
preparation stage of change, 206
Pressman, Robert M., 114
problem solving, 46–47, 67, 190–191, 196
Prochaska, James O., 206
productive versus unproductive anger, 6–7
protecting yourself from hidden anger, 49–50, 139–140
protecting yourself with hidden anger, 10–14
psychology, nonlinear nature of, 11–12
Psychology and Aging, 134
Psychology Today, 127
Psychosomatic Medicine, 30

reactions: choosing your, 173–181; to control, 178–179; to depression, 181–182; getting out, 181–182; to immature behavior, 179–180; to manipulation, 179, 182–185; out-of-proportion, 13–14, 120–122, 144–152; as result of hidden anger, 50–51; to self-absorption, 180–181
reading recommendation lists, 215, 222, 224, 225, 226–227
Real, Terrence, 151
reconciliation, 98
Reichman, Nancy, 95
relationships. *See* couples; families; fractured relationships
research on passive-aggression, 6, 211–218
resolution techniques, xv–xvi, 89–91, 178
responses. *See* reactions

revenge, 22–23, 68–69
Robinson, Clyde, 129
Rogers, Fred, xviii, 50, 54
Rost, Kathryn, 64

sadomasochistic people, 217
SAD (seasonal affective disorder), 147
sarcasm, 15, 70–71, 120, 167–168, 184, 216–217
school issues: academic achievement, 35–36; academic environment, 62; anger types, 67–72, 75–81; classroom manipulation, 183–185
"The Science of Happiness *(Time),* 34
seasonal affective disorder (SAD), 147
The Secrets of Happily Married Men (Haltzman), 181–182
self absorption, reacting to, 180–181
self absorption and vanity, 77–81, 113–116, 197–198
self-assessment, 16–18, 60–62, 65, 191–192
self-care during depression, 152
self-esteem, 47, 72, 183–184, 198–199
self-fulfilling criticism, 172
self-help strategies, 192–193
self-injury, 153–154
Seligman, Martin, 34, 134, 191–192
Shaeheli, Jean Coppock, 97
silence versus feedback, 76–77
Silver, Larry B., 51
social heroes, 113
societal conditioning, 32–33, 53–54
spark stage of anger, 44
Spector, Paul E., 68
Spitzer, Robert, 213
the star personality type, 77–81
stress, 36–37, 63–66, 93–94, 105–107
Successful Problem Solving (McKay and Fanning), 191
suicidal ideation, 148
Surviving Separation and Divorce (Oberlin), 27, 136, 139

taking it personally, 207
the target, 10–14, 130, 169–170
teenagers. *See* adolescents
tenor of the workplace, 63
termination stage of change, 206
Thase, Michael E., 151–152

therapy for anger issues, 105, 160, 201–205
Therapy with Difficult Clients (Hanna), 206
thought process of an angry mind, 29–31, 46
time bomb problem, 26
Time magazine, 34, 153
Toxic Coworkers (Cavaiola and Lavender), 80
triangulation: in families, 79, 118–119; gossip,
    170, 172–173; infidelity, 97–98; of parents,
    with children, 115, 124; recognizing as
    anger, 133; of star personality type, 79;
    therapy as healthy form of, 181; time-
    consuming hobbies as, 98–99; at work, 177
triggers. *See also* buttons: addiction-based, 105;
    fear as, 71; identifying, 85, 99, 104,
    119–121, 170, 189, 192; out of proportion
    responses and, 62, 126
troubled family, 104–105

undifferentiated people, 87
unmasking anger, 18–20
unproductive versus productive anger, 6–7
unrealistic expectations, 85–86, 88, 92, 158
U.S. War Department Technical Bulletin, 211

vacillation, 9, 216
Values in Action Strength Test, 191–192
vanity, 77–81, 113–116, 197–198
victim mentality: abrasive negativism,
    214–216; blaming as, 10, 46, 75–76; gossip
    as sign of, 172–173; increasing anger over
    time, 41–42; overview, 71–72; pseudovic-
    tims, 169
victims of hidden anger, 10–14, 130, 136–139,
    169–170

Waite, Linda J., 84
Washington, D.C., xv, 27
weight gain, anger-related, 25, 31–32, 99
Wetzler, Scott, 50, 72, 215, 217, 218
When Friendship Hurts (Yager), 127–128
Whose Life Is It Anyway? (Brown), 166
Williams, Janice, 31
Williams, Redford, 30, 32
workaholism, 64–66
Working with the Self-Absorbed (Brown), 78–79
workplace culture, creating a better, 66–67,
    81–82
workplace issues: anger types, 67–72, 75–81;
    blaming, 76; cost of hidden anger, 36–37;
    dealing with hidden anger, 81–82; getting
    back at the boss, 3; overview, 59–62; the
    star personality type, 77–81; stress, 36–37,
    63–66; triangulation, 79; workaholism,
    64–66

Yager, Jan, 127–128